E.B.White

The Emergence of an Essayist

E.B.White

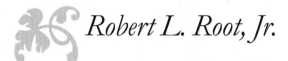 *Robert L. Root, Jr.*

UNIVERSITY OF IOWA PRESS Ψ IOWA CITY

University of Iowa Press, Iowa City 52242

Copyright © 1999 by the University of Iowa Press

All rights reserved

Printed in the United States of America

Design by Richard Hendel

http://www.uiowa.edu/~uipress

Printed on acid-free paper

Library of Congress Cataloging in Publication Data

Root, Robert L.

E. B. White: the emergence of an essayist / by Robert L. Root, Jr.

    p.   cm.

Includes bibliographical references and index.

ISBN 0-87745-667-4 (cloth)

1. White, E. B. (Elwyn Brooks), 1899–1985.—Criticism and
interpretation.   2. American essays—20th century—History and
criticism.   I. Title.

PS3545.H5187Z86   1999

818'.5209—dc21   98-48375

99 00 01 02 03 C 5 4 3 2 1

TO CARL KLAUS,

educator, editor, essayist

"It is encouraging to see how perfectly a book,
even a dusty rulebook,
perpetuates and extends the spirit of a man."

CONTENTS

ACKNOWLEDGMENTS

This book as been a long time in the making and I am grateful to those who have aided its completion. The project was launched with a research professorship at Central Michigan University and extended with a sabbatical leave from the department of English; the examination of manuscripts in the Rare Books and Manuscripts Division of Cornell Library was partly funded by a travel to collections grant from the National Endowment for the Humanities. My relations with Cornell University library personnel have been cordial and productive, and over a ten-year period I have been assisted by Lucy Burgess, Katherine Reagan, and Laura Linke. When I left the University of Iowa for Michigan in 1976, I was beginning work on my first book, a study of the Restoration dramatist Thomas Southerne, to whom I had been introduced in Carl Klaus's Restoration drama course; now I return to Iowa through its Press and fittingly publish on another author to whom Klaus introduced me. My interest in literary nonfiction stems from postdoctoral work in composition, rhetoric, and discourse theory at the University of Iowa in the classes of Carl Klaus, Richard Lloyd-Jones, David Hamilton, and Paul Diehl. Klaus's writings on prose style, the essay, and E. B. White have been continuing touchstones for my thinking. This book has benefited not only from his advice but also that of Michael Alpert, Samuel Pickering, Scott Elledge, and an anonymous but sage reviewer. Thanks to Holly Carver at the University of Iowa Press and to Carolyn Brown, copyeditor — as E. B. White says, "An editor is a person who knows more about writing than writers do but has escaped the terrible desire to write." Finally, my love and gratitude to my wife, Sue, who traveled by train to share an overheated room in Willard Straight Hall at the beginning and who knows what it means to have reached the end.

E.B.White

"THE FAINT SQUEAK OF MORTALITY"
The Emergence of an Essayist

I don't remember now how I happened to be reading *One Man's Meat* or even whether I'd read E. B. White before, but I remember the effect that "Once More to the Lake" had on me. I was the recent father of a son, visiting friends who also had a new son. I was reading in bed, in the guest room of their old farmhouse near Lake Ontario, the house quiet, everyone else asleep. When I came to the ending of the essay — "As he buckled the swollen belt suddenly my groin felt the chill of death" — I gasped and choked up and tears pooled in my eyes. In that instant I felt more in touch with another writer than I had ever felt in my life. In the morning, as I packed my family to leave, I left my copy of the book behind, with pages dog-eared, telling Bill emphatically, "You *have* to read this essay."

I bought another copy for myself but put off reading it until I could give it undivided attention. I hoped to discover more essays like "Once More to the Lake" and wanted nothing to interfere with my connecting with the author again. Eventually, I read all of E. B. White's nonfiction and found other essays that reverberate with a similar sensibility and authorial presence — "The Ring of Time," "Death of a Pig," "The Flocks We Watch by Night," "Morningtime and Eveningtime." But what surprised me in all that reading was how often I encountered nonfiction that seemed to be something other than an essay. Despite the similar sensibility, despite the authorial presence, so often what I read seemed to come short of an essay — a miniessay, perhaps, or a protoessay or an essayistic . . . something else. If White was an essayist, he seemed not to be writing essays as I'd come to think of them or as anybody else had written them before. But if he wasn't an essayist, I didn't know a satisfactory term that would describe what he was.

I have been a long time trying to figure out what it was about E. B. White's nonfiction prose that unsettled me. Now, after reading and rereading his magazine publications, books, letters, and manuscripts, I think I know why, as he himself might have put it, a careful search of his premises reveals far fewer essays than the admiring reader of "Once More to the Lake" might reasonably expect. His nonfiction is less influenced by the grand tradition the term "essay" conjures up and more influenced by popular journalistic forms outside that tradition; the literary forms in which he worked spilled over into one another in ways almost impossible to separate or isolate. E. B. White was not simply, in Irwin Edman's phrase, "our finest essayist, perhaps our only one" ("Earthy" 2) but instead was unique among American essayists. He did not start his nonfiction writing career as an essayist but rather emerged as an essayist from the career he had already established. The influences of the other nonfiction forms in which he worked suffused his writing of essays, and he broke free only in a handful of them. Yet the work he did under those influences not only challenges literary classification but also points the way toward nontraditional forms of the essay, forms whose limits are still being tested.

The image of E. B. White as an essayist really centers around "Once More to the Lake." Even Joseph Epstein, who once identified White and Ralph Waldo Emerson as "two American essayists who are elsewhere much revered but to whose virtues I am apparently blind" ("Writing" 33), singled out "Once More to the Lake" as "his most beautiful essay" and described it as "dazzling and devastating, art of a heightened kind that an essayist is rarely privileged to achieve" ("E. B. White" 316–317). Phillip Lopate, although leery of what he calls White's "sedating influence on the form," has also declared, "No one has written more consistently graceful, thoughtful essays in twentieth-century American language than White" ("What" 80). Both essayist/editors include "Once More to the Lake" in their large anthologies of historic and essential personal essays. This essay and a few others widely reprinted in trade anthologies and classroom collections have secured E. B. White's place as an essayist, reinforcing it with a tower of authenticating reprints and scholarly articles.

Because White has been so venerated, and because certain of his essays have been so universally used to exemplify the form, readers perhaps tend to assume that the rest of his essays are similar to "Once More to the Lake" — that is, unified in design, theme, and tone, with a similar authorial voice. To identify a writer as an essayist is to locate him in the essay tradition of Montaigne, Emerson, Thoreau, Lamb, Hazlitt, and Woolf, a still viable and presently flourishing tradition with which White only identified himself late in his career. The various influences upon the style, structure, and voice of his writing came principally not from the practitioners of the self-contained familiar essay but from the columnists and commentators of periodical journalism. His more immediate predecessors and contemporaries, whose work has faded into obscurity, provided the context out of which White's career blossomed. His essays are intimately related to other forms of nonfiction writing that he wrote regularly. When we encounter his essays in isolation, one or two at a time in massive anthologies, or when we read them in his own collections, we have little sense of the milieu in which they were originally published; such encounters give us no understanding of the ways their shape and substance were influenced by the kinds of writing he did and the conditions under which he wrote. An approach to the essays as monuments on display ends up overlooking the question of how any of these works came into being. It reduces the value of these essays as models for aspiring essayists and obscures a richer understanding of the breadth and complexity of White's nonfiction art.

E. B. White did not begin his writing career as an essayist, nor did he particularly set out to become one. Rather, he emerged as an essayist through a variety of interrelated journalistic forms. To appreciate fully the kind of essayist he became, it is necessary to understand how he worked in such initially distinctive forms as the paragraph (the form of the early Notes and Comment page), the column, the editorial, and the *New Yorker* Letter (or correspondent's department). When we trace the path of his development we see that his work in the essay was more random and more confused with other forms than we might have expected. Only in his later years was his identification as an essayist unquestionable; throughout his career the boundaries of White's essays were blurred with the boundaries of other forms.

White seems to have first revealed himself as an essayist not in the literary forms of his published work but rather in the sensibility or the attitude he brought to much of his writing. In his foreword to *Essays of E. B. White*, a retrospective collection published in 1977, he defined the essayist in terms of his own example: "The essayist is a self-liberated man, sustained by the childish belief that everything he thinks about, everything that happens to him, is of general interest. He is a fellow who thoroughly enjoys his work, just as people who take bird walks enjoy theirs. Each new excursion of the essayist, each new 'attempt,' differs from the last and takes him into new country. This delights him.

Only a person who is congenitally self-centered has the effrontery and the stamina to write essays" (vii). The self-deprecation of "childish belief," "congenitally self-centered," and "effrontery" masks the more elevated implication that the essayist is a kind of "Everyman." This concept is as old as Michel de Montaigne's admonishment to his own readers. It was Montaigne who established the essay's freewheeling form: a shifting combination of autobiography and memoir, literary and cultural criticism, personal narrative and philosophical treatise. His term, *essai*, meaning an attempt or a trial, identified the essay as a tentative, speculative form. Montaigne also established the tone of modest demurrer, the open admission of self-involvement and ego, the atmosphere of introspection and reflection. "I am myself the matter of my book," he wrote to the reader. "I want to be seen here in my simple, natural, ordinary fashion, without straining or artifice; for it is myself that I portray" (2). Like Montaigne, White too takes the pose of self-involvement, of ordinariness, artlessness. It was a pose similar to the self-effacing posture of the humorist, a role he was also familiar with from his early prose and poetry.

More tellingly, White identifies the essayist as a writer capable of many roles — "The essayist arises in the morning and, if he has work to do, selects his garb from an unusually extensive wardrobe: he can pull on any sort of shirt, be any sort of person, according to his mood or his subject matter — philosopher, scold, jester, raconteur, confidant, pundit, devil's advocate, enthusiast" (vii). The pairs of opposed personalities in this list suggest not only the various roles White recognized himself as having played but also the oppositions and range that may appear in any individual role.

White sees these roles as dimensions of a "self-liberated" and "self-centered" writer. He worries that some people may think it "presumptuous of a writer to assume that his little excursions or his small observations will interest the reader." He admits: "I have always been aware that I am by nature self-absorbed and egotistical; to write of myself to the extent that I have done indicates a too great attention to my own life, not enough to the lives of others. I have worn many shirts, and not all of them have been a good fit. But when I am discouraged or downcast I need only fling open the door of my closet, and there, hidden behind everything else, hangs the mantle of Michel de Montaigne, smelling slightly of camphor" (viii). The allusion to mothballs is a typical White turn toward self-deprecation following a serious remark, yet the allusion to Montaigne protects White against the charge of egoism and self-absorption. It aligns him with the principal progenitor of this literary form, the identity behind all of any essayist's assumed identities.

In addition to associating himself with his literary forebears, White also acknowledges the impulse to take an essayist's approach from the very beginning of his writing life. At one point he writes: "I like the essay, have always liked it, and even as a child was at work, attempting to inflict my young thoughts and experiences on others by putting them on paper. I early broke into print in the pages of *St. Nicholas*. I tend still to fall back on the essay form (or lack of form) when an idea strikes me" (vii).

As a child White had published in the children's magazine *St. Nicholas*; he wrote about the experience in a 1934 *New Yorker* article, "The St. Nicholas League," but never reprinted the piece until *Essays of E. B. White*. As he compiled the collection, White may have retrospectively recognized the essayistic impulse as a dominating one in his writing. In this sense, his pushing other forms toward the essay was a consistent, if not always self-conscious, attempt to draw upon his instincts toward the personal, the familiar, the pronounced first person singular. These instincts underlay most of his impulses toward writing (including his semiautobiographical children's books).

White recognized this impulse early in his career. In a January 1929 letter to his brother Stanley White he observed:

> I discovered a long time ago that writing of the small things of the day, the trivial matters of the heart, the inconsequential but near things of this living, was the only kind of creative work which I could accomplish with any sincerity or grace. As a reporter, I was a flop, because I always came back laden not with facts about the case, but with a mind full of the little difficulties and amusements I had encountered in my travels. Not until *The New Yorker* came along did I ever find any means of expressing those impertinences and irrelevancies. . . . The rewards of such endeavor are not that I have acquired an audience or a following, as you suggest (fame of any kind being a Pyrrhic victory), but that sometimes in writing of myself — which is the only subject anyone knows intimately — I have occasionally had the exquisite thrill of putting my finger on a little capsule of truth, and heard it give the faint squeak of mortality under my pressure, an antic sound. (*Letters* 84–85)

Written only a few years into his career at the *New Yorker*, these comments reverberate in the comparisons with Montaigne in the introduction to *Essays*, nearly fifty years later. The "small things of the day, the trivial matters of the heart, the inconsequential but near things of this living," the "writing of myself . . . the only subject anyone knows intimately" all sound the Montaignian note ("I am myself the matter of my book").

They also echo the opening pages of Henry David Thoreau's *Walden*. Thoreau warned the reader, "We commonly do not remember that it is, after all, always the first person that is speaking. I should not talk so much about myself if there were any body else whom I knew as well." He added, "I, on my side, require of every writer, first or last, a simple and sincere account of his own life, and not merely what he has heard of other men's lives" (3). Thoreau was the one major literary figure to whom White referred throughout his writing, and his centennial essay on *Walden* was one of the major catalysts for the turn toward the essay that dominated the last portion of his career. White himself would later couch some of his career decisions in terms of a "search for the first person singular." The impulse toward the essay may have arisen early, but the emergence of the essayist within White was in some sense the labor of his whole writing life.

While White's comments about being an essayist may help explain what he thought, retrospectively, he was doing in the form, they do not reveal what he thought the nature of that form was. It is a truth too seldom appreciated by scholars and critics that writers themselves do not have to define or delineate the forms in which they work — they simply have to follow their best instincts about what satisfies their sense of unity or design and fulfills their need to write at all. Scholars and critics are the ones who worry about definitions and categories; they are the ones who try to establish boundaries between forms and to notice when the borders have been either crossed or straddled. Aristotle's rules for tragedy are not those Euripides would have written. Perhaps then it is not surprising that White should realize in retrospect how often the essayistic impulse had motivated his writing throughout his career and yet almost never use the term "essay" to describe his writing before that realization. It also is not surprising that, at the time White began his career, hardly anyone noticed that the essay was in a period of transition.

From very early on essayists themselves had tried to differentiate their essays from their other nonfiction writing. Montaigne and Bacon both distinguished between essays and more scholarly writing; Joseph

Addison claimed his essays differed from his "methodological discourses"; Samuel Johnson defined the essay in part by what it was not — he called it "an irregular, undigested piece, not a regular, orderly performance." But because the essay allowed for considerable latitude, most practitioners simply let their own idiosyncratic examples serve for definition, as Charles Lamb did. By the turn of the twentieth century, scholars and critics had a wealth of material that they could use to categorize and subcategorize the form, to draw up its borders, and to illustrate or exemplify their definitions.

Collections published as White finished college and began searching for a career offer instructive illustration of how editors interpreted the essay. A typical example is Benjamin A. Heydrick's categorizing in *Types of the Essay* (1921). He exemplifies the personal essay with work by Steele, Lamb, and Hazlitt; the descriptive essay with work from Ruskin, Stevenson, and Thoreau; the character sketch with Goldsmith's "Man in Black"; editorial essays, which "are really brief arguments," entirely from Addison and Steele; the reflective essay ("its subjects are general, often abstract, and its tone is serious" [xiii]), with Bacon on studies, Emerson on self-reliance, and Carlyle on books. Heydrick clearly identifies the essay with the great tradition and defines it partly by citing Bacon's distinction between the essay and the treatise and by insisting that the essay "is brief, and does not attempt to treat a subject either completely or systematically" (vii).

Similarly representative of this approach is Bernard L. Jefferson's *Essays and Essay Writing* (1929), which extends the great tradition on the British side from Montaigne (in Florio's translation) and Bacon to Maurice Hewlett, Hilaire Belloc, Robert Lynd, and G. K. Chesterton, and on the American side from Franklin, Irving, and Emerson to Agnes Repplier, Samuel McChord Crothers, Robert Cortes Holliday, and Henry Seidel Canby. Jefferson emphasizes personal or familiar essays in which "we may expect to find the minds of interesting men unfolding themselves in various engaging moods" and writing "of their fireplaces, their gardens, journeys they have made, their experiences in childhood, their views of men and of the universe, or of anything which they love or hate" (xii). The emphasis here, as so often in discussions of the essay, is on the identity of the essayist, whom Jefferson views as someone with "a warm, human quality — . . . courtly grace, or an aristocratic mental outlook, or a care-free gallantry, or an all-pervading whimsicality, or an idealistic fire, or some other engaging quality or mixture of qualities." The form is identified as "the *familiar* essay" because the essayist "makes familiar to us the peculiar stamp of his personality and the rarities of his temper" (xiii). Typically, Jefferson finds in these essays "an individualistic touch which one does not find in the informative article and in the scholarly or scientific treatise," which are "impersonal, . . . dispassionately correct and systematic" (xiii). His most interesting assertion, in the light of White's comments about the essayist rather than the essay, is that it is possible to write "in the essay spirit, although, strictly speaking, it may not be in the essay form" (xiv).

Heydrick and Jefferson are representative of a number of editors and compilers who regard the essay as a current and continuing genre, extending a long tradition. They present the writers in this tradition as if their currency were timeless, unaffected by changes in world view, prose style, or literary form. Even when such editors take a less historical approach to the essay, the essayists selected tend to be squarely in the tradition, writing of personal experiences, travel, books, and occasional subjects. For example, in *The Writing of Informal Essays* (1928) editors Mary Ellen Chase and Margaret Eliot MacGregor collect such traditional practitioners as Agnes Repplier, Hilaire Belloc, G. K. Chesterton, Robert Lynd, and Alice Meynell; Charles Lamb and Michel de Montaigne are each subject of an essay.

Although such trade or textbook anthologies resolutely reinforce the traditional models, these collections are misleading about the state of the essay in their own time. Their emphasis on traditional approaches tends to eliminate examples that conflict with, or at least fail to conform to, the models of the historical masters. In actual practice the decline of the literary periodical and the rise of popular journalism had put pressure on the essay as a literary form, and editors who emphasized current practitioners provide a more immediate context for the ways essays were being written at the time.

For example, the two collections edited by Christopher Morley, *Modern Essays* (1921) and *Modern Essays, Second Series* (1924), are made up of pieces selected to fit Morley's concept of the essay. He claims in the preface to the first volume that the essay "may be severely planned, or it may ramble in ungirdled mood, but it has its own point of view," and that it can be identified by "a tendency to generalize, to walk around the subject or the experience, and view it from several vantages" (v). He also identifies the persona of the essayist as a requisite component: "The fine flavor and genius of the essay . . . is the rich bouquet of personality. But soliloquy must not fall into monologue. One might put it thus: that the perfection of the familiar essay is a conscious revelation of self done inadvertently (vi)." Morley asserts that "as brilliant and sincere work is being done to-day in the essay as in any period of our literature" and identifies the diversity of the pieces: "There is the grand manner; there is foolery; there is straightforward literary criticism; there is pathos, politics, and the picturesque." Claiming that "every selection is, in its own way, a work of art," he makes an important distinction about the authors: "the greater number of these essays were written not by retired aesthetes, but by practicing journalists in the harness of the daily or weekly press" (vii).

Morley was himself a practicing journalist, with a popular column called "The Bowling Green," then running in the *New York Evening Post* and soon to be transferred to a new weekly magazine, the *Saturday Review*. He was a prolific writer, producing novels and short stories (he is best known for *The Haunted Bookshop* and *Kitty Foyle*), poems, plays, prefaces, and introductions (including one for *The Complete Sherlock Holmes*), edited works (such as *Modern Essays* and two editions of *Barlett's Familiar Quotations*), and various other nonfiction books. He collected sixteen volumes of essays and related material from his newspaper and magazine work, principally reprinted from his columns. His familiar essays ran the gamut from literary criticism to travel, from character sketches to memoirs — in fact, in their more traditional anthology Chase and MacGregor reprinted Morley's essays in four different subcategories.

Modern Essays is made up of both British and American authors and includes a number of names recognizable more for work in poetry or fiction — Rupert Brooke (on "Niagara Falls"), Joyce Kilmer, Joseph Conrad, A. A. Milne, James Branch Cabell, Stewart Edward White, Willa Cather, Sherwood Anderson, John Crowe Ransom — as well as many obvious choices in nonfiction — William Allen White, Hilaire Belloc, Stephen Leacock, Max Beerbohm, H. M. Tomlinson, Louise Imogen Guiney, Robert Cortes Holliday, W. H. Hudson, Maurice Hewlett, Alice Meynell, and Llewelyn Powys (with an essay on Montaigne). Among the journalists, Morley includes Alexander Woollcott, Henry Seidel Canby (his editor at the *Saturday Review*), Simeon Strunsky (his editor at the *New York Evening Post*), and two important fellow columnists, Heywood Broun (with "The Fifty-First Dragon") and Don Marquis (with "The Almost Perfect State").

The emphasis that Morley places on the current state of the essay and his insistence on locating it in "the daily or weekly press" are suggestive for the course the essay would take for the next several decades and for establishing the context of E. B. White's writing during that period. The popular magazines eventually became the principal outlet for the essay in all its forms. A number of magazines published literary and cultural criticism, political and social analysis, observations on current events and daily living, and regular columns in more-or-less-specific subject areas. The increasing competition among magazines tended to highlight popular writers and repeat popular features, and a number of writers found themselves writing weekly or monthly columns rather than randomly composing essays. The nature of periodical journalism imposed exigencies on writers that affected the kind of prose they produced. Because most of E. B. White's writing was done for a weekly or monthly magazine, as part of a regular department or feature, it is not surprising that his approach to writing tended to be journalistic rather than literary and that the way he composed had to adapt to various kinds of constraints of form, content, audience, and time imposed by his employment.

Morley's selections also help us understand how some journalistic elements influenced the development of the twentieth-century essay by loosening its already flexible concept of unity and coherence. Many of the columnists of the period did not simply fill their columns with essays but rather included essays among the components of their columns. We will examine in more detail some specific habits of the columnists and "colyumists" in the next several chapters, but for now it should be said that the demands of filling weekly or monthly column space made the writers in charge of them (often referred to in the period as "colyum conductors") draw upon a freewheeling sense of structure, not only writing essays but often appending unrelated notes and comments to them to fill up the assigned space in the newspaper or magazine — indeed, some colyums may have been nothing but notes and comments. This "disconnected" series of items paved the way for the "disjunctive" essay now widely practiced and discussed, and opened the door for the essay to turn away from the single-unit form, whether tightly argumentative or ramblingly reflective.

Morley points the way for this shift in structure with two selections in the first volume of *Modern Essays*. For the most part the selections are single, unified works, even if some have the sort of Roman-numerated sections typical of longer and more argumentative essays and articles. But the selection by Don Marquis is introduced not as a unified work but as "two of Mr. Marquis's amiable meditations on the 'Almost Perfect State'" taken from his "Sun Dial" column. The two are printed as sections I and II and could be taken as two linked parts of a single work, but they were not necessarily printed consecutively in Marquis's column or in his later collection of all the column items on that theme. The other "disjunctive" selection is titled "Trivia," made up of several "miniature essays" taken from a "remarkable little book" of that name by Logan Pearsall Smith (297). The selection includes several individually titled sections: "Stonehenge," "The Stars," "The Spider," "L'Oiseau Bleu," "I See the World," "The Church of England," "Consolation," "The Kaleidoscope," and "The Poplar"; each runs from one to three paragraphs in length. They have been assembled at random by Morley and are not necessarily consecutive in the original book.

The idea that a selection may be tentative or inconclusive is not a new one — the traditional essay has almost by definition been that way. The idea of printing a partial essay is not new either — excerpts had been popular in much earlier textbooks, and through our own time college anthologies have routinely reprinted sections of essays and articles or have presented portions of book chapters as if they were self-contained essays. But it is new to draw together tangential or disconnected elements and present them as a satisfactory representation of a whole; that is, to offer a collection of comments and paragraphs as the equivalent of an essay. In the anthologies mentioned earlier, few selections are segmented in any way, and then only as subdivisions of a larger argument. Heydrick presents only two essays with subdivisions; Chase and MacGregor, only one. All use Roman numerals to set off distinct sections of a unified and lengthy whole, and two of the pieces are from recent magazines. Jefferson cites "an interesting development . . . in the direction of a kind of essay sequence comparable to a sonnet sequence" in which the writer "composes a series of brief essays somewhat loosely strung together in the development of a common theme or of somewhat related themes. The different divisions may be set apart from one another by some such transitional device as Roman numerals" (xv). His chief example is two sections taken from "First Study" in Charles Dudley Warner's *Backlog Studies*, but because both are about the pleasures of sitting by a fireplace, they read very much like a subdivided whole. Morley's collection is the only one to present essays as segmented, even fragmented, compositions.

The milieu of the essay that White was introduced to at the end of his college years and the beginning of his writing career was in transition; the most influential voices were those of essayists in the popular press, usually the celebrated and established columnists. White's emergence as an essayist would be shaped by these forces, these voices, and they would make him a distinctly individual voice in the long history of the essay.

❧ E. B. White's essays form a smaller portion of his nonfiction than his reputation as an essayist might suggest. He worked prolifically in other parallel or tangentially related forms and was principally a paragrapher or columnist or editorialist for most of his career. He emerged as an essayist sporadically, intermittently, usually within or alongside those other forms. White often created essays that are unlike the work of any other essayist, and their uniqueness, their idiosyncratic nature, often arises from the circumstances under which he wrote them. To understand those circumstances we will have to follow two alternate and interwoven strands: the first is the trajectory of White's career as a nonfiction writer during four distinct periods of magazine writing; the second is the manuscript evidence, where we can find it, of White's composing processes for representative works in each period.

E. B. White was born on July 11, 1899, in Mt. Vernon, New York, and died on October 1, 1985, in Maine. For most of his eighty-six years he was a writer, beginning with the journal he kept in childhood and a poem published at the age of ten in *Ladies' Home Journal* and ending with correspondence to family and friends and an occasional letter to the editor of his local paper or the *New York Times*. A bibliography of his writing compiled by Katherine Romans Hall lists 2,242 items, including poems, short stories, parodies, sketches, parables, editorials, paragraphs, essays, introductions, reviews, articles, advertisements, obituaries, children's novels, and a textbook. With only a few important exceptions, most of his writing appeared first in magazines and newspapers. White periodically reprinted the best of it in a series of "clipbooks." The three most prominent collections, *One Man's Meat, The Second Tree from the Corner*, and *The Points of My Compass*, together only include 157 items out of that bibliography, and White's two retrospective anthologies, *Essays of E. B. White* and *Poems and Sketches of E. B. White*, contain mostly previously collected work. White lived a writing life, begun at a very early age and carried on through every event of his life, defining his work, his play, his relationships with his wife and family, his public and private life.

The major portion of White's work was written for the *New Yorker* magazine, to which he began contributing in its first year of publication, 1925. Hall has observed that, during the fifty-three-year period of *New Yorker* publication her bibliography covers, "the magazine has used approximately 450 signed EBW pieces, 1,350 identifiable unsigned pieces, and hundreds of anonymous remarks in the form of Newsbreaks, Answers to Hard Questions, captions to drawings, etc." (226). It was from the beginning of White's regular employment at the magazine that his career really began. Working there set in motion habits of thought and expression, ways of working at writing and shaping individual pieces, that influenced his development as a nonfiction writer and his emergence as an essayist.

White's nonfiction career can be divided into four fairly pronounced periods. They are differentiated by the kind of magazine writing he was doing, the voice or personality he adopted for it, the constraints of form and writing circumstances that were imposed on it. The periods are generally summarized in the anthologies or "clipbooks" of previously published work that he occasionally compiled. One question that runs through this book is, How do the essays of E. B. White differ from the other forms of writing in which he routinely engaged? A related question is, How did those other forms influence White's essays? To pursue these questions, it will be necessary to explore the nonfiction forms that predominated in White's writing in each of these periods and to determine the forces that influenced how he handled these forms. Both manuscript evidence (when available) and testimony from White and his fellow practitioners will help uncover how he composed his nonfiction — that is, the sources of his subject matter, the nature of his drafting and revising, the constraints of specific assignments and work circumstances on what he wrote.

The first nonfiction period encompasses the first dozen years of White's employment at the *New Yorker*, from 1926 to 1938. Almost all of White's writing in this period appeared first in the *New Yorker*, except for poetry published intermittently in "The Conning Tower," Franklin P. Adams's *New York World* column, and in *Is Sex Necessary? or Why You Feel the Way You Do* (1929), a parody of psychological and sexual self-help books cowritten with James Thurber. His other books of this period reprinted previously published material: *The Lady Is Cold* (1929) collected poems from the *New Yorker* and the *New York World*; *Ho Hum* (1931) and *Another Ho Hum* (1932) collected newsbreaks (comic column filler reprinting or reacting to mistakes in newspapers) from the

New Yorker, in both cases with a foreword from White rather than credit for authorship; *Alice through the Cellophane* (1933) reprinted a three-part series commenting satirically on business. The later poems of the period were collected in *The Fox of Peapack and Other Poems* (1938), and his best stories and sketches were published in *Quo Vadimus? or The Case for the Bicycle* (1939). Most of this work established and maintained his reputation as a humorist — he and Thurber were both strongly influenced by Robert Benchley and Clarence Day in their early work for the magazine, and as a writer of light verse White was ranked with Dorothy Parker and Ogden Nash. His editing of *A Subtreasury of American Humor* with his wife, Katharine, was in many ways a capstone for this period, but by the time it was published in 1941, he had essentially shifted both the tenor and the temperament of his writing.

In spite of the notable light verse and humorous or satirical prose he produced in the period, his most constant and prolific work was the widely admired paragraphs published anonymously in the *New Yorker*'s Notes and Comment section each week. In 1934 he compiled and published a generous sampling of them in *Every Day Is Saturday*, a collection that helped identify him as the principal author of that section. The Comment paragraphs established White's reputation as a wit and as a prose stylist, and they also influenced much of the longer writing he did over the years.

The ways in which writers compose and the nature of the writing they create are strongly influenced by the circumstances in which they work. White's circumstances changed several times during his career. His first decade at the *New Yorker* demanded that he be witty, concise, current, and prolific. As both rewrite man and original composer of the Notes and Comment page, his productivity was aided by the demands of the paragraph form: lightness of tone allowed for slightness in focus and thought; brevity restricted the complications of development and argument; currency prevented the need for sustained identification of subjects and encouraged highly spontaneous and extemporaneous responses; volume demanded both speed in achieving an acceptable draft and a willingness to accept a certain level of unsustained archness as sufficient. White's ability to adapt to the demands of the Comment page made him its preeminent paragrapher; it also locked him into habits of writing that both frustrated and sustained him throughout his career.

In this early period White published only two essays, "Onward and Upward with the Arts: St. Nicholas League" and "Onward and Upward with the Arts: Farewell, My Lovely!" He would later include both in *Essays of E. B. White*. The second essay was published as a small illustrated book, *Farewell to Model T* (1936), and its popularity may have encouraged White to write longer, more personal, and less formulaic nonfiction than paragraphs.

The second period of White's nonfiction career is essentially coterminous with his column for *Harper's Magazine*, which ran from 1938 to 1943, although in truth most of the periods overlapped with one another. Throughout the 1930s occasional hints of dissatisfaction appeared in White's Notes and Comment writing, and evidence in his letters reinforces the sense that the anonymity, tone, and format of Comment writing were becoming increasingly difficult for him to live with. In 1937 he took a leave of absence from the magazine in order to give himself what he liked to term his "sabbatical." White and his family moved to a farmhouse on the Atlantic coast of Maine that they had owned since 1933. There he began contributing a monthly four-page column titled "One Man's Meat" to *Harper's Magazine*.

The weekly deadlines of the *New Yorker* paragraphs were replaced by the monthly deadlines of the *Harper's* column, which wrought changes in White's composing concomitant with the changes in his circumstances. Most important of those changes were the development of an authorial identity more reflective of his own personality — the column was written in first person singular instead of the first person plural required of the Comment — and the tendency to write items that were more personal, introspective, and sustained than the Comment paragraphs had been. The column provided the space and the freedom to write single essays that could fill the department, an option White took less often than he composed multiple-item columns. The items themselves were less formulaic, longer, and more often thematically linked to one another than the items of his usual Comment page had been. His location on a Maine farm rather than in Manhattan made his daily work environment less concerned with the currents of city affairs and urban living than with personal affairs and rural living; when he turned his columnist's eye on public events, he focused on topics of national or even global concern rather than on merely metropolitan (and thus essentially local) concerns. Nonetheless, throughout this period White continued to rely on current stimuli to provoke his composing for the column. The monthly deadline was still a regular deadline, even if the format of the column allowed more latitude than the format of Notes and Comment.

The "One Man's Meat" columns were a popular feature of *Harper's* and established White's reputation as an essayist. How many of the columns actually *were* essays is open to question. Many of them were collected into a book published by the parent company, Harper and Brothers, first in 1942 and then in 1944 in a "new and enlarged edition." In March 1943 White stopped writing for *Harper's*. Soon after, the Whites closed up their Maine home and returned full time to New York.

The third period of White's nonfiction writing overlaps with the second period and centers again on Comment writing. White had continued to contribute newsbreaks and comment to the *New Yorker* throughout his time in Maine, and, as the war continued, his pieces for "Notes and Comment" began to appear more regularly and to sound less like the voice of the 1930s *New Yorker* and more like the voice of "One Man's Meat." During the course of the war White's Comment for the *New Yorker* gradually expanded into full-fledged editorials. Their subject often was the need for a global perspective and a world government after the war. Although they were often witty and wry, they were seldom lighthearted or whimsical, as his earlier Comment had been. Their seriousness followed White's own bent toward taking more of a stand on current issues. White's arguments in favor of world government were collected first in a *New Yorker*–published promotional pamphlet entitled *World Government and Peace: Selected Notes and Comment 1943–1945* and then more completely in *The Wild Flag* (1946). After the war White continued to write *New Yorker* editorials on current affairs, attacking McCarthy era witch-hunting, the nuclear arms race, DDT and other pesticides, and pollution.

White's return to the *New Yorker* and his abandonment of the *Harper's* column marked another change in his work circumstances. While ostensibly he was back in the weekly work of the Comment page, he brought to it the tendency toward more sustained items, an insistence on a more editorial slant to at least some of the items, and a more personal presence even within the constraints of the first person plural. White's acceptance of the Comment page as the site of his regular forum on the need for world government allowed him to accumulate the series of editorials that became *The Wild Flag*, but it also limited the development of any one segment of that sustained argument. As the Comment items became longer, they also demanded more attention to overarching structure and thematic development. Nonetheless, the regular production of editorials aided his composing by requiring a similar tone, voice, and format.

With the exception of two children's books, *Stuart Little* (1945) and *Charlotte's Web* (1952), White settled into the routine of writing for the *New Yorker*. His most notable essays of this period were written for other magazines, "Here Is New York" for *Holiday* (later published — like "Farewell, My Lovely!" — as a small book) and "Death of a Pig" for *Atlantic Monthly*. In 1954 he collected an assortment of poems, stories, essays, and Comment pieces for a new anthology of his writing, *The Second Tree from the Corner*. More than any other collection, it shows the range of White's writing during a roughly twenty-year period.

This period of White's writing ends with the retirement of both E. B. and Katharine in 1957, when Katharine was sixty-five, and their return to their home in Maine to live year-round. By this time, however, White had already entered the final period of his nonfiction writing. Throughout the 1950s White had begun to write less regularly for Notes and Comment and to publish a series of longer pieces at irregular intervals, beginning with a centennial reflection on Thoreau's *Walden* for the *Yale Review* and "Our Windswept Correspondents/The Eye of Edna" in the *New Yorker*, both published in 1954. Others appeared in the *New Yorker* under the title "Letter from the ———." Because these were more infrequent, the writing circumstances for them were less predictable than for the earlier writing, and the complications of their composing were increased.

The format, resembling that of the *New Yorker*'s regular featured articles by far-flung correspondents, allowed White great latitude in terms of length and voice. Some were made up of one fully developed essay, some assumed the chatty discursiveness of correspondence, and some expanded on the format of the Comment page by developing multiple items. White sometimes imitated the format and attitude of other correspondents to the *New Yorker* and sometimes ironically undercut the Letter conventions by imitating the tone of a more personal correspondent, as if he were someone who really was writing a letter instead of writing a Letter. These vagaries make the Letter format less confining and less predictable than the various incarnations of the Comment page, and White allowed himself the freedom to draw on all the forms he had experience with — multiple-item Comment, correspondence, editorial, personal essay — to complete the entries in the Letters series. By 1962 there were enough of them to publish the collection, *The Points of My Compass*. This collection, as well as his revision of William Strunk's *The Elements of Style* (1959), with an additional chapter titled "An Approach to Style," were significant confirmations of White's status as an essayist and prose stylist.

White's retirement brought changes in his work circumstances. With less frequent demands for his writing, he often found himself unable to draw on habitual resources. When asked to provide an obituary or commemorative editorial, he did not have the persistent readiness of the regular editorialist to draw on, and his composing challenges were compounded by having to rediscover his editorial voice at the same time he wrestled to discover his attitude or opinion. While regular and prolific production under deadline would have quickly resulted in usable copy of some kind, irregular and random production made his composing of individual essays more arduous and more complicated.

White's writing life tapered off after Katharine's retirement, and the fourth period of his nonfiction writing concludes with the publication of *The Points of My Compass*, although he continued to contribute Comment (mostly obituaries for old friends and public figures) and to write a handful of further Letter pieces. Except for *The Trumpet of the Swan* (1970), a final children's book, his energies centered on retrospective collections of his writing, beginning with *Letters of E. B. White* in 1976. *Essays of E. B. White* (1977) collected some new material published after 1962 but also included some of the best essays of *One Man's Meat*, *The Second Tree from the Corner* and *The Points of My Compass*. *Poems and Sketches of E. B. White* (1981) selected from both the collected and the uncollected poetry and fiction. The final books published in White's lifetime were new editions of *One Man's Meat* (1983) and *The Second Tree from the Corner* (1984). His last essay, the introduction to the new edition of *The Second Tree from the Corner*, was written in February 1984.

Having constant circumstances for composing — familiar and regular work habits, consistent audiences, and a similar persona or voice from text to text — reduces the constraints on a writer's ability to write. It allows greater focus on considering ideas and finding language that expresses and delineates subject matter. Writers of occasional (in either the sense of infrequent or event-inspired) essays for a variety of publications need to reinvent themselves as well as to create a more or less original form for each essay; regular writers of essays similar in tone and format for the same publication can draw automatically on predictable resources and do not need to spread their energies as far. Occasional essayists are encouraged by the composing circumstances to reinvent themselves with each essay, while regular essayists are both supported and constrained by their task environment. Throughout his career, whatever the subgenre or form in which he worked, White tended to have constant and regular composing circumstances that were simultaneously liberating and confining — liberating in the sense of giving him a certain rhythm of production to draw on and thus freeing certain aspects of his composing, confining in the sense of restricting him to limited flexibility of form, approach, and execution.

Changes in White's composing circumstances altered the processes by which he wrote and also altered the way he understood the forms in which he was working. His paragraphs, the form of early Comment, became more personally charged and essayistic. His column for *Harper's* was subsequently influenced by the shape and tenor of his early Comment, as well as by the urge toward longer, more substantial, and more personal pieces like "Farewell, My Lovely!," yet in response to world events it eventually took on more forthright, argumentative, and impersonal tones. When White shifted his attention back to Comment writing, sometimes he brought to it the assertiveness of his argumentative columns and pushed it toward the outright editorial, and sometimes he brought to it features of his personal columns and pushed it toward the miniature familiar essay. When he turned to the Letter series, he did not abandon the earlier forms he had worked in but continued to draw upon them or fall back on them; a Letter could be like an essay, an editorial article, or an extended Notes and Comment page.

In terms of defining White's work as an essayist, then, the problem is knowing the point at which a distinctive literary form, such as the paragraph, has been stretched to such a degree that it transmogrifies into a different literary form, such as the essay. The Sisyphean labor of classification in White's case is further complicated by the ways in which other forms blend into one another as well as into the essay. "The Age of Dust" is a five-paragraph comparison of a report from the *Bulletin of the Atomic Scientists* with the behavior of a little girl on a swing. Is it an editorial or a Comment (it was the entire Notes and Comment page for 16 August 1950) or an essay (Ken Smith discusses it as one, 178–181) or a sketch (White included it in *Poems and Sketches*, not in *Essays*, and Edward Hoagland comments in his review of *Poems and Sketches of E. B. White* that "the sketches which resemble short stories are nowhere near the caliber of those which amount to short essays," 59)? As multiple items make up the Comment page, so they also sometimes make up the column and the Letter, and in every sub-genre they range from the tightly unified to the wholly independent — although sometimes choosing which is which depends on how seriously the reader thinks some segues and token transitions should be taken. As a further complication, the paragraphs of some pieces that lack asterisks or spacing breaks have only the rambling linkage of an informal letter or stream-of-consciousness essay; they *seem* more unified than some of the more segmented columns and Comments but are logically and thematically less unified.

No other essayist I can think of labored under such circumstances. Most of the contemporary essayists with whom White is anthologized are represented by single-subject works written expressly to explore that subject. Even such columnists as Lewis Thomas, in his collections *The Lives of the Cell* and *The Medusa and the Snail,* and Stephen Jay Gould, in any number of his collections, write individual columns that are completely about a single topic; even other essayists who appear in such popular magazines as *Harper's, Atlantic, Esquire,* and the *New Yorker* or in such literary magazines as the *American Scholar, Commentary, Georgia Review,* or *Antaeus* all write single-topic essays, often their sole appearance in the publication or completely independent from any of their other essays in format and theme. Very few of White's essays were written and published under these circumstances.

Because White wrote most of his nonfiction under the constraints of weekly journalism, form is not merely an academic question in a discussion of his writing — in fact, it has a considerable role to play in determining the nature of his nonfiction and the conditions under which it was composed. We need to look closely at the forms of nonfiction that dominated each of the major periods of E. B. White's writing life. If we examine the general context in which his writing took place, as well as the work circumstances in which he wrote, we can trace the trajectory of his career as an essayist. In particular we can look at representative works-in-progress over these periods, drawing on manuscript evidence, supporting material such as letters, and research in literary composition. We can also determine the ways his work circumstances changed over the years and the influence of those changes on his work habits.

Similar studies have been done of manuscript evidence, perhaps most notably with the work of Henry David Thoreau. In *The Making of*

Walden, J. Lyndon Shanley examines the progression from journals kept during and after Thoreau's stay on Walden Pond through multiple revisions to final published text. Similarly, Lauriat Lane, Jr., examines the textual evidence for the composition of Thoreau's essay "A Walk to Wachusetts," and William Howarth compares versions of drafts of a lecture and essay entitled "Moonlight." In such studies the scholar's job is to reconstruct as much as possible the contents and sequence of various drafts of a single work, and then to compare changes among them, trying to ascertain the effects of — and as much as possible the motives behind — such changes. Sometimes, by seeing what an original passage was like and comparing it with a revised, published passage, we come to understand how the earlier passage was inadequate in the author's view and why the later passage better served his purposes.

There are problems inherent in such reconstruction, of course. Authors do not always keep all the materials they create — some drafts and notes may be wadded up and thrown away at the time, or used later for kindling or more frugally for drafting of a totally different work on the verso. Thoreau's drafts, for example, sometimes indicate passages torn from journals (early in his writing he tended to cannibalize his journals physically; later, he more scrupulously copied material and left the journals intact) and the cutting and pasting of earlier drafts into later drafts, as well as the tendency to use the back side of pages from one draft when composing a later draft.

In the case of White's manuscripts, some difficulty surfaces from the unavailability of his personal journal, which he indicated should be destroyed after his death and which would undoubtedly have given indications of considerable work in progress. We have some sense of the journal from the excerpts he provides in the essay "First World War" in *One Man's Meat*, where he shares his youthful concerns about World War I in the early days of World War II, and we know it was useful to him in such works as "Farewell, My Lovely!" and "The Years of Wonder." White himself kept relatively little of his work-in-progress before his retirement, when he began to donate his papers to Cornell University and tried to collect the existing manuscript evidence. Thus, most of the fullest manuscript evidence comes from a period of White's least active and perhaps least typical composing. White's children's books have been examined in manuscript by Peter Neumeyer, and his editorial on the first manned moon landing in 1969 has been followed through several drafts by Scott Elledge, in an appendix to his biography of White, and subsequently by Douglas Hunt, in the introduction to a college textbook. The drafting of a late sketch — "Dear Mr. ⁞⃘0 2 ⁞⃘⃘⃘⃘ ⁞⃘063⁞⃘ ⁞⃘0 2⁞⃘ ⁞⃘0730⁞⃘8⁞⃘" — has been examined in the introduction to another college anthology by Nancy R. Comley and others. But manuscript evidence for some of his most admired essays — "Once More to the Lake," "The Ring of Time," "Death of a Pig," and "Farewell, My Lovely!" — is missing, leaving the researcher in the realm of purest conjecture about their composition.

Without such manuscript evidence, and in conjunction with the manuscript evidence that does exist, it is still possible to talk about how White wrote by examining what we know of other evidence concerning his composing — his letters, for example, are very suggestive about the circumstances under which he worked — and comparing that to what we know of composing processes in general. A great many complications attend such an examination, not the least of them the uncertainty and incompleteness of the manuscript record. It is a tricky endeavor to read the mind of an author primarily on manuscript evidence, and some would argue that the creative process is too complex or too mystical to be comprehended by the creative person experiencing it, let alone by an academic kibitzer trying to reconstruct it after the fact. But, in truth, what writers go through does not vary much from one writer to the next, and one writer's experience is never completely alien to other writers. We may not be able to know exactly and ultimately, but we can understand approximately and sufficiently. The evidence of White's manuscripts will reveal considerable insights into his composing processes, generally giving us more evidence about the impact of work circumstances and form on composing, and specifically giving us insight into White's emergence as an essayist.

"LITTLE CAPSULES OF TRUTH"
White as Paragrapher

When *Harper's Magazine* published the first installment of "One Man's Meat" in October 1938, a section of the contributors' column was devoted to introducing "E. B. W., otherwise E. B. White, otherwise Elwyn Brooks White, of the *New Yorker*." It led off with his most immediately recognizable and significant accomplishment: "Most of our readers are familiar with Mr. White's brilliant paragraphs in The Talk of the Town pages of the *New Yorker* and the sketches he has contributed to that magazine" (561). Although it mentioned next the satirical manual with Thurber and two books of poems, it also highlighted two clipbooks from the *New Yorker*: *Alice through the Cellophane* and *Every Day Is Saturday*. Until this moment, when White was in transition from one phase of his writing life to another, his chief accomplishment clearly had been his writing for the *New Yorker*, especially the paragraphs on the Notes and Comment page. To understand how he arrived at this point, it is necessary to consider White's development as a writer and the forces that influenced it. Because some of these forces also helped to shape the *New Yorker* itself, they had a role in determining the ways magazine and writer meshed at the start of his career.

In the biographical sketch that White provided for his debut in *Harper's*, he wrote: "I was born of respectable people in Mount Vernon, New York, in 1899. There was an iron vase on the lawn and a copy of *Wet Days at Edgewood* on the library table. My parents came from Brooklyn; I presume they moved because Mount Vernon sounded tonier and would be better for the children" (561–562). White was the son of Samuel Tilly White, the president of a piano firm, and Jessie Hart White, both in their forties when he was born. He was the youngest of six children; the eldest child, Marion, was married and a mother by the time her brother Elwyn was four years old. Only the youngest daughter, Lillian, was close to him in age. White has written of his childhood:

"Being the youngest in a large family, I was usually in a crowd but often felt lonely and removed. I took to writing early, to assuage my uneasiness and collect my thoughts, and I was a busy writer long before I went into long pants" (*Letters* 1).

According to White, when he was in kindergarten his brother Stanley, eight years older, taught him to read by showing him how to sound out words in the *New York Times* (*Letters* 6). He also claimed in the *Harper's* autobiographical note, "My brother had an Oliver typewriter, and it was the noisy excitement connected with borrowing and using this machine that encouraged me to be a writer" (562). Early reading and writing and a habit of self-reliance gave White maturity and independence beyond his years, although it did not fully encourage his social growth. Throughout his life White had a tendency to avoid social interaction, particularly public appearances, and preferred even in interviews to provide written responses rather than extemporaneous conversation.

White's early habit of frequent writing influenced his development as a writer. The earliest letter in *Letters of E. B. White*, dated 21 October 1908, when White was nine, was written to Albert, his older brother, then away with Stanley attending Cornell University. Corresponding with adults, White developed an appropriate diction, which allowed him to play with language in ways that simultaneously suggested his youth but also demonstrated his control of language. His prose was conversational, relaxed, and occasionally mimetic, as when he wrote, "he s'posed he'd never been brought up that way" (*Letters* 11) or "Well there haint much more to say" (*Letters* 12) in imitation of colloquial speech. Not only in his early letters but also in the prize-winning prose published in *St. Nicholas* in 1911 and 1914, when he won a silver badge at the age of eleven for "A Winter Walk" and a gold badge at the age of fourteen for "A True Dog Story," White demonstrated considerable control over his writing and an ability to achieve a range of effects.

White's powers of imitation and parody extended to prose examples in the culture around him. In 1904, when White was five, his family began taking the train from New York to Maine to spend summer vacations at Belgrade Lake. White described the era of those vacations as "sheer enchantment" and in 1976 claimed that "the delicious smells and sounds of Belgrade Lake are still with me after many years of separation" (*Letters* 9). Although he later would write about it in "Once More to the Lake," he first celebrated Belgrade Lake in 1914, in a handmade promotional pamphlet he wrote for a neighborhood friend. In the pamphlet's prose he imitated the tone of commercial brochures and provided his own illustrations. While his love of animals, passion for boating and camping, and interest in the natural world remained with him throughout his life, he stayed equally attuned to the varieties of language use, particularly those that opened themselves up to parody.

In his senior year in high school White published poems (including a parody of Longfellow's "Song of Hiawatha"), stories, and editorials in the *Mt. Vernon High School Oracle* and served as its assistant editor. In 1917 he went to Cornell University and in his freshman year began writing for the *Cornell Daily Sun*. As editor-in-chief during his senior year, he wrote all or part of 180 editorials, some arguing for the establishment of a school of journalism at Cornell; one of them — on "The King's English" — won a writing award judged by New York columnist Arthur Brisbane. Although White was an English major, his grades were not particularly distinguished in the literature classes he took; in later life he would assert of himself, "I'm not a reader. I've never been much of a reader, and I don't know much about literature" ("Interview with Susan Frank" 7). The center of his activities at Cornell was his journalism, and it tended to make a particular kind of journalist out of him — not a reporter but an observer and commentator.

As a writer White received encouragement and support at Cornell from three faculty members in particular: William Strunk, Bristow Adams, and Martin Sampson. Will Strunk's advanced writing class, English 8, was taught out of his privately printed textbook, *The Elements of Style*, which White would revise forty years later; White received A's in both semesters of the course and later wrote memorably of Strunk's attitude toward writing. Adams, known as B. A., taught in the College of Agriculture but hosted gatherings of students in his home on Monday nights; the conversation was often wide ranging. White was a frequent visitor, making the Adamses a surrogate family with whom he corresponded often after college.

More immediately influential on White's writing were Saturday night meetings of the Manuscript Club at the home of Sampson, the chair of the English department. "Each member arrived bearing something he had written — a sketch, a poem — which was then deposited, unsigned, in a cardboard box. After a round of shandygaff and some light conversation, Professor Sampson would open the box and read the compositions, a ritual followed by a discussion period" (*Letters* 18). White once quoted Sampson's description of the Club's "creed": "To be frank, to use one's brains, to write what is in one to write, and never to take oneself too damned seriously or too damned lightly" ("Manuscript Club"). According to White's biographer, Scott Elledge, Sampson encouraged members to "avoid the expression of excessive emotion, to understate their feelings in witty or comic statements, and to aim for the tone of world-weary, supercilious elegance, like that of *Smart Set* magazine" (Elledge 56). That creed no doubt influenced the form and content of much of White's early poetry, some of which appeared in "The Berry Patch," a feature of the *Cornell Daily Sun* modeled after the columns of Franklin P. Adams, Christopher Morley, and Don Marquis in New York City newspapers. The association with all three professors and with the community of writers and journalists around him strengthened White's concept of himself as a writer, and the Cornell experience overall encouraged him to seek brevity, immediacy, wit, and self-expression in his writing.

After graduating, White declined an offer to teach at the University of Minnesota and instead tried his hand at writing for a living. In rapid succession he worked for the United Press, a silk-mill house magazine, and the American Legion News Service. (Coincidentally, he worked for the American Legion at the same time that Harold Ross, his future editor at the *New Yorker*, was editing the *American Legion Weekly* in the same building, although the two never met.) White's major accomplishment during his first year after college was having a poem published in Christopher Morley's "Bowling Green" column in the *New York Evening Post*. Discouraged by his lack of success in New York City, in the spring of 1922 he and Howard Cushman, a friend from Cornell, set out across the country in White's Model T Ford, which he christened "Hotspur." When they eventually reached Seattle, Cushman turned back.

White took a job as a reporter for the *Seattle Times*. During his brief employment there he had a two-month's stint writing a column of short items disguised as personal ads in the classified section. Despite the curious location of the column and severe constrictions on its format — "almost every sentence had to be enclosed between rules" (Hall 223) — White managed to develop the column along the lines of Morley's, Marquis's, and F. P. A.'s columns. He mixed poetry and paragraphs and developed humorous departments whose "standard headings were the forerunners of *New Yorker* newsbreak heads — 'Answers to Hard Questions' was one" (Hall 223). He was not well equipped to be a reporter and lost his job in June 1923. In response he boarded a cruise vessel bound for Alaska with only one-way fare and talked his way into a job on the return voyage to pay for the cruise. The experience was the end of his adventuring. Later that year, he returned to New York, where he took a series of jobs in advertising and contributed poetry to F. P. A.'s column, "The Conning Tower."

By his twenty-sixth birthday, in 1925, White was fairly discouraged about his career. He loved New York City, found it a stimulating place to live and explore, and enjoyed appearing frequently in F. P. A.'s column, but advertising, like reporting, was not a job to which he was suited. He wanted to make his living as a writer, but the kind of writing he most wanted to do, the kind at which he was then most successful, poetry, was not bringing in any money, and the kind of writing he was being paid for, advertising, made him morose and unhappy. It is interesting to speculate about what would have happened to White's writing during the next fifty years if the *New Yorker* had not come along.

Although the *New Yorker* itself and E. B. White's association with it both began in 1925, many of the influences that shaped the early magazine, particularly in the sections that he would eventually dominate and that would steer him in the direction of the essay, had also been long-standing influences on his own writing. He identified those influences in *Here Is New York*:

> When I first arrived in New York my personal giants were a dozen or so columnists and critics and poets whose names appeared regularly in the papers. I burned with a low steady fever just because I was on the same island with Don Marquis, Heywood Broun, Christopher Morley, Franklin P. Adams, Robert C. Benchley, Frank Sullivan, Dorothy Parker, Alexander Woollcott, Ring Lardner, and Stephen Vincent Benet. I would hang around the corner of Chambers Street and Broadway, thinking: "Somewhere in that building is the typewriter that archy the cockroach jumps on at night." New York hardly gave me a living at that period, but it sustained me. I used to walk quickly past the house in West 13th Street between Sixth and Seventh where F. P. A. lived, and the block seemed to tremble under my feet — the way Park Avenue trembles when a train leaves Grand Central. (31–32)

This homage confirms the varied influences that seem so evident in the writing White did through the twenties — indeed, in the writing White had done in college as well.

Especially important for both White and the evolving Talk of the

Town feature of the *New Yorker*, particularly the Notes and Comment page, were the first four figures on White's list. Franklin Pierce Adams (F. P. A.), Christopher Morley, Don Marquis, and Heywood Broun were the preeminent columnists of the day and had dominated the field for nearly a decade.

"What is a colyum?" Alexander McD. Stoddart asked rhetorically in 1918. "It is merely a space set aside appearing in a regular column every day" and containing a "daily melange of paragraphs, jokes, verse, reprint, contributions, letters and even illustrations" (274). Stoddart traced the form back to two Chicago columns: Eugene Field's "Sharps and Flats" and Bert Leston Taylor's "A Line O' Type or Two" (published under the byline B. L. T.). Before coming to New York, F. P. A. had succeeded B. L. T. at the *Chicago Journal,* and certain elements of Adams's column can be traced back to Taylor's and its predecessors, especially the use of poetry, paragraphs, and contributions from readers. One of Taylor's recurring features drew upon items in country newspapers that gave him "the opportunity to write a headline that will cause a chuckle" (Stoddart 289), an early model of the *New Yorker*'s "newsbreaks."

Don Marquis claimed that "when I was a kid I read, every day, Eugene Field's column in a Chicago paper, and later, George Ade's sketches, and I decided that I wanted to do something like that" ("Confessions" I, 6). Marquis wrote that his column in the *New York Evening Sun* really began when he was an editorialist for the paper:

> The editorial paragraphs in the *Evening Sun* had from time immemorial followed the editorials under a small separate headline: Notes and Comment. I deliberately wrote more Notes and Comment every day than they had ever had before, and after a few weeks, suggested that the Notes and Comment Department be lifted to another part of the page. . . . Then I gradually began to run in more and more verse, more and more comment and features of an entirely different character. Before the editor and proprietors were aware of what was going on I had a column of my own. ("Confessions" II, 59).

Notes and Comment was eventually titled "The Sun Dial" and Marquis's byline was added. Marquis included "verse, paragraphs, sketches, fables and occasional serious expressions of opinion," as well as continuing characters, such as Archy the literary cockroach, Mehitabel the cat, Hermione the Modern Young Woman, and the Old Soak (62).

Marquis also printed contributions from readers ("a great tempta-

tion when one wants a day off," 62). He noted that "a surprising number of the best, and best-known, poets of the day used to send me
stuff for nothing that they would have got well paid for if they had sent
it to the magazines" (53). Christopher Morley and Franklin P. Adams
also regularly printed contributions from readers. While the contributors were never paid, the columns were showcases for their work and
put them prominently in the company of better-known, more well-
established writers. After Morley discontinued his "Bowling Green"
column in the newspaper, he edited an anthology of poetry by contributors, including Stephen Vincent Benét, Edna St. Vincent Millay,
and Elinor Wylie. It is not surprising that White was eager to be among
this company and would continue to contribute to them, particularly
F. P. A.'s column, throughout their publication.

According to Marquis, showmanship was an important ingredient
of the column: "A column must have plenty of white space, a challenging make-up, constant variation in typographical style; not only must it
catch the eye but it must have points and corners and barbs that prick
and stimulate the vision, a surface and a texture that intrigue and cling
to and pull at the sight. Franklin P. Adams, of the New York World,
is the master hand at this sort of thing. Heywood Broun, now [1928] on
the New York Telegram, usually neglects it" (60). The variety of items,
the use of contributions, the tossed-off air about the column — all encouraged a daily schedule that was grueling under the best of circumstances. Marquis claimed that on some occasions "one gets up a column in thirty minutes, depending largely upon contributions; at other
times I have worked twelve and fifteen hours on them" (53).

In a 1916 *Scribner's Magazine* short story, Arthur Chapman described
the title character of "The Colyum Conductor" in these terms:

> Daggett ran a column of verse and paragraphs on a New York news-
> paper. It was an interesting column — "clever" was the word that
> fell oftenest on the ears of the bored Daggett — and thousands
> turned to it before they so much as glanced at the portentous head-
> ings on the front page. Daggett drew a big salary, but he was worth
> it and more. Many of his quips crept, or rather jumped, into the
> common speech of the day. Comedians and monologists made free
> use of the material in the "On the Face of Things" column. Dag-
> gett's work was steadily clipped by watchful exchange editors every-
> where, and the changes on his jests were rung by other column con-
> ductors, but before a "wheeze" had percolated to Biloxi or Yakima,

the resourceful humorist had caught the public fancy with something new. (210–211)

Daggett, Chapman tells us, "was content to put his modest initials, A. S. D., at the bottom of his column each day" (211) and had no aspirations to write a play or a novel. The success of Chapman's story depends on wide familiarity with "colyum conductors" among his audience; by the time it was published, many newspapers across the country had their own local version. In 1920, when *Everybody's Magazine* ran a monthly series called "The Colyumists' Confessional," only four of the twelve columnists it featured were from New York City, and three of them were Marquis, Morley, and Adams.

The continuing popularity of the columns induced some writers to try to explain or analyze the form. The anonymous commentator in the *Saturday Review of Literature* (probably the editor, Henry Seidel Canby), noting the colyum's popularity and variety, suggested that "under all styles its conductor's fundamental attitude is this, 'it is my daily (or weekly) endeavor to conceal from you the fact that I take myself at all seriously'" (37). He thought of it as a particularly American form: "The American mind savors much more richly the fascination of seeming to make a fool of one's-self. And then there is a lack of order and proportion, a certain wild spontaneity about the paragraphing of a Colyum, that fits well with American recklessness" (37). Mary Ellis Opdycke observed in the *New Republic*:

> It is the intimacy of detail, the naked bits of autobiography, that establish the colyum of America.
>
> These privacies take on a national importance as soon as they leave the composing room. The Pacific coast knows what the colyumist likes for breakfast, almost before he has ordered his supper; his secret sins are syndicated from Texas to Maine. Everything the New York colyumist does becomes his copy. He eats at one restaurant and notes down the menu in a rondeau; he plays poker or pool and adds up his winnings in his colyum. . . . He meets a girl on the street and quotes what he says to her, and if she is very bright what she says to him. The capital for his colyum is the order of every waking minute of his day, as well as what he has dreamed the night before — if it was fit for print. (16)

Morley, who was perhaps the most literary oriented of the major colyumists, believed that "the more a colyumist is out on the streets, making himself the reporter of the moods and oddities of men, the better his stuff will be" ("Confessions" 39). As he saw it, the "colyumist's task" was "to present a few scrawled notes of the amazing interest and colour of the city's life, . . . a task not a whit less worthy, less painful, or less baffling than that of the most conscientious novelist." It was accomplished, he said, "in surroundings of extraordinary stimulation and difficulty. It is heart-racking to struggle day by day, amid incessant interruption and mêlée, to snatch out of the hurly-burly some shreds of humour or pathos or (dare one say?) beauty, and phrase them intelligibly" (40).

Marquis and Morley took column conducting to be something of a calling, but Mary Ellen Opdycke had reservations about the columns, particularly their unevenness of quality (especially in the selection of contributed material) and their inordinate influence. "Chiefly are the colyumists popular for their charm, their wit, their brisk novelty. But a sinister hint of their power as advertising agents hangs about their attractiveness. It is fun for the young writers to know them, but it is also good policy" (17). She questioned the need of readers to feel a sense of intimacy with the social circle described or invented by the columnists.

The column tradition was sufficiently well established that Charles L. Edson could write *The Gentle Art of Columning* in 1920, with "prefaces" by Marquis, Adams, Morley, and George Horace Lorimer. The greater portion of the book illustrates successful and unsuccessful elements of columning, such as "The Punning Paragraph," "The News-slant Paragraph," "Paragraphs that Jingle," and "The Humorous Editorial." "The News-slant Paragraph is the essence of comic journalism," Edson wrote. "Timeliness is its essence, and therefore the News-slant Paragraph is journalism literally. Journal means daily, and the News Paragraph is a midge whose life cycle is a day. Its twin sisters, the Pun and the Epigram, may live for days or forever" (41). Adams is quoted frequently to exemplify "the art of columning," and he, Marquis, and Morley are meant to exemplify the best and most current models of "comic journalism."

In a 1923 article Carl Van Doren identified Franklin P. Adams of "The Conning Tower," Christopher Morley of "The Bowling Green," Don Marquis of "The Lantern," and Heywood Broun of "It Seems to Me" as "the most widely known columnists of the period" and labeled them "the Town Wits." He defined them as columnists who "retail the gossip, promulgate the jests, discuss the personalities, represent the manners of New York. . . . Nothing is too great for them to bring it before the bar of laughter; nothing is too small for them to flash a beam of light upon it" (310). Van Doren identified them as descendants of the periodical essayists of earlier times: "They are town wits, as Addison and Steele were in their merry London, as Irving and Paulding were in the New York of a hundred years ago." He pictured them, like "their elder prototypes," "foregather[ing] in what might once have been called taverns or coffee-houses, or sit[ting] each in his favorite haunts with his friends and hangers-on." The things they say are not "caught up and spread by the gossip of the listeners"; instead, their "daily columns [are] yawning to be filled with light, gay, personal by-products of such conversations." Although Van Doren recognized a change of medium in the transition from periodical essay to newspaper and a change of audience as well, he nonetheless declared that "by virtue of their essential qualities these column-conductors, closely as they fit their times, continue a tradition which goes back to one of the earliest moments in the history of human fun — the moment when cities began to demand of their wits a more edged, more sophisticated, more varied, and more continuous entertainment than had been demanded among the farms and villages" (315). Especially pertinent in this praise are such terms as "human fun" and "continuous entertainment," a decidedly slanted interpretation of what the periodical essayists were doing, but Van Doren's smug approval of the cosmopolitan columnists — "more edged, more sophisticated, more varied" — suggests the impact they had on their readers, not only displaying "sophistication" but also bestowing it.

The colyumists were never more popular and influential than in the years immediately following World War I. Even for the best of them, however, the exhausting demands of column conducting were hard to maintain. Morley's "Bowling Green" column for the *Evening Post* ran from 1920 to 1923; in 1924 he took it to the new weekly magazine, *Saturday Review of Literature*, where he ran it as a chiefly literary column until 1941. Marquis gave up writing a daily column in 1925; even though he felt that, in the two and a half years of "The Lantern" in the *New York Tribune*, "I did better stuff than I'd ever done before," eventually "I got to seeing that column as a grave, twenty-three inches long, into which I buried a part of myself every day — a part that I tore, raw and bleeding, from my brain. It became a nightmare" (62).

When E. B. White came to write for the *New Yorker*, he would have the opportunity to draw upon the experience and the expression of the columnists he admired. Particularly in the 1920s the verse he wrote (usually under the byline E. B. W., frequently in F. P. A.'s column) and the casuals he published can be placed in a thriving comic tradition. Several critics have placed White in the context of American humorists, including Mencken, Lardner, Benchley, Marquis, and his friend and *New Yorker* colleague James Thurber (see especially Blair and Hill; Yates), but it is essentially the columns of the Town Wits — Adams, Morley, and Marquis — that influenced his work on the "Notes and Comment" page of the *New Yorker*, the writing that led eventually to his work in the essay. In some ways, during his first decade with the magazine, he took the paragraph form they had modeled to its most brilliant level of accomplishment, but he also felt the dispiriting weight of its regular and unrelenting obligation. The years writing Notes and Comment under the influence of the colyumists would color the writing he did for the rest of his career.

The New York in which the *New Yorker* first appeared, the literary/journalistic milieu that E. B. White was prepared by his reading tastes and college writing experience to join, had a recognizable atmosphere and influential writers modeling the most popular forms. Its creator, Harold Ross, had been an itinerant reporter around the country and had worked with Franklin P. Adams and Alexander Woollcott on the *Stars and Stripes*, the military newspaper, during World War I. After the war Ross, Adams, and Woollcott maintained their friendship in New York. Ross was editor first of the *Home Sector*, an attempt at a postwar *Stars and Stripes*, and then the *American Legion Weekly*; Adams continued as conductor of his highly successful colyum, "The Conning Tower," which he had been running before the war; Woollcott worked as a journalist for the *New York Times*. Eventually, beginning in 1919, all three became part of a literary/journalistic social circle that came to be known as the Algonquin Round Table. The group that met frequently at the Algonquin Hotel was, as Thomas Kunkel points out, "mostly young — late twenties and early thirties — not terribly accomplished, and little known beyond their circle" (77). F. P. A. was the oldest and the most established figure, and the group included Adams's fellow columnist, Heywood Broun, who had not yet reached the status he would soon share with Adams, Marquis, and Morley. Other figures just making their mark were two writers for *Vanity Fair*, Dorothy Parker and Robert Benchley; the future playwrights George S. Kauffmann, Marc Connelly, and Robert Sherwood; the novelist Edna Ferber; and Harpo Marx. After Ross began the *New Yorker* in 1925, a number of these figures eventually became contributors — for example, Parker "supplied about the only readable material there was in the first two issues" (pseudonymous theater reviews and a satire) and later was acclaimed for her verse, fiction, and literary column, "Constant Reader"; Woollcott provided an anonymous profile in the third issue and eventually wrote a one-page column, "Shouts and Murmurs," from 1928 to 1934; Benchley wrote a humorous essay the first year and also served as a reviewer; others contributed at least occasionally, and some of them frequently. The *New Yorker* was partly spun out of the atmosphere around the Round Table, although Kunkel is surely right to note that Ross knew "he couldn't build the magazine on his famous friends — which in the long run was a blessing since it forced the *New Yorker* to find fresh voices of its own" (104–105).

Far more significantly, the magazine also came out of the milieu of such earlier humorous and satirical periodicals as *Life*, *Judge*, *Vanity Fair*, *Smart Set*, *American Mercury*, and the British periodical *Punch*. Ross himself briefly edited *Judge* in 1924, while he was planning and promoting his own magazine. At *Judge* Ross found elements that he "would appropriate for, or refine in" his own magazine, including "casuals, 'Newsbreaks' (those column-ending tweaks of newspaper mistakes), movie reviews, celebrity news," and several of the writers and artists he published there later wrote or illustrated for the *New Yorker* (Kunkel 90). When the *New Yorker* began it was closer in spirit to those humor magazines, particularly in its cartoons and jokes, than to the more literate and sophisticated magazine it became. Scattered throughout its pages were also such regular components drawn from the colyumists as "punning paragraphs," "news-slant paragraphs," epigrams, as well as light or satiric verse and jibes about language usage (the stuff of newsbreaks).

The *New Yorker* first appeared in February 1925. Ross had hoped to create a weekly magazine of wit and style, directed at sophisticated readers in New York City rather than general readers across the nation. In spite of the lower-level humor of the *Judge* tradition, Ross seemed to extend to the magazine Carl Van Doren's identification of the Town Wit columnists with the literary tradition of Addison, Steele, Hazlitt, Irving, and Paulding. It was an identification the columnists themselves made: Morley was a self-conscious antiquarian; Adams filled his column one day a week "with a first-class parody of Samuel Pepys's diary, filled with trivia, name-dropping, and comic contretemps" (Blair and Hill 410). Its first cover (and the anniversary cover each year thereafter) pictured a Regency fop of the age of Hazlitt and Lamb, later identified as "Eustace

Tilley," replete with top hat, high collar, and monocle. The very title itself, the *New Yorker*, was a hearkening back to the literary periodicals of the eighteenth century — *The Tatler, The Spectator, The Guardian, The Rambler, The Idler, The Connoisseur.* The casual tone of the Notes and Comment page as well as the rest of Talk of the Town section recalled Hazlitt's idea of essays as "table talk." The Talk section, Ross insisted, "should be like dinner-table conversation" (Thurber 102) and depended upon a sense of immediacy and locality: "'Talk' was to be an entertaining miscellany of anecdotes about interesting people and events on the New York scene. It needed an easy informal style, blending the reportorial and the essayistic, and a strict economy of means" (Holmes 107).

Talk of the Town items were published anonymously under the collective byline "The New Yorkers" and, together with Notes and Comment, would establish the tone and style generally identified with the *New Yorker.* Despite the raggedness of the initial issues and the changes that the magazine continually made over its first year, "one cannot help but be struck by how many of the now-familiar elements were in place from the start" — that is, were part of Ross's original design (Kunkel 105).

Ross's prospectus for the magazine was emphatic about its tone and perspective: "*The New Yorker* will be a reflection in word and picture of metropolitan life. It will be human. Its general tenor will be one of gaiety, wit and satire, but it will be more than a jester. It will not be what is commonly called sophisticated, in that it will assume a reasonable degree of enlightenment on the part of its readers. It will hate bunk" (Kramer 61). He referred specifically to the sections of the magazine that would become the Talk of the Town:

> There will be a page of editorial paragraphs, commenting on the week's events in a manner not too serious.
>
> There will be a personal mention column — a jotting down in the small-town newspaper style of the comings, goings and doings in the village of New York. This will contain some josh and some news value.
>
> *The New Yorker* will carry each week several pages of prose and verse, short and long, humorous, satirical and miscellaneous. (Kramer 62)

He concluded: "*The New Yorker* is a magazine avowedly published for a metropolitan audience and thereby will escape an influence which hampers most national publications. It expects a considerable national circulation, but this will come from persons who have a metropolitan interest" (Kramer 62–63). These qualities of the magazine as Ross imagined them were closely related to the qualities that distinguished the columnists and earlier humor magazines. However the magazine would change over the years, the initial prospectus was grounded in a milieu familiar to Ross — and to White as well.

The first issues were unexceptional and the reception by readers was lackadaisical at best.

> Ross's problem was not so much *The New Yorker's* format, which was slowly gelling, but its execution, which wasn't. It wasn't that he didn't know what he wanted. He dreamed of toppling conventions. He envisioned news and comment and a dash of gossip, delivered with cheek. He wanted the *New Yorker* to be informed but off-hand ("We were on our way to the Winter Garden when we overheard . . .") and humorous throughout. And he wanted it all bent to his own peculiar notion of a sophisticate's world. (Kunkel 107)

The magazine began to evolve and improve only as it developed a stable of writers and editors whose unique talents were matched to the magazine's needs.

All accounts of the *New Yorker's* history identify four people as particularly important: Katharine Sergeant Angell, who was hired in the summer of 1925 and became one of its most influential editors; E. B. White, who began contributing in the first year, joined the magazine full time in 1927 and eventually assumed responsibility for its opening Notes and Comment page — playwright Marc Connelly credited him with bringing "the steel and music to the magazine" (Kunkel 147); James Thurber, whose responsibility for the Talk of the Town section meshed perfectly with White's opening page; and Wolcott Gibbs, a versatile writer and editor. Except for Thurber, the involvement of these people with the magazine continued throughout their careers — Angell and White married in 1929 and retired together three decades later — and their early work for it helped to establish its tone and sensibility. In addition, particularly in the case of both White and Thurber, whose work would eventually go beyond the *New Yorker*, the magazine established them in the front ranks of contemporary wit and humor.

🐝 The path that led E. B. White to the essay proceeded through a long period of writing paragraphs for the Notes and Comment section of the *New Yorker* in addition to other forms of writing: the poetry for F.P.A.'s column and the magazine, the casuals (humorous fiction and sketches), the occasional theater or film or book review, the rewrites of Talk of the Town features, the continual production of newsbreaks by the thousands. In sheer volume, however, White's Comment pieces constitute the major writing of his career, and, in spite of the attention he received by the end of the 1920s as a poet of light verse and as a humorist, his anonymous paragraphs in Notes and Comment had the largest and most dedicated readership. During the early 1930s, when White was virtually the sole author of the feature, he produced what came to be identified as the *New Yorker* style. His success in that form was such that other writers, such as James Thurber and Wolcott Gibbs, tended to emulate White in their own contributions to the feature, although each surely had his own unique voice in the other writing he did.

White had been familiar with the paragraph as a literary form from the brief editorials he had written in college, the reading he had done of the columns of F. P. A., Morley, and Marquis, and his brief experience developing a column in the personals section for the *Seattle Times*. But when he came to write Comment for the *New Yorker*, he was strongly influenced by his success writing humorous casuals. Most of these revealed an individual perspective that identified them as White's writing.

"A Step Forward," his first accepted publication in the *New Yorker*, drew upon his experience in advertising as well as his interest in the turning of the seasons. It consisted of a series of brief advertisements for Spring, such as:

New Beauty of Tone in 1925 Song Sparrow
Into every one of this season's song sparrows has been built the famous VERNAL tone. Look for the distinguishing white mark on the breast. ("Step" 21)

Spring would be virtually an annual subject in White's writing. "A Step Forward" appeared in the ninth issue of the magazine. A clever but unexceptional piece, in retrospect it suggests something uniquely White — the juxtaposition of the commercial world to which White objected (and in which he made his living) with the natural world that he valued (and in which he felt more comfortable). White's touch is delicate, the tension of the piece arising from juxtaposition of its elements rather than explicit commentary.

At the heart of most of White's early casuals is an incident or observation identifiable as an actual event. For example, White's second *New Yorker* acceptance, "Defense of the Bronx River" (published 9 May 1925), is a whimsical piece in which the humor arises from exaggeration ("the Bronx River goes virtually dry every Sunday afternoon from so many motorists using it to fill their radiators") and from the narrator's obvious attempt to drag in facts at the expense of logic ("When Pola Negri first came to New York a million people awaited her opinion of the skyline. Yet how many of these million know that the Bronx River is wider than the Hutchinson and not so wide as the Ohio?"). Yet the article actually does trace the flow of the Bronx River and includes detail drawn from actual observation ("In Spring the willows along the shore turn a pleasant yellow, and the stream takes their color, and the little tributaries of the Bronx come rushing down from the hills in pipes and empty into the main stream, augmenting it and causing white rapids at Bedford Park").

In the other casuals of the period White focused on an observed tableau or vignette: a janitor polishing a fireplug with liquid from a Gordon's Gin bottle, an unemployed man idling on the street, an old drunk on the subway, noises of New York City, a fantasy drawn from elements observed from an apartment window. As he wrote to his brother Stanley, these were "the small things of the day," "the trivial matters of the heart," "the inconsequential but near things of this living," the "little capsule[s] of truth" continually important as the subtext of White's writing.

The "faint squeak of mortality" he listened for sounded particularly in the casuals in which White used himself as a central character. The persona varies from piece to piece, but usually the first-person narrator is someone struggling with embarrassment or confusion over trivial events. In "Garter Motif," subtitled "An Author's Caprice in the Presence of a Haberdasher," he struggles with his attempts to assert himself and buy flashier garters; in "No Hat," he enjoys befuddling customers in a department store who mistake him for a clerk; in "Open Letter to My Burglar," he critiques the performance of someone who robbed his apartment. In all these cases, though the casuals may range from light whimsy to madcap farce, they center on the sort of commonplace incidents that anyone living in New York City might experience or observe.

One of the best examples — and in some ways a turning point for his writing — is "Child's Play," in which a waitress spills another customer's buttermilk on him and he considers how to make the incident an occasion for mildly heroic behavior. At one point he writes:

> As a matter of record, I was doing pretty well. I hadn't jumped; I hadn't sworn; I hadn't burst into tears; I hadn't made a wry face. I was just sitting there, all buttermilk, patting my stomach in a desultory fashion with paper napkin — which, I leave it to my readers, is about all you can expect of a man. I was even fairly content with the world. "Perhaps," I mused, "this is one of those 'smart backgrounds' THE NEW YORKER is always talking about." ("Child's Play" 17)

The significance of the piece is White's discovery of a particular voice. As his biographer, Scott Elledge, has observed, with the publication of this "self-mocking story of a 'personal triumph'" White "had found a way to make a living by writing about himself — briefly and frequently, like other journalist-essayists, beginning with Addison and Steele. He liked to 'write short'; he liked the freedom to report whatever most interested him at the time; and he liked to be published promptly" (*E. B. White* 107). In the beginning of his relationship with the magazine it seemed like an ideal place for him to work, and it gave him an outlet that initially increased his range as a prose writer. It also helped give him a persona he could carry over into writing Comment.

White's first paragraph for Notes and Comment appeared in the issue for 2 October 1926:

> The only thing more fun than eating a ham sandwich in a polo box at Meadow Brook is paying for a purchase in Woolworth's with a ten-dollar bill. They ring a bell. They actually do. It seems that sales girls may not handle such large sums, for no sooner had we tendered the pretty black and yellow ten-dollar note in payment for a red mouse trap than the girl pounded on a bell and shrilled loudly for Mr. Kempler, Mr. Kempler. Pretty soon Mr. Kempler came, took hold of the situation, and in less than five minutes, we fought our way out through admiring throngs, with nine dollars and ninety cents in change, half expecting the crowd to break out and cheer us to the echo. (17)

As in such casuals as "Child's Play," White projects a commonplace situation in almost heroic terms. His persona is again that of a merry individual delighted by the trivial event, and the narrative is again developed up to the point of the narrator's exit. The tone of the feature is embodied in the use of the first person plural, the editorial or clinical "we," and the deliberate conversational preciosity of "They actually do."

Under the system in place at the magazine, this paragraph was published with a number of other paragraphs by other authors and assembled on the Notes and Comment page by the Comment editor. But this piece bears the hallmark of White's writing, and later, when White as Comment editor was rewriting paragraphs proposed, suggested, or drafted by other writers, he was so able to make the pieces his own that it is nearly impossible to tell which is a piece originated by White and which is a piece he rewrote and shaped from another source. Eventually, as White took over more and more responsibility for the feature, the original source for the majority of items was White himself.

The first Notes and Comment page entirely composed by White was published 26 February 1927. It contains five paragraphs, one about encountering author Rupert Hughes in a bookstore, one about a stationer selecting Christmas card stock in February, one on the Museum of Natural History, one on an expensive basketful of orchids in a shop window, and one about the reasons people buy question-and-answer books. The only connections among the five items are the general tone and the authorial persona, the fact that only one item begins with a straightforward declarative sentence, and the twist in the endings of all five. The beginnings run, in order, as follows:

> Always moderately willing to flex the knee in the presence of greatness, we found our genual tribute somewhat painfully protracted the other day in Brentano's.

> To witness, on a very cheerless day, a very solemn man examining a card which read "Merry Christmas and a Bright and Happy New Year" was our solemn, cheerless experience yesterday.

> Quite well aware that most persons, in their earthly glee, are too forgetful of the heavenly bodies, we are greatly pleased to hear that plans are under way for a stargazing wing at the Museum of Natural History.

> Wicker and small is the basketful of orchids in a Madison Avenue florist's window. Terse and to the point is the tag, $100. Moody and thoughtful are we, who stand each day and survey the luxurious

nosegay for no more reason than we hope to be lucky enough to see who buys it.

Our report is now ready on why people are so delighted to ask and answer questions that a book full of them has been published. (17)

Three of the five focus on the narrator as bystander — someone who happens by a place where he observes something curious or someone else doing something. Two of the pieces arise from news items about construction plans and book publication. There is no common thread to the paragraphs, other than the persona of the commentator, who is projected as someone curious, observant, supercilious, and whimsical, with facility and delight in language. These characteristics are made clear by the endings of the paragraphs, which are, in order:

> We hereby notify all concerned that twenty minutes is longer than we commonly defer to an author, unless it be a woman and pretty.

> To us the whole greeting card industry has the artificial aspect of a marriage arranged by the parents of the couple. Merry Christmas in February. How stuffy!

> We are inordinately fond of the Natural History Museum, partly from childhood memories, partly because the Museum — besides being fearful and wondrous — is a hospitable place to go, and managed with intelligence.

> It is such window displays that keep us from Getting Things Done.

> That is our report. Ask us another.

The opening paragraph recounts how the narrator is first prevented from carrying out his business by the arrival of a famous author and then unable to get the clerk's attention; the emphasis is really on the gulf that separates the famous author and the narrator, particularly as represented by the attentiveness of the clerk, but the final phrase undercuts the hauteur of the narrator by revealing his weakness. In the second paragraph the criticism of the greeting card industry is undercut by the stuffiness of the narrator's disdain. In the fourth the concluding sentence, with its capitalized "Getting Things Done," turns the reader's attention to the narrator and away from the implicit social criticism of the paragraph. In the fifth the conclusion circles back to the opening remark about the report and implicates the author as one who delights in answering questions. Only the third ending is really an endorsement of something, yet it too provides a personal focus that makes the item something more than a bit of news or an editorial statement in favor of building a planetarium.

From this beginning White went on to write Notes and Comment in its entirety with increasing frequency; occasionally, he wrote all but one or two items every week. By the end of 1926 White had contributed one paragraph apiece to each of three widely separate Comment pages; in 1927 he contributed to twenty-two Comments and wrote all of twenty-nine; in 1928 he wrote all of forty-one and contributed to seven others. From 1929 on the number of Comments solely written by White increased steadily from twenty-nine to thirty-six in 1930, thirty-nine in 1931, forty-seven in 1932, fifty in 1933, and fifty-two in 1934 and 1935; in those years most of the other Comments to which other writers contributed were largely written by White. Between 1930 and 1936 White wrote the bulk of Notes and Comment between fifty and fifty-two weeks — more than 250 paragraphs — a year (see Appendix 1). At the same time his bylined articles and his contributions to Talk of the Town, as well as his poetry, decreased. His chief work had become the writing of paragraphs.

3 &

"A FLOW OF UNCANCELED CLAUSES"
Composing Early Comment

The Notes and Comment page of the *New Yorker* evolved very slowly over the decades that White wrote for it. Because he was instrumental in guiding that evolution, a history of the page is also, to some extent, a history of White's metamorphoses from paragrapher to editorialist to essayist. Influenced by such shaping events as the Roaring Twenties and Prohibition, the Depression, the Second World War, and the Cold War, the *New Yorker* responded to changing times by slowly making the "editorial paragraphs" of Notes and Comment more editorial and less paragraph. But in the magazine's first decade, especially after White became the principal writer for the Comment page they were closer in tone, format, and pace to the paragraphs of the popular colyumists.

The first page of the Talk of the Town section of the *New Yorker* set the continuing tone for the magazine. It had originally been a page of gossip but quickly was modified into a series of five to ten paragraphs called Notes and Comment. Under the system that developed, any number of writers were responsible for the paragraphs. They could also contribute the news items that made up the titled features in Talk, though none of the pieces were bylined. Often staff writers were responsible for taking the rough reports of the Talk features and the general ideas in a contributors' file and working them up into publishable Comment. White did his turn as rewrite man for Talk, which for most of the 1930s was principally the responsibility of James Thurber, but eventually his chief duty was Comment. The popular view that White in Notes and Comment and Thurber in Talk of the Town created the consistent, identifiable "voice of the *New Yorker*" is essentially accurate.

In the first decade of the *New Yorker*, anyone on the staff could contribute to Notes and Comment, either by discussing a subject with whoever was going to write the page that week — a Thurber drawing shows White scowling at a man barking a Comment idea at him — or by writing up a paragraph and submitting it to a Comment "bank" from which another writer could draw individual items and rewrite them. For Notes and Comment both the contributor of the original idea and the eventual paragraph author were credited and paid; more than most magazines the *New Yorker* had a tendency to pay for promising ideas and undeveloped drafts that never led to publication. White referred to the system under which he wrote Comment in his preface to his first clipbook of paragraphs, *Every Day Is Saturday* (1934).

> It should be clear at the outset that [these paragraphs] lack a kind of purity of origin; that is, although I wrote them (or seem to remember having written them), other people contributed in some degree to their content. This is embarrassing, but I don't know what to do about it. I would like to credit everybody with an assist, but there are no records which might make this possible; and, anyway, the thing isn't as clear cut as all that. A commentator, working anonymously under cover of the editorial "we," isn't choosy where he picks up his ingredients. He gets them from a thousand mysterious and unremembered sources, the way a country dog gets his breakfast. (vii)

Actually, the payment records of the *New Yorker* are an invaluable source of information on who wrote which anonymous item, and White and Thurber scholars in particular have consulted them. Manuscripts of White's held in the collection at Cornell University routinely credit originator as well as writer of items that White himself did not originate. White may have been uncomfortable about the nature of this haphazard form of collaboration; in 1941, when he and Katharine completed *A Subtreasury of American Humor*, he was insistent that every writer in the anthology should share in the royalties for the book.

The Comment bank was initially an attempt to assure a backlog of material to draw on because in the early days of the magazine the shortage of copy led to the inclusion of weaker pieces than Ross and his staff would have preferred. Ross and his successor, William Shawn, were noted for maintaining exceptionally large backlogs of material. In the case of Comment, the bank assured that there would always be something to draw on if the Comment page writer ran out of fresh observations or came up against the deadline with too few items to make up a page. Sometimes the paragraphs that came from the bank had lost their freshness and relevance. The page was rather like a buffet that prided itself on fresh ingredients but continually resorted to left-overs, items repackaged from the back of the refrigerator and occasionally well past their expiration date. Given the circumstances of its preparation, the page could often offer wildly varying levels of quality. Even in Comment pages conceived and written entirely by White, as so many eventually were, paragraphs published consecutively could have been composed months apart. The pool of paragraphs he could draw on was necessarily larger than the number he printed. Much material ended up unused and discarded because it was no longer timely or pertinent or because no one was able to work it up into a publishable paragraph or find a place for it among more pertinent and more polished pieces.

Timeliness was an important element of Notes and Comment. In order to stay timely a writer had to be in touch with the currents of daily affairs in New York City and, to a lesser extent, the nation. White's method of gathering material frequently resembled that described by Christopher Morley in "Confessions of a Colyumist": "But it is fun. One never buys a package of tobacco, crosses a city square, enters a trolley-car or studies a shop-window without trying, in a baffled, hopeless way, to peer through the frontage of the experience, to find some glimmer of the thoughts, emotions, and meanings behind. And in the long run such a habit of inquiry must bear fruit in understanding and sympathy" (40). This meant constant attention to likely material for Comment, either droll observations of the passing parade, arch responses to the daily headlines and recent news events, or trenchant reactions to political, cultural, and social affairs; in a word, commentary on whatever New Yorkers might be — or might like to feel they were — conversant with. Such currency gave the Comment page considerable liveliness, even if it diminished its shelf life. A generally admiring review of *Every Day Is Saturday* in the *New York Times Book Review* noted that paragraphs in the collection suffered not only from variations in "the amount and quality of their humor" but also were "handicapped somewhat by being deprived of their association." The review continues: "Humor has an unscrupulous trick of evaporating from human happenings, as juice evaporates from a Fall apple during Winter months and leaves it dry and flavorless. So Mr. White had the stars against him when he sat down to make this compilation, and readers must not think the fault is his if they fail to find in some of these paragraphs the amusement the fresh pages of the *New Yorker* afforded them" ("Paragraphs" 9).

Every Day Is Saturday collected 229 paragraphs published between 7 January 1928 and 11 August 1934. They make reference to such current figures as Coolidge, Hoover, Roosevelt, Mrs. Roosevelt, Jimmy Walker, Arthur Brisbane, Dorothea Dix, Ed Sullivan, Walter Lippman, Ring Lardner, H. L. Mencken, George Bernard Shaw, Dorothy Parker, Edna St. Vincent Millay, James M. Cain, William Faulkner, Ernest Hemingway, Eugene O'Neill, H. G. Wells, Father Coughlin, Charles Lindbergh, Gene Tunney, Max Baer, the Ziegfield Follies, the Depression, Prohibition, the CCC, Texas Guinan, Helen Morgan, Helen Kane and Betty Boop, the Dollar Book Club, Rockwell Kent, Knute Rockne, Einstein, and Prince Michael Romanoff. Generally, the references assume shared knowledge with the reader; an item titled "Interpretation" begins with the sentences: "The failure of La Willebrandt to put Mistress Guinan and Mistress Morgan in jail must have saddened her heart. Hostesses are still at large, where they can get at Methodists" (*Every Day* 30). Although Morgan is later identified as "Helen Morgan," the identification is not enlarged upon or intended to clarify the identities of the principals. White's comment on the outcome of the Morgan trial assumes that the reader knows the context of the comment, including the principal players; the reader is assumed to be current on the same affairs that the commentator is. Thus, when one comment begins, "Mr. Morgan, of Madison Avenue, pointed out over the radio the other night . . ." (124), and another begins, "The text of the Morgan inquiry would make a Primer of Power" (180), only the informed contemporary reader can be certain of the identity of these Morgans. (In uncollected Comment White had a habit of joking about Otto Kahn, the Donald Trump of his day. How long will this very sentence remain intelligible?)

Part of the sense of purpose to the Notes and Comment page is its role as both chronicle and commentary. *Every Day Is Saturday* reprints several paragraphs expressly written to catalog current events. The opening Comment, "Threshold," originally published in the first issue of 1928, sounds the theme that no "semblance of unity," no "identifiable rhythm," appears in the "affairs of the spinning world." The paragraph then lists seemingly random and unrelated items:

A hundred feet below the sea, dead men lie in a sunken submarine. In the sky above Guatemala, a boy flies a plane and writes signed stories for the *Times* about good will. In the Gulf Stream off Miami, the champion prizefighter of the world is out fishing with William Lyon

Phelps. At the piers in the Hudson River, ladies are sailing to look at Malta and Crete who have never looked at Rivington Street, Goerck Street, or Tompkins Square. On Sixth Avenue, half an hour ago, a man who looked like a seaman asked us for a quarter for a flop. Love ends at thirty, says Will C. Durant. Everyone should leave money to Columbia, says Nicholas Murray Butler. The sentiment of the country is for peace, believes Calvin Coolidge. In Washington, chemists are threatened with arrest for analyzing liquor which citizens are afraid to drink till they make sure it isn't poison. Just before sunrise, astronomers scan the heavens for a comet which has failed to show up, confounding science if not the Creator. In jail a young man regrets having killed a girl, and everyone knows his name, has seen his picture, has read his story. On a belt that never stops turning, Fords are being produced that have gears instead of bands, and everyone knows that too. Bells ring. It is the New Year. Possibly a happy one. Certainly a frantic one. (1–2)

The ending of the piece draws no conclusion, reaches no point, and could well end paragraphs detailing the beginning of almost every year; the body of the paragraph is a catalog of current events apparently selected for their contrast with one another: the death of the men in submarines with the flight of the young aviator, the fishing of the boxer with the cruising of wealthy women and the poverty of the seaman asking for a handout, the problems of various scientists with the mass knowledge of a lurid murder case and well-advertised business developments. The paragraph could have been written by thumbing through a few recent newspapers and writing down whatever items seemed sufficiently random or juxtaposed spontaneously with one another.

At various times throughout the book similar catalogs appear: "Great Days of 1928" recites a number of recent events and ends inconclusively with the sentence, "Put them all together, they spell something" (8); "Grace Notes" begins with the heading: "Grace notes for an unborn historian" (165), then catalogs a series of unconnected declarative sentences about the start of 1933, and finally breaks off after a declaration rather than a conclusion; "1933" declares: "In many ways, 1933 was our most immemorial year. . . . It was the year when a dwarf sat in J. P. Morgan's lap" (203), repeats that second sentence several times as a motif amid otherwise unconnected tidbits and observations, and ultimately ends with it.

One of the most intriguing catalog items is entitled "Chair Car," from the first issue of 1932. "Train thoughts are best," it opens; "the thoughts of travelers are long, long thoughts" (102), a copychange of well-known lines from Longfellow's "My Lost Youth," "A boy's will is the wind's will, / And the thoughts of youth are long, long thoughts." The item fills the entire Notes and Comment page of the issue by purporting to be the random observations of a passenger on a train: "In a parlor car the mind gets its second wind. Trains are useful, too, to minnesingers; from the soft monotony of rail travel comes a metrical distillation. Inner thought: it is easier to make rhymes on a train; the lines come out the right length because the wheel clicks never miss their count. Idea: if we were a poet we would spend all our time on trains" (102–103). Labels for some sentences ("Inner thought," "Idea") echo a favorite device used by Don Marquis. The Comment suggests common elements of composition for such paragraphs — reliance on echoes of familiar phrases and devices that come readily to hand, close observation of commonplace occurrences, personal reflection couched as disinterested generality ("if we were a poet" — White had already published his collection *The Lady Is Cold*).

The piece reads like a journal entry composed over the course of a journey by train. In fact, it may well have been. The catalog items may seem to be collections of "grace notes for unborn historians," but they are also easier columns to write because they are about disconnectedness. White once observed in a Comment about former president Calvin Coolidge's daily column: "Every writer of paragraphs or columns knows that his best stuff is apt to be not the finely chiseled piece, but the occasional flow of uncanceled clauses — the regurgitated spirit — words that run to paper swift as rain" (*Every* 78). It is arguable whether a Comment like "Chair Car" represents White's best stuff, although it has a vitality and energy some of the more well turned pieces lack, but the catalog Comment, the descriptive observation, may be valued more highly for its pertinence in the writer's mind. At any rate, such items — arising from "a flow of uncanceled clauses" — allowed some relief from the rigors of finely chiseled pieces.

Few of the paragraphs in *Every Day Is Saturday* originally made up an entire Notes and Comment page in the *New Yorker*. Rather, they were selected from a vast array of unconnected paragraphs. The collection makes no attempt to give representative items from each issue. Sometimes the dates at the start of each selection (every one of them a Saturday, the day the magazine was published) indicate that several in a row have come from the same issue, but an examination of those original issues reveals the tenuousness of the occasional interconnections. For example, both "Below Fourteenth," about the effect of prosperity on Greenwich Village (23–24), and "Hoboken," about the growing theater district in Hoboken (24–25), are from the 30 March 1929 *New Yorker*, but the opening sentence of "Hoboken" ("It's really too bad that we got started on the subject of success, because that leads us by easy stages to Hoboken") is more of a facetious pretense at a segue than an actual transition to a related paragraph. Another linked set in *Every Day Is Saturday* is the series containing "Dollar Books," about the intention of publishers to market books outside bookstores; "Emotions of Artisans," about Rockefeller's attitude toward cathedral workmen; and "The Origins of Poetry," about poetry written in prison. They are all connected by their concern with creativity on some level and the environments in which it emerges, but they are not explicitly related and seem to be more a felicitous juxtaposition of paragraphs than an expressly thematic unit.

More often, the items from a single issue are even less connected than these. Paragraphs from the 28 December 1929 issue are about humor, the passenger who fainted when a luxury liner sank, and the nature of art and antique auctions; the 4 October 1930 paragraphs are about a yachting award, the heaven of the spiritists, and the month of September; the 29 August 1931 paragraphs deal with cellophane, the Physical Culture Hotel of Bernarr McFadden, and the Empress Eugenie Hat. Harold Ross objected to the idea of developing interrelated paragraphs throughout the page; White had sometimes found a way around Ross's rules by writing long single paragraphs with distinct subdivisions marked by ellipses, which in effect created subparagraphs within a paragraph. It was not until 1935 that Ross — still insisting that Notes and Comment should be an anonymous, first-person-plural opening page — allowed White himself, rather than the Comment page editor, to decide in what order the paragraphs would appear. As Elledge notes, "this concession gave White the opportunity to develop loosely structured essays from a series of self-contained paragraphs, all more or less related to one theme" (193). However, the key terms in that judgment are the qualifiers: "loosely structured," "more or less related," "self-contained paragraphs."

Most of the items in *Every Day Is Saturday* are slight, often drawn from other media, reacting to reports on recent events, contemporary personalities, fads, fashions, and foibles of one kind or another. Many comment on the literary scene of the day, such as the notice of George Bernard Shaw's much publicized visit to the United States or the lecture tours of popular authors like Louis Bromfield.

Nonetheless, the paragraph form itself did not demand frothy writing or light thinking. In remarks no doubt meant to include White's late Comment writing as well, W. W. Watt observed:

> In the slightest of his "Notes and Comments," the note is likely to be a description of an acute social symptom, the comment a critical diagnosis.
>
> This means that White's reader is never floated for long on the surface of current events. Sooner or later he is carried into the broader and deeper currents where the themes are no longer topical but timeless: the cycle of birth and death; the arrival and departure of the seasons; the memories of youth; the ecstasy of love; the sacraments of Nature; the magic of language; the folly of Homo sapiens, unaware of the erosion of freedom; the ignorance of Homo faber, who prefers the finny monsters of the thruway to the Model T, and remains equally indifferent to the menace of the bomb and the miracle of the egg. (Watt 259)

Some of the early Comments dealt with subjects White would return to over the years, in even weightier pronouncements. He repeatedly attacked censorship, pollution of the environment, militarism, nationalism, the crassness of politicians, publicists, and propagandists. For example, two Comments in *Every Day Is Saturday* treat the popularity of sport. One refers to the adulatory eulogies that had poured forth on the death of Notre Dame football coach Knute Rockne:

> Rockne, so far as we know, was everything everybody said he was; yet it seems only fair to other upright members of college faculties to recall that that was not the reason he was famous. He was famous because he was a pillar of big-time football: he could look a million-dollar gate in the face, and at the very time of his death he was on his way to fulfill a motion-picture contract and to attend a sales-promotion meeting for Studebaker automobiles. He was in the big money, and that was why Hoover happened to know about him. We see nothing wrong in the President's expressing grief over the loss of a beloved football coach, but from a diplomatic angle it seems to leave out certain other deceased members of college faculties, men who worked with undergraduates in groups other than groups of

eleven. In our unofficial capacity, therefore, we take this opportunity to express the nation's grief in the death of all the other upright members of college faculties who died during the past year. We are sorry we don't know their names. (68–69)

The paragraph perhaps illustrates White's loyalties to academic professors — he continued to correspond with some from Cornell and would later write glowingly of his teachers — but it also suggests an unwillingness to overvalue celebrity and a desire to step back from the public response to events and evaluate them on their own terms.

When, later that same year, a right end on the West Point football team died on the playing field, White noted that "the death of Cadet Sheridan brought forth almost as much sentimental slop in the newspapers as did the death of Knute Rockne." After citing the ways the papers were "investing the incident with a peculiar kind of glory usually reserved for war heroes," he refers to the *Evening Post*'s description of "the clean, brave death of this man" as something (White's italics) *"which might so readily have been turned into a dreadful thing, had possible motive been added to circumstantial evidence."* White observes: "We notice that it is always the people with whole necks who think that broken ones are so glorious" (99–100). In neither of these paragraphs does White step back from editorializing, although he chooses to do it not in direct declarations but by comments from the side.

The indirectness of his conclusions was one of the aspects of White's writing that some readers most admired — the wry, unexpected fillip at the end — but it was also the aspect that some criticized most strongly, since it stepped back from outright condemnation. For example, in a 1931 paragraph on the radio broadcasts of the Detroit-based priest, Father Coughlin, who "speaks against birth control, pacifism, and internationalism," White notes that he "gets as many as three hundred and ninety thousand letters a day . . . [and] employs eighty-three secretaries to handle his mail" and then observes:

Talking against internationalism over the radio is like talking against rain in a rainstorm: the radio has made internationalism a fact, it has made boundaries look so silly that we wonder how mapmakers can draw maps without laughing; yet there stands Father Coughlin in front of the microphone, his voice reaching well up into Canada, his voice reaching well down into Mexico, his voice leaping international boundaries as lightly as a rabbit — there he stands, saying that internationalism will be our ruin, and getting millions of letters saying he is right. Will somebody please write us one letter saying that he is wrong — if only so that we can employ a secretary? (70)

The ending, while making an amusing contrast to Coughlin's success, tends to undercut the authority of the speaker, making him seem more hapless and insignificant, at the same time that it reinforces an appreciation of his ironical wit.

The endings of White's paragraphs were unpredictable, but the likelihood of a twist in the ending was very predictable. The structure of the paragraphs could be depended upon generally to start with a remark about where the speaker was or how he happened to learn about a particular occurrence. It would be followed by some sort of explanation focusing the reader's attention on a particular aspect of the occurrence and then shift to the speaker's reaction, usually one that, if disagreeing, provides an alternative interpretation or, if agreeing, provides an unexpected rationale for agreement. The concluding sentence is usually surprising in focus.

Although most of the paragraphs cited so far would demonstrate this structure, we can also consider as an example White's second-to-last paragraph in *Every Day Is Saturday*, which opens with the notice that Michael Gold of the *New Masses* had reviewed Ring Lardner's book, *First and Last*. The comment cites Gold's faulting Lardner's work because he wrote for magazines that wanted nothing that "'criticizes a fundamental capitalist institution'" and then turns to analyze Gold and his magazine as belonging "to the literary order whose art is identified with the worker. Their cry is that if it isn't propaganda, it isn't art." White claims that "Mr. Gold finds that [Lardner's writing] wasn't art because it wasn't about miners. 'Even in the realm of pure nonsense, his work was frustrate.'" White concludes: "Give us another orange frustrate, will you, Ring?" (240–241). As argument, the conclusion endorses without explaining the endorsement, and the word play (frustrate/phosphate) perhaps unintentionally characterizes Lardner as fizzy and unnutritious; at the same time, it supports Lardner in a memorable, clever phrase.

To some degree, the voluminous demands of Comment writing led White to develop paths of little resistance, such as drawing frequently from his own interests. Ralph Ingersoll, a former editor at the *New Yorker* who had been embroiled in a fierce and tangled relationship with Ross before leaving to edit the new magazine *Fortune*, credited White, with Thurber, as "the soul" of the magazine and claimed that "the record of E. B. (Andy) White's absorptions is written for all to see in 'Notes and Comment': first his Scottish terriers, then his guppies, more recently a serious interest in economics — his crusade is against the complexity of life — and a continuation of his long campaign against war" (85–86). The claim, made in 1934, is somewhat erroneous, since some of those items appeared in humorous casuals rather than in Comment, but it is accurate to observe that White's preoccupations surfaced frequently in his paragraphs, especially since they were expressly meant to be light observations rather than pointed editorials.

John Wesley Fuller, examining White's prose style, has observed that White "work[ed] out many minor techniques for himself" in order to meet the challenge of Comment writing for the *New Yorker*:

> Among these techniques were the use of an informal, sometimes slang-like diction, counterbalanced by knowledgeable control of clarity and grammatical nicety; the casualness of his organizational methods; the use of an irony subtle enough to pay readers the tacit compliment that they were quick enough to catch what lesser wits might miss; the satirist's assumption of a norm of sanity on the writer's and reader's part against which to judge the foolhardiness of the world; the strategy of satiric attack that holds up the other fellow's generalizations for inspection and minimizes the need of asserting one's own; the affectation of ironic naiveté coupled with a willingness to mock his own occasional confessions of sentiment. (11–12)

Throughout his writing of Comment White used these techniques to maintain a persona — a sense of the writer's identity or personality — that conforms to Ross's conception of "the New Yorker." It is successful with readers largely because of the way White inhabits that persona, to some degree subtly subverting it with his own particular interests and perspectives at the same time that he holds back from creating a voice he himself would identify as his own.

Evidence of the ways in which Comments were composed can be found in the White collection at Cornell. The most complete series of notes and drafts are usually those from the later part of White's career; to illustrate White's composing processes, both Scott Elledge in his biography of White and Douglas Hunt in the introduction to *The Dolphin Reader* offer drafts of his Comment on the first moon landing, published 26 July 1969. When White first began to donate his papers to Cornell, he explained to George H. Healey, the curator of rare books, that the "*New Yorker* has saved all the original material that went into its issues as far back as 1934. (The stuff from 1925 to 1934 was presented to the Paper Drive during the Second War by a patriotic, if slightly insane, member of our advertising department)" (*Letters* 484). The recycled paper included all of the original material represented in *Every Day Is Saturday*, as well as the larger mass of uncollected material. When White had the staff collect the material still extant in *New Yorker* files, he wrote Frank Sullivan that "I now have a stack of Notes & Comment manuscripts, or typescripts, that is, literally, two feet high. This ought to stop Healey, but he seems ready for anything. Actually, the comment manuscript originals are, in the aggregate, as like as two peas. They simply show that I was, in the final draft, a neat typist, that I spelled most of the words right, and that I got almost everything into the confines of a single sheet of yellow paper" (*Letters* 519). Most of the entries designated "MS in Cornell" in Katherine Romans Hall's bibliography simply refer to the final typed draft that was sent to the printer, complete with copyediting directions and proofreading marginalia. By and large, White discarded all the remaining drafts of his writing until the time he began to donate his papers to Cornell; from that point on he tended to save everything.

Very little evidence of White's composing from his early period survives. Nonetheless, there are substantial clues to be found when some of the existing final drafts are placed in the context of remarks about paragraph writing he made in letters and published comment. For example, although Hall's bibliography credits White with all of the 27 July 1935 Notes and Comment section, the typescript evidence demonstrates that White's role was chiefly to write up or to revise ideas that others had submitted. The typescripts credit the phonebook item and the Jones Beach item to Graham, the work projects item to Ross, the tenants item to Horn, the Washington item to Close, and the food-color item to Coates — none of the original ideas were White's. Comments for 2 February 1935 and 7 March 1936 written entirely by White have only three items each that originated with White. On many Comment typescripts White is identified as the originator as well as the writer of all items.

One Notes and Comment page credited entirely to White in this way ran 2 May 1936. Although White may be said to put his stamp on most of the paragraphs he wrote, regardless of the source, these paragraphs are made identifiably his pieces by the particular perspective he brings to each of them. For example, the first item merely juxtaposes two things observed: a Pierce automobile with chauffeur in front of a bank with a "little pair of lady's drawers — pink as the eye of Russia" drying on a clothesline on the roof; the observation about the color of the underwear concludes the piece with the hint that the underwear is a proletarian symbol subverting the pomp of capitalist pretensions (although my explicit explanation does little justice to White's ironic implication). The second item contrasts a public relations announcement of an indoor ice season in Lake Placid with White's own memories of a Lake Placid summer in his youth. The third item discusses the brochures of the French Line, a transatlantic steamship company — they extol ship-to-shore multiperson radiophone service, but White pooh-poohs it in favor of "an old Liggett's phone booth. It may smell of last year's grippe germs, but it is all, all our own." The fourth item, begun with a lament for the lack of leisure on May Day, deals with the problem of unemployment, "a state of 100-per-cent mechanical ingenuity and 100-per-cent manual idleness," and takes the view that "the things the race has built with its hands . . . are still the abiding satisfactions and the immediate insurance against madness"; White's distrust of technology and endorsement of simpler, more rewarding living echo a persistent theme in his writing, one whose literary source he identifies in the paragraph: "Thoreau saw it a hundred years ago — we begin to see it dimly now." The fifth and last item refers to the May Day festival at Bryn Mawr, Katharine's alma mater, and notes in passing that the proceeds are "to go to a new chemistry building." The paragraphs are bound together by White's observations and perspective and deal with some of his favorite themes.

In the Cornell file the pieces of this particular Comment page give some indication of the way White composed such paragraphs. Three of the five paragraphs are typed and two are handwritten. The typed drafts bear the marks of the compositor — indicators of hyphens and upper-case letters, font size and spacing, corrections of spelling errors — but they also indicate changes made by the author. In the first paragraph about the bank and the underwear the word "ladies" is followed by the word "lady's" before the word "drawers," clearly recognition of a misspelling by the writer during typing. The third paragraph, about the French Line, has only compositor's changes, but the fourth paragraph, about work, changes an original passage — "although, considering the havoc it has wrought, there has been curiously little opposition to it. At any rate, the people gradually" to "to which, anyway, there has been curiously little opposition, considering the havoc it has wrought. The people"; later on in the paragraph a phrase is added in longhand and a sentence deleted, suggesting last minute changes by the author rather than the compositor.

More revealing are the two handwritten items. The fifth and shortest paragraph, a comment about a May festival at Bryn Mawr, is not only in White's handwriting but shows minimal changes throughout.

> *Even at Bryn Mawr, where May*
> > *still*
> *Day revels ^ have an essentially Elizabethan flavor*
> *(although the money is to go to a new chemistry*
> *building) trouble has raised its head. The*
> *committee in charge of the festival dug up a*
> *yoke of white oxen for the traditional parade*
> *and it turned out that the brutes were*
> *suffering from an odd, unhealthy condition*
> *known to ~~oxherds~~ drovers as "perishing*
> *hip and shoulder." ~~The college has been~~*
> *~~in as deep a quandary as revolutionaries~~*
> *~~agitated over this as~~ May is a month*
> *of many agitations, all of them*
> *severe.*

White took two passes at a simile to describe the college's agitation before giving up and trying a different tack in the concluding sentence. The indications in the text and in the use of this sheet as the compositor's copy suggest that the paragraph was hurriedly composed.

Similarly, and more obviously, the second handwritten item was apparently composed in a single draft. The item as published reads:

> Our life would be a drab thing were it not for the vivid material which we receive all the time from romantic press bureaus, to whom life is rich and charming and real. We get daily bulletins from night clubs, health resorts, radio stations, hotel bars, dry-cleaning establishments, publishers, railroad and steamship lines, and a hundred other concerns and enterprises. They tone us up and keep us alert and informed. One of our most faithful correspondents is a man who describes himself as News from Lake Placid in-the-Adirondacks. We have no doubt mentioned his letters before. Not a drop of snow falls, not a sled turns over, but we know of it in great detail. Today comes an Adirondack announcement to the effect that July 4th is the date of the opening of the midsummer indoor ice season. It

makes us realize how the world changes. Once upon a time (and this will come as a surprise to News from Lake Placid in-the-Adirondacks) we spent a summer working as a caddy in Lake Placid in-the-Adirondacks. Long afternoons we sat in the caddy house and learned about life from the town boys. In those days July 4th wasn't the beginning of the ice season — it was the day the black flies came out of the woods onto the eleventh fairway and held their Annual War Games. The only indoor ice in those days was in the tall glasses of the golf players from whom we used to get 35 cents for nine holes, 70 cents (with 5-cent tip) for eighteen holes. (*New Yorker*, 2 May 1936, 11)

It uses the occasion of a press release to compare an adolescent memory with the circumstance in the publicity, virtually free associating to link an indoor ice rink with a summer spent caddying. The handwritten draft of that item is a single page that reads as transcribed.

> *Our life would be a drab thing indeed*
>   *vivid*
> *were it not for the* ^ *material which we receive all the time*
>   *& real.*
> *from romantic press bureaus, to whom life is rich & charming* ^^
> ~~*One of*~~ *We get daily bulletins from night clubs, health resorts,*
>   *publishers*
> *radio stations, hotel bars, dry cleaning establishments,* ^ *railroad*
> *& steamship lines, & a hundred other concerns & enterprises.*
>   *tone*   *up*
> *They* ~~*chase*~~ ^ *us* ^ *& keep us alert & informed. One of our most*
>   *a man who describes himself as*
> *faithful correspondents is* ^ *News from Lake Placid in-the-Adirondacks.*
>   *his letters*
> *We have no doubt mentioned* ^ ~~*it*~~ *before. Not a drop of snow falls, not*
> *a sled turns over, but we know about in great detail. Today*
>   *Adirondack*   *date*
> *comes an* ^ *announcement that July 4 is the* ~~*[illegible]*~~ *of the opening of*
> *the*
> ^ *midsummer indoor ice season.* ~~*It*~~ *It makes us realize how*
>   ~~*In 1915*~~ *upon a time*
> *how the world changes. Once* ^ *(and this will come as a surprise*
>   *[illeg.]*
> *to News from Lake Placid in the Adirondacks) we spent a summer*

working for a surveyor   *& caddying on the side* ⸺

^ *& caddying in Lake Placid in the Adirondacks* ^ . *In those days July 4 wasn't the beginning of the ice season — it was day the black flies came out of woods onto the 11th fairway & held their Annual War Games. The only indoor ice* w *in those days was in the, highball*

tall glasses of the   *Long afternoons we sat with the town boys*
    players
golfers from whom   *in the caddy house & learned about life*
we used to get
35 cents for 9 holes,   *from the town boys.*
70 cents (with 5 cent tip)
for 18 holes.

There is considerable evidence in this sheet that we are looking at a first and final draft. For one thing, most of White's final drafts are typescripts, not manuscripts, and even in the occasional case of a holograph final draft, the neatness and the lack of revisions indicate that the copy was prepared by hand for the printer, perhaps in the absence of a typewriter, rather than composed on the spot. The manuscript for the Comment page of 21 March 1936 is just such a page — the holograph copy seems merely an example of penmanship rather than of composition. In the item about Lake Placid, however, internal evidence suggests that this is the only draft.

For example, the beginning of the fourth line ("One of" crossed out) suggests a change during composition rather than a revision during copying, as does the false start in line 7 ("they chase us" changed to "tone us up," a phrase that was probably in place before "and keep us alert and informed"). So does the fumbling with the placement of "caddying" in line 15 (first changing "spent the summer caddying" to "working for a surveyor & caddying" and then moving "& caddying" to the end of the sentence and adding "on the side," a more accurate representation of what he was doing at the time). The paragraph apparently originally ended with the phrase "Annual War Games," but White must have read the draft through and then added the sentence about "long afternoons in the caddyhouse with the town boys." The addition was probably in place before he added the new final sentence about the "only indoor ice" being in highballs, although there is room in the manuscript for it to have come later. Either way, the decision to add the phrase beginning "the tall glasses" in place of "highball" as a way of ending the piece had to come after the "Long afternoons" addition in order to account for the placement of the concluding phrase on the page. Perhaps White discovered the tenuousness of the connection between his memory and the news release and revised the paragraph to hearken back in some way to the original item (although the ice cubes may link them only slightly less tenuously).

The manuscript also leaves a few "the's" out as well as some punctuation and challenges a compositor to follow the revisions. Thus, while this probably was the copy that went to the printer, it certainly was not a final draft that had gone through the process that made so many of White's typescripts evidence of the neatness of his typing. Given the nature and extent of the revisions, there is simply nothing here to suggest that there were earlier drafts.

The manuscript copies of White's Comment on the moon landing, discussed and reprinted by both Elledge and Hunt, show a careful, painstaking craftsman continually revising, rethinking, editing, tinkering with his prose. But that writer was also one who had retired from the regular schedule of Comment writing. His was the voice of the *New Yorker* for some of its most crucial or powerful editorials — the moon landing, the assassination of John F. Kennedy, the death of Harold Ross — but he had long since ceased to labor under the conditions that had won him a regular audience in the 1930s. In the same year that he wrote the paragraph on News from Lake Placid in-the-Adirondacks he was responsible for all of fifty weeks of Comment and contributed to a fifty-first. That left one week of non-White Comment in 1936; it meant that White had contributed between 250 and 300 paragraphs that year. In contrast, he wrote only three widely spaced Notes and Comment pages in 1969 and very little else, and the moon landing Comment — a single paragraph that made up the entire page — was the only focus of White's writing for five days. In this light it is hard to imagine that the painful process of the moon landing manuscripts was typical of his composing in the 1930s; rather, given his own remarks on the need for volume and speed in the production of paragraphs, the Lake Placid comment seems far more likely to be typical of his composing in that period.

The regular, relentless, timely production of paragraphs for Notes and Comment demanded the ability to generate material rapidly, without long periods of gestation, without multiple revisions, with only cursory reflection. It rewarded immediacy as well as grace under extreme pressure. It was designed to meet the current reader on the grounds of currency. The regular output helped generate regular output. The conventions of form, audience, and persona, because they were recurring, became automatic; the regular production kept the writer continually generating ideas and searching for subjects. The reward for this kind of writing was a contemporaneous link with the reader; the difficulty was its limited staying power. Like the writing of others much read and admired in the period (such as members of the Algonquin Round Table and the popular "colyum conductors"), White's Comment paragraphs tended to be ephemeral; as one commentator had noted about the writing of Marquis, Morley, and Adams: "Necessarily the Colyumist must strike at many things ephemeral with ephemeral phrases. A great deal of his writing is for the day only" ("Colyums" 43).

Other writers have commented on the limitations regular and prolific writing imposes on the work itself. For example, *New York Times* political columnist Tom Wicker, looking over his career in *On Press*, observed, "Just as Detroit sometimes has to recall its cars, not everything I or any columnist turns out is up to scratch." He estimated that "about one-third of my columns [came] reasonably close to meeting my personal standards" and represented "the kind of work in which I could take real satisfaction." He admitted, "As for the rest, some aimed high but missed the mark, which is neither surprising nor deplorable; but more have been the kind of hackwork any demanding schedule is likely to produce" (178). Based on conversation with colleagues, Wicker felt his experience was typical of columnists.

The *Times* theater critic Walter Kerr once recounted his dismay over the unevenness of the work he produced in his voluminous reviews. He had been rereading his past reviews to collect into a new clipbook, an anthology of his best newspaper work written since his previous clipbook.

> I get one year's worth of material every five years, as nearly as I can figure it. I was shocked. I started one of them, which one I do not remember for sure now, but it was while I still on the *Tribune*. I started to go through the pieces and I went through two years without finding even one that I wanted to reproduce, and I thought, Jesus, have I been this bad this long without realizing it and am I going to get a book here at all? Or do I send the advance back or what? Fortunately, in the next year, the third year, they started turn-

ing up usable again, but there was actually two years worth of material that I ended up throwing away. (Root, *Working* 155)

Although Kerr was surprised by how much of his regular newspaper reviewing it took to give him enough material for a new book, it should be remembered that the work was probably sufficient for the day it was published and only in retrospect — read separately from the immediate context in which it first appeared — did it appear inadequate. Kerr's clipbooks then, such as *Journey to the Center of the Theater*, tend to be made up of more enduring, less ephemeral pieces. Wicker found that his pieces were so time bound that he was unable to collect them into a clipbook, even though the work was effective as a regular newspaper column.

In light of these comments it is easy to see why White's two clipbooks made up exclusively of Comment writing — *Every Day Is Saturday*, containing his earliest paragraphs, and *The Wild Flag*, reprinting his most timely paragraphs about the end of World War II and the establishment of the United Nations — have not been reprinted in the last several decades. Only the relatively few paragraphs in *The Second Tree from the Corner* have been reprinted in successive editions of the book, which is itself a potpourri of genres. (The paragraphs collected in the posthumously published *Writings from the New Yorker 1925–1976* [1990] were selected by the editor, Rebecca M. Dale, from material White had repeatedly rejected for inclusion in clipbooks in the past.)

It is also easy to see why White became so discouraged by his prolific output. The Comment writing was a mixed experience. White's prolific production of paragraphs encouraged glibness at the same time that it made consistency possible; it rewarded him with immediate and continual publication but prevented him from developing more sustained, more reflective, more carefully fashioned, and more universal work. At the same time, it should be said that White's *New Yorker* Comment pieces represent some of the finest examples of the paragraph as a literary form. Morris Bishop declared that they "represent the apotheosis of the paragraph. E. B. White makes a note on human behavior or on an occurrence of the week; he meditates upon it and adorns it with comment, witty, paradoxical, or merely true. He pours his sentences into the molds of speech, and inserts two or three unexpected words, like raisins. His paragraphs have an opening quality; they seek to break a hole in the texture of time which confines us; they hint of eternity. It is the poetic substance in these paragraphs which makes them still radioactive in many memories" (vii).

Reviews of *Every Day Is Saturday* were generally favorable: William Rose Benét in the *Saturday Review of Literature* observed, "Many of us have marveled that one man could conduct the procession of those paragraphs every week with such sapience and humor as Mr. White has evinced" (40); the word "conduct" aligns White with Marquis, Morley, and Adams. Benét felt that "the force of Mr. White's comments has not depended so much upon his material as upon his way of using it . . . , his civil way of presenting some of the most astonishing phenomena of our time." He appreciated the quiet tone of the paragraphs: "The beauty of Mr. White's comments is never garish or flaunting" (40). The anonymous review in the *New York Times Book Review* quoted liberally from the book to illustrate its comparison of White to Thoreau ("Thoreau on a Roof Garden"), a comparison that must have particularly pleased White. William Soskin in the *New York American* identified White as "The Perfect Modern Skeptic" and aligned him with Montaigne and Pepys, declaring: "Mr. White writes with constant and patient attention to form, with a cutting conciseness, with an inventive and infinitely varied sense of situation, with a sweet gift for the precise and nice phrase" (quoted in Elledge 191). The comparisons to Thoreau and Montaigne surely must have bolstered White's sense of what he was capable of, but the largely favorable reviews at the same time confirmed his métier as the paragraph.

From before the publication of *Every Day Is Saturday* White was dissatisfied with the *New Yorker* paragraph and continued to chafe under its constraints. He was not alone in his fatigue and frustration. Don Marquis had explained in his "Confessions of a Reformed Columnist" that he "never knew but two columnists who said it was easy": Frank L. Stanton of the *Atlanta Constitution* and Franklin P. Adams. For himself, "while it ruined me, I loved it. It sapped my vitality, made corns and bunions on my brain, wrecked my life, and I adored it" (6). Christopher Morley in his own "Confessions of a Colyumist" described a colyum conductor suffering from its effects:

> You may know him by a sunken, brooding eye; clothing marred by much tobacco, and a chafed and tetchy humour toward the hour of five P.M. Having bitterly schooled himself to see men as paragraphs walking, he finds that his most august musings have a habit of stew-

ing themselves down to some ferocious or jocular three-line comment. He may yearn desperately to compose a really thrilling poem that will speak his passionate soul; to churn up from the typewriter some lyric that will rock with blue seas and frantic hearts; he finds himself allaying the frenzy with some jovial sneer at Henry Ford or a yell about the High Cost of Living. Poor soul, he is like one condemned to harangue the vast, idiotic world through a keyhole, whence his anguish issues thin and faint. (41)

These were sentiments with which E. B. White the paragrapher could identify.

By the time *Every Day Is Saturday* appeared, White had written more than 1,500 paragraphs for the department. While the title of the book ostensibly refers to the datelines on each piece, which carry the date the magazine was published, it may also have been an oblique comment on the way the demands of the department made him feel. Part of the reason White decided in 1937 to take a leave from the *New Yorker* was the relentlessness of the deadlines and the productivity. In a March 1937 letter to his brother Stanley, White explained, "Some time this summer I am quitting the *New Yorker* for at least a year — sort of a delayed sabbatical — and am looking forward to it with some relish. I want to see what it feels like, again, to let a week pass without having an editorial bowel movement. It is terrible to have to write down one's thoughts before they even get their pin-feathers, and I have been doing that for quite a while" (*Letters* 151). Explaining to Harold Ross why, at the end of his sabbatical, he had chosen to do a monthly department for *Harper's* rather than the same number of words for the *New Yorker*, he wrote in September 1938 that "a monthly department gives me about three weeks of off time, which I can devote to a sustained project, like shingling a barn or sandpapering an old idea. I want this interval during which I do not have to produce anything for publication. I cannot get it with Notes & C. because they come along every Friday, rain or shine" (*Letters* 180). Like the colyumists before him, White had written most of his Comment from the headlines or chance observation. The unremitting production of paragraphs gave him little time for more reflective writing.

The Comment page was voracious, demanding not merely five to ten random items but items that were timely, sprightly, and well expressed. The "comment bank" White and Ross had established was an attempt to keep ahead of the demand: "Every week I write and turn in more stuff than can be used, so that I can pick what seems best (and what seems to run together best) and stow the rest away to die or to wait." Often a paragraph "becomes timely by circumstance, or becomes apropos a new comment," but most became outdated and unusable. White preferred writing more than he could use rather than relying on "the old way of having a third party make up the department hit and miss, with the bank as the chief source of supply" (*Letters* 126). The demands this system made on White are made clear in a letter prompted by the publication, while he was on vacation, of a paragraph in the bank that he himself would never have used. He complained to Ross:

> It was probably my fault that the St. Anne comment got into the book, because I should have killed it and many other bank comments long ago, but just let it slide. Anyway, seeing it in print gave me quite a turn. In my letter asking for two weeks vacation, I thought I made it clear that I wanted time off only if the substitute stuff was to be either original new stuff, or the extra comments which I had turned in the week before. If I had known you were going to resurrect my out-dated and oddly inept remark about Catholicism, I would gladly have forsworn any vacation. I regard the bank (as it exists now) as a somewhat expensive concession to my perhaps overdeveloped sense of perfection (or timeliness). . . . The weakness of the system is that, on very infrequent occasions, such as last week, some very ripe paragraph gets into the book. (*Letters* 126)

The demands of the department were constant and regular and, much too often in White's view, inescapable.

The need to stay current with the affairs of the city and its cultural milieu was a continual cause of pressure in White's Comment writing. When he moved to Maine his output decreased in part because he felt himself too much out of the current of affairs in New York City; he wrote Ross in 1938 that "I have not been getting many comment ideas here on my own hook, and probably won't until I take to reading the papers again" (*Letters* 181). He later turned down the opportunity to run the Comment page again because, he writes, "I don't want to sign myself up to a specified amount of comment as long as I am living 500 miles from first base, because it is too difficult, sometimes, to turn out anything at all, much less a specified amount. In New York I could always dig up a department, by looking around in an old folder or a new barroom, but here the situation is different" (*Letters* 241). Only when White returned to New York City late in World War II was he able to again assume responsibility for the Comment page.

Comment made demands on White beyond relentless productivity and immediacy. He had long felt a gap between his writing and his sense of himself as a writer. Part of the disengagement lay in the format of the Comment paragraphs, especially the insistence on the use of the first person plural. In 1934 he wrote to Gus Lobrano, "It is almost impossible to write anything decent using the editorial 'we,' unless you are the Dionne family. Anonymity, plus the 'we,' gives a writer the cloak of dishonesty, and he finds himself going around, like a masked reveler at a ball, kissing all the pretty girls" (*Letters* 121). To Ross in 1938 he justified his move to *Harper's* by explaining that "in a department like N & C there are certain limitations in subject matter and in manner of expressing yourself which, after ten years, become formidable and sometimes oppressive. With a signed department, using 'I' instead of 'we,' I can cover new ground, which is necessary at this stage" (*Letters* 180). Composing Comment pages imposed a number of limitations that a writer had to overcome, not the least of which was a certain surrendering of his own identity.

White's disenchantment with Comment was not a recent development but a sore point continually exacerbated by the demands of constant production over the years. The sense that Comment was something other than meaningful writing was hinted at even in the material collected for *Every Day Is Saturday*. "Radio Novel," dated 19 August 1933, opens with the line, "Of paramount interest to the writing profession, of which we are no longer one" (185). "Sloth" (25 November 1933) was even more pointed:

> As the year goes into its dying phase, the thing that most distresses us is the paucity of our literary output. Other than these few rather precise little paragraphs, into which we pour the slow blood of our discontent, we never get around to writing anything at all, in a world when not to write is considered irregular. Though we brood a good deal about writing plays and books, and speak familiarly of it at lunch to our friends (as though we were in the middle of it), a careful search of our premises at the end of a year reveals no trace of a manuscript — merely a few notes on the inside flap of paper-match packs.

From this beginning White continues in a more ironic tone: "When we look around and see the output of other writers we grow faint. Both President and Mrs. Roosevelt, to name only two other literary people, have published a book in the past year; and to realize that they, who are really busy, can do it, while we, who seldom have anything pressing on hand, cannot, is extremely discouraging. Literary jealousy is probably at the bottom of many of our anarchical impulses" (197–198). The reference to the literary productivity of the Roosevelts is amusing irony, but it hardly mitigates the gloom of the first half of the paragraph.

A few months later White was observing, in a piece he titled "Career," that "students in 'Appreciation of Humor' should be warned right at the start that humor has no social standing in letters. It should be made clear to any student who might be considering a career of humor that after he has written his arm off, for funnier or for worse, even his best friend will still ask, 'When are you going to do something really important?'" (214–215). He would later observe in his introduction to *A Subtreasury of American Humor*: "The world likes humor, but it treats it patronizingly. It decorates its serious artists with laurel, and its wags with Brussels sprouts. It feels that if a thing is funny it can be presumed to be something less than great, because if it were truly great it would be wholly serious" (xviii). Surely one of the influences on White's decision to leave Comment writing was his sense of pressure to do something more important.

Some of that pressure came from White's own sense of the limitations of the Comment page as a response to current affairs and issues. While the magazine prospered throughout the Depression, its drollery was a weak weapon to combat the economic and social dilemmas people were facing. The Comment page demanded that paragraphs maintain a jocular air and end with an unexpected twist, both of which tended to deflect the thrust of any criticism within the paragraph. The tendency annoyed Ralph Ingersoll, who used a 1934 *Fortune* article to complain that "the *New Yorker* has become gentler and gentler, more nebulous, less real" partly because of Katharine's "civilizing influence on Ross" and especially because of White's "gossamer writing, in his increasingly important 'Notes and Comment'" and "flavoring of the whole magazine with captions and fillers" (97). He claimed that White's approach made the magazine battle "nobly if ineffectually . . . with its delicate barbed quill" (152). Ingersoll's turbulent relationship with Ross as well as his own commitment to confrontation as a political strategy may have encouraged the sharpness of tone in his complaint, but the criticism stung White.

Ingersoll was even more negative a few years later, when White characterized Roosevelt's criticism of those opposing his attempt to stack the Supreme Court as "the utterances of a petulant savior" and concluded his 13 March 1937 Comment with: "America doesn't need to be saved today; it can wait until tomorrow. Meanwhile, Mister, we'll sleep on it." Although, as Scott Elledge points out, *Time* called the piece "an unusually earnest thrust from the White rapier" and "a pinking far more effective than the bludgeonings of his customarily solemn critics" (198), Ingersoll wrote White a personal letter claiming to be enraged by his "gentle complacency" and harshly asking: "Doesn't that well-fed stomach of yours ever turn when you think what you're saying? Let us sleep on suffering, want, malnutrition. Let us sleep too on young men who are so fond of phrasing things exactly that humanity never troubles them" (Elledge 199). Almost immediately after an interchange of letters with Ingersoll, White decided to stop writing "Notes and Comment." When he returned to regular writing, he did so in a context in which he could identify himself with his opinions, have more time to consider what he wrote, and fit the length of the piece to the thought, instead of the other way around.

Undoubtedly all these reasons are related: the difficulty with the pressures and anonymity of Comment, the inability to write for himself, the need to attempt something more ambitious, the feeling that the *New Yorker* — begun as a magazine of sophisticated wit — was unable to address the hard issues of the age (the Depression, the political scene in Europe), to which can be added the simple weariness of having done essentially the same thing for nearly a decade. For the purposes of following E. B. White's emergence as an essayist, however, the limitations of early Comment help us to understand some of the constraints on his composing processes and the influences he brought with him to the kinds of writing he was to do in the future.

In a letter to Katharine clarifying "the whole subject of my year of grace — or, as I call it, My Year," White explained first of all why he was quitting his job at the *New Yorker*: "I am quitting partly because I am not satisfied with the use I am making of my talents, such as they are; partly because I am not having fun working at my job — and am in a rut there; partly because I long to recapture something which everyone loses when he agrees to perform certain creative miracles on specified dates for a particular sum" (*Letters* 154). Although elsewhere in letters and in print he would give somewhat varying reasons for his taking "a sabbatical," his explanation to Katharine seems the most accurate. He would return to the paragraph — in fact, would never really leave it — but by 1937 he was ready to move on, and the choices he made about his writing led him toward the essay.

4

"IT IS NOT ALL VELVET, THIS MONTHLY LIFE"
White as Columnist

Leaving his weekly deadline at the *New Yorker* first for a period without
deadlines and then for monthly deadlines at *Harper's Magazine*, White
considerably altered the circumstances in which he wrote and entered
a new period of his emergence as an essayist. In the "One Man's Meat"
column he expanded and redirected his Comment paragraphs. He fore-
grounded his own presence in the writing through the use of the first
person singular and a greater emphasis on the private and personal
than on the public and impersonal (the Comment emphasis). He also
took advantage of the greater allotment of space in the magazine to
extend his short items beyond the single paragraph. Sometimes he took
up the entire department with a single essay; other times, as he had
done with the Comment page, he interlinked essentially separate items
or resorted to expedient assemblages of entirely unconnected items.
Some of his most enduring and artful essays came out of the "One
Man's Meat" period, but through it all, and in the overwhelming majority of the columns he produced, he relied upon the resources and
strategies of the paragrapher/columnist to generate the writing.

In the period before and around the time White took up the *Harper's*
column, popular magazines regularly carried (in addition to feature articles, letters from readers, and reviews of books or the arts) two kinds
of column. One was the kind of column we have been referring to as
"the colyum," made up of multiple items, usually gathered around the
magazine's editorial interests (literature, politics, social life) and often
provided by multiple contributors, including readers. This is the basis
for a page like Notes and Comment in the *New Yorker*, but it did not
originate there. For example, at the turn of the century, the *Bookman*, a
monthly literary magazine published by Dodd and Mead (many of the
leading magazines were divisions of book publishers), ran an opening
section called "Chronicle and Comment," which reported on the lives

of authors and publishers and provided paragraphs on current books and plays. *Century Magazine* in the first quarter of the century ran a department that hearkened back to the journalism of William Hazlitt, titled "Table Talk" and composed of seven to ten separate segments run over four pages. *Saturday Review* ran a department called "Trade Winds," which was eventually conducted by Christopher Morley. A one-page series of political comments ran in the *Nation* under the title "In the Driftway," with the byline and third-person-singular persona, the Drifter. *Atlantic Monthly* opened with a four to five page department of unsigned comments called "The Shape of Things." And *Scribner's* ran "As I Like It," a literary department signed by William Lyon Phelps that sometimes extended for a dozen pages.

The other kind of column was the "signed" department: single authors were given a set space each week or month to write about their particular concerns from their particular viewpoint. Most often these columns were composed of single essays or editorial-like articles. *Harper's* had a long-running department called "The Easy Chair," which had been written by its editors since the mid-nineteenth century; Donald Grant Mitchell, George William Curtis, William Dean Howells, and, in E. B. White's time, Bernard DeVoto had all taken a turn in the Easy Chair. The long-lived traditions of the column perhaps showed themselves most obviously in the third-person-singular manner by which the author referred to himself: for example, "The Easy Chair's visits to one mill in particular have not been pious pilgrimages" or "more than once the Easy Chair's rumble seat has been filled with anticipation of Christmas, months away" (DeVoto, "Letter" 445–446).

At about the same time, Oswald Garrison Villard wrote a one-page political column, "Issues and Men," for the *Atlantic Monthly*; Heywood Broun wrote a similar column, "Shoot the Works," for the *New Republic*; and Christopher Morley continued his "Bowling Green" column with a literary emphasis in the *Saturday Review*. In the *New Yorker* itself, Alexander Woollcott had been given a single-page column called "Shouts and Murmurs" (today run as a final page department open to contributors). White, then, could find considerable precedent for a signed column that served as a forum for personal reflections and essays running the length of the department.

But in practice the distinctions between these two types of column were anything but rigid. For example, William Lyon Phelps's "As I Like It" department in *Scribner's* was always composed of multiple items, but the number of pages Phelps was routinely allotted gave him the room to develop one item to considerable length. Frequently, the lead item would be a critical essay in itself, followed by an unpredictable number of items that ran from a sentence or two to a few paragraphs. Such was the size of his department that Phelps had no reservations about reprinting letters from readers or lengthy excerpts from works under discussion as a way of filling his designated pages. The reader response column was a common device of the daily newspaper colyum conductors (and still is, as anyone who subscribes to a paper with a daily columnist can attest).

If the multiple-item columnists could occasionally develop an item into an essay, the single-item columnists could occasionally fall back on multiple items as a way to fill the department. Christopher Morley, whose reputation as an essayist was such that his work was frequently reprinted in college composition anthologies, wrote the majority of his essays for his newspaper and magazine column, "The Bowling Green." In moving from the daily grind to a weekly one, Morley decreased the demands on his writing, but the *Saturday Review* version of the column was longer than the newspaper version, and Morley often resorted to printing long excerpts from the writers he was discussing and regularly ran a column made up entirely of letters from readers. Because the "Bowling Green" was routinely segmented by three or four paragraph breaks as a way of filling the space, Morley sometimes linked three or four disparate items with a common theme or recurring motif so that they read as more or less unified. Particularly in Morley's hands, the distinctions between the two types of column and the boundaries between what might be called the essay proper and the *faux* essay are difficult to determine.

Morley frequently collected his essays from the "Bowling Green" column and other sources and published clipbooks at a regular rate. For example, *Pipefuls* (1921) was "edified (for the most part) out of the ribs of two friendly newspapers," the *New York Evening Post* and the *Philadelphia Evening Public Ledger*, as well as out of the *Bookman, Everybody's,* and *Publisher's Weekly.* The reprinted selections function like essays to the naked eye; that is, they run for several pages and each covers pretty much one topic. It is only in a section called "A City Notebook (Philadelphia)" that Morley reprints a series of paragraphs separated by asterisks that read like Notes and Comment, collecting bits and pieces of the colyum to form a segmented whole linked chiefly by setting rather than by subject.

Columnists regularly wrote columns made up of randomly arranged paragraphs or comments, and Morley was not alone in wanting to include his paragraphs as well as his essays in his hardcover collections. The much-admired literary essayist Frank Moore Colby, who joined the *Bookman* as an editor in 1904, published only a few clipbooks in his lifetime. His final (posthumous) publication, drawing from all his work, was the two-volume collection, *The Colby Essays*. The first volume was subtitled "The Pursuit of Humor and Other Essays," and the second volume was subtitled "Tailor Blood and Other Notes and Comment." Most of the material in the second volume was collected from the anonymous paragraphs that had appeared in the *Bookman*'s "Chronicle and Comment" department. In his preface to *A Subtreasury of American Humor*, White called Colby "one of the most intelligent humorists operating in this country in the early years of the century" and quoted a lengthy passage from "The Pursuit of Humor"; he also reprinted two essays by Colby, "Confessions of a Gallomaniac" and "When Nature Lovers Write Books," and two Comments, "Novels and Hats" and "The Loeb Classics." Although Colby's chiefly literary interests as an essayist were quite different from White's, *The Colby Essays* would have sanctioned the treatment of Comment writing as an essayistic enterprise.

In both his own writing and in his editing of others, Christopher Morley contributed to that sanctioning. As noted earlier, in his anthology *Modern Essays* (1921) he reprinted as essays work by Don Marquis and Logan Pearsall Smith that were really multiple items. The sections that Morley reprinted from Smith's collection, *Trivia*, were not published in that order in the original, and no two of them appeared sequentially there. They were really a series of individual paragraphs accumulated and arranged by Morley.

Morley's reprint of two sections of Marquis's *The Almost Perfect State* was even more editorially altered. Marquis had run his comments on the "Almost Perfect State" over many entries in his newspaper column and eventually collected them into a clipbook. The two sections that Morley reprinted actually reverse the order in which they appeared in the book, as two separate chapters (37 and 39). Moreover, Morley took out most of the indicators that the material had appeared in a colyum. His first section dropped the second segment of the original, captioned "A Motto for Your Desk" and running for several lines of upper-case, centered verse. His second section omitted the poem that started Marquis's book chapter and altered the format of the page. Compare, for example, the following excerpts. The first comes from Marquis's book (177):

*   *   *

OPTIMISTIC THOUGHT

Men could not think of the Almost Perfect State if they did not have it in them ultimately to create the Almost Perfect State.

*   *   *

The second comes from Morley's anthology (45):

> Men could not think of THE ALMOST PERFECT STATE if they did not have it in them ultimately to create THE ALMOST PERFECT STATE.

In Morley's version it is simply a one-sentence paragraph without a heading or separation from other paragraphs. Throughout his version Morley has removed all asterisks and segmental formatting, making the pieces read as much like cohesive traditional essays as possible. Only a close reading discovers the abruptness of shifts from paragraph to paragraph, the disjunctiveness of the segmented column at odds with the linearity of the unsegmented essay, and makes the reader at all suspicious of the original form of the piece.

The tinkering that Morley does with Marquis's columns suggests his reluctance to run even so thematically linked a series of segments as these in a disjunctive format, a format at odds with the traditional concept of the essay. In its original form the "amiable meditations" on the "Almost Perfect State" are clearly loosely related, at times random paragraphs, not essays. The changes Morley makes also raise the question of the difference between a cohesive, unified, "conjunctive" essay and a disparate, segmented, "disjunctive" essay; it is not merely, as he treats it here, a matter of typography and compositor's preferences — simply getting rid of the asterisks, italics, and paragraph breaks. This will be more of an issue when we examine White's most Marquisian columns.

Morley himself was well aware of the difference between the traditional essay and the multiple-item column. When the essays in his clipbooks are compared against their sources in his columns, it is clear that the white spaces and breaks that he edits out for book publication were chiefly space fillers in the original. The assemblage of paragraphs of "A City Notebook (Philadelphia)," noted earlier, is a relatively rare occurrence in his collections. However, two years after the publication of *Modern Essays*, he assembled a clipbook of his own work that illustrates how much his column writing could resemble that of Marquis. *Inward Ho!* (1923) is made up of notes from his *New York Evening Post* column. It is arranged into fifteen chapters of random observations ostensibly made up of thematically linked materials discussing poetry and the creative impulse. Like Marquis's observations on the Almost Perfect State, the disjunctive nature of the material arises from the widely scattered circumstances of its composition, as individual items appearing intermittently in the column over a long period of time. The book is chiefly a means of collecting loose ends and forming them into a kind of less transitory whole. The act of collecting them in one place itself confers at once a kind of tenuous unity to them.

The title comes from the final segment of the first chapter:

Loud sang the hearts of the Freudian adventurers — Inward . . . Inward Ho! (11)

While this little segment is separated by a row of asterisks from the segments preceding it, lines within segments are often equally disjunctive. One segment reads:

It seems to me interesting that the book with the most vegetarian title is, of all others, the most carnal — Leaves of Grass.

There are no strict vegetarians. Even Bernard Shaw eats eggs.

I had a million questions to ask God: but when I met him, they all fled my mind; and it didn't seem to matter.

But even Abraham Lincoln returned from Gettysburg murmuring that he had forgotten the things he Really Wanted to Say.

Truth and Beauty (perhaps Keats was wrong in identifying them: perhaps they have the relation of Wit and Humour, or Rain and Rainbow) are of interest only to hungry people. There are several kinds of hunger.

If Socrates, Spinoza, and Santayana had had free access to a midnight icebox we would never have heard of them. (9–10)

The surrounding segments may be either more or less connected to the individual segment than the items in a segment are connected to each other. Except for chapters called "Moby Walt" (which has been reprinted elsewhere), "Catching Up with the Past," and "At Home, Four to Six," which are all unbroken chapters, all the other dozen chapters are made up of segments, usually at least one division per page, often more than that. A typical sequence of segments reads (40):

* * *

How dull and flat, however, life would be if all our follies and errors were laundered and ironed. How few poems would be written; how miserable the idealists would be.

* * *

The difficulty with ecclesiastical creeds is not that they are too hard to believe, but too easy.

* * *

If you believe a thing, it is true.

* * *

The chambered nautilus is a lovely creature; but I would not trust him as a hydrographer.

* * *

The asterisks were the part of Don Marquis's standard approach to colyuming that Morley edited out of the Marquis excerpts in his anthology. Morley assembled segments he wanted to preserve and fashioned them into a little book. What he has not done is reproduce the entire columns in which the segments appeared, which would more nearly allow us to read them as the daily newspaper reader first encountered them, mostly in isolation from one another over intervals of days, weeks, even months.

As we move to an examination of E. B. White's work in his *Harper's* column, we will discover that his writing there came out of the columning tradition rather than the essay tradition — most of the entries in the magazine show all the elements of the column and relatively few display the traditional elements of the essay. We will also discover that something transforming happens when the column is "edified" for publication in a book; editing and revising alter our sense of what we have read in the column. That too is part of White's emergence as an essayist.

White did not intend to become a monthly columnist when he took his year off; rather, he hoped to escape the limitations he felt on the Comment page and to write something of more personal — and probably more literary — significance. In his letter to Katharine about his sabbatical, he explained, "I have some pilgrimages to make. To the zoo. To Mount Vernon. To Belgrade, and Bellport, and other places where my spoor is still to be found" (*Letters* 155). His intention then was to write a long autobiographical poem (a fragment of which survives as "Zoo Revisited" in *The Second Tree from the Corner*). Increasingly, he felt he could only do that away from the city life that the *New Yorker* represented for him.

In the opening installment of his *Harper's* column in October 1938 he identified two reasons for his "removal" from New York to Maine. The first is deliberately reminiscent of Thoreau: "Some months ago, finding myself in possession of one hundred and seventeen chairs divided about evenly between a city house and a country house, and desiring to simplify my life, I sold half my worldly goods, evacuated the city house, gave up my employment, and came to live in New England" (553–554). Later in the same issue, he acknowledges that "an urge to reduce my chattels" was "only half the story." He identifies his move as an "abdication," a flight from the tenor and tone of the times, yet in his explanation, which leads to a long condemnation of a pernicious and pervasive advertising culture, he also suggests a dissatisfaction with his own role in that culture.

> What was it? What did it? What finally was too much to bear? It would be hard for me to put my finger on any one thing; rather it was an accumulation of things and the total effect inimical to health and happiness. A certain inflection in the Voice of Radio. A certain capitulation to the moral level of a phrase of swing. A certain easy virtue in everyone, myself included, and the willingness to accept the manner and speech of the promoter and the gossip writer. A certain timbre of journalism and the stepping up of news, with the implication that the first duty of man is to discover everything that has just happened everywhere in the world, as though one couldn't scratch his own mosquito bite till he first discovered who won the tennis in the antipodes. (555)

The item eventually connects the "compromising spirit" of advertising and gossip to the "willingness to accept a somewhat attractive hoax for the sake of being with the mob" preponderant in European politics of the time, but his implicating himself in his condemnation speaks directly to the constraints he had accepted in writing the Comment page. The very column title, "One Man's Meat," emphasized White's desire to get out in front of his prose and take responsibility for it more emphatically.

Some of the more positive incentives for striking out on his own as a writer and for trying to tap his personal past and present may have come from success of one of his earliest essays, "Farewell, My Lovely!" As White pointed out in his "Note" to *The Second Tree from the Corner*, and again in the acknowledgments to *Essays of E. B. White*, "Farewell, My Lovely!" was "a collaboration with Richard L. Strout," originally published in the *New Yorker* (16 May 1936). It was then enhanced by drawings by Alain and printed as a small book by G. P. Putnam and Sons under the title *Farewell to Model T*. Both the original essay and the book were published under the pseudonym "Lee Strout White." The note attached to the essay in *Second Tree* claims that the piece "was suggested by a manuscript submitted by" Strout; there is no evidence that Strout's collaboration was more than a suggestion — certainly the essay drew heavily on White's own experience with the Model T, corroborated by letters and notes about his cross-country trip in "Hotspur" after college.

White had written a similar reminiscence, "Onward and Upward with the Arts/The St. Nicholas League," in 1934, but that essay was chiefly focused on all the contributors to the children's magazine, *St. Nicholas*, who had achieved some celebrity as adults. The essay on the Model T connected with a wider span of readers, drew more directly on his own experiences, and distanced itself from the humorous sketches in which he exaggerated for comical effect both his own character and the mundane events he observed. "Farewell, My Lovely!" is amusing, but it is not comical; it is also affectionate, observant, reminiscent, and personal. In it White had the opportunity to write about a subject of interest to himself, without the spur of timeliness, and to draw upon his own past to make contact with the reader. Unlike Comment, which depended on freshness of subject matter and recentness of observation, "Farewell, My Lovely!" drew on considerable knowledge of the topic stored in his own memory and rehearsal of the language and ideas (White had already written about these experiences in his journal and in his letters to family and friends while traveling). Out from under the protective cover of his humor and his prose style, White was able to share something of value to himself with his reader. Although he had certainly developed a distinct and individual persona in his Comment and sketches, it had clearly been a literary persona, an assumed identity, a variation on the role of Eustace Tilley; in "Farewell, My Lovely!" White revealed an authorial persona closer to that of his personal letters and his private journal.

Although the desire to discover himself in his writing, to speak in the first person singular in both the figurative and literal sense, had animated much of his discontent with the *New Yorker* before his sabbatical, the success of "Farewell, My Lovely!" may have been another impetus in his striking out on his own. Elledge observes, "In 1936 his *New Yorker* essay 'Farewell, My Lovely!' had brought him a greatly increased readership, a large payment from *Reader's Digest* for permission to publish a condensed version of it, and an invitation from the editor of the *Saturday Evening Post*, the highest paying magazine in the country, to submit future pieces" (212). The book version sold well. Except for his collaboration with Thurber, *Is Sex Necessary?* — which went through eleven printings of its first edition (45,000 copies) in 1929 and was reprinted twice, in 1931 and 1936 — his other books had not been very successful. His first book of poetry, *The Lady Is Cold* (also 1929), went through a single printing of 1,392 copies. *Every Day Is Saturday* — which, he wrote Gus Lobrano, was "a sort of a book" but "I don't think a great deal of it" (*Letters* 121) — also had a single printing in 1934, producing 1,750 copies. *Farewell to Model T*, on the other hand, went through three printings within a year of publication. Not only was it popular, it also gave White a substantial literary identity — not the humorist of the Thurber collaboration and the *New Yorker* sketches or the versifier of "The Conning Tower" or the anonymous paragrapher of Notes and Comment and compiler of newsbreaks and Comment paragraphs. The essay was another encouragement for White to look inward in his writing and to give up his faithful but confining service to the *New Yorker*; its success may have made him more restless to branch out in 1937.

White may have also been encouraged by the publication of "You Can't Resettle Me" in the *Saturday Evening Post* later in 1936. The piece is essentially a paean to New York City, taking off on a controversial proposal by Dr. Rexford G. Tugwell to "move people out of crowded cities into model villages where they will be comfortable" (36). It is a rather weak piece, lacking the liveliness and warmth of "Farewell, My Lovely!" and straining to expand what might have made a lively paragraph into a thorough essay. White never reprinted it, possibly out of dissatisfaction, possibly because he eventually wrote the much better essay, "Here Is New York," which superseded this one. Nonetheless, its publication held out the hope of freelancing, and during his year off he wrote another essay, "Memoirs of a Master," also drawing on personal experience.

White wrote Comment for the *New Yorker* through July 1937, then left the magazine and the city in hopes of working in new directions. But his sabbatical was neither as long nor as productive as he had hoped. After a period of idleness and reflection, he made little progress on new material, particularly the poem, and the rejection of "Memoirs of a Master" by the *Saturday Evening Post,* for whom he had intended it, put a damper on his hopes of a freelance career. By the following summer he was contributing paragraphs for the Comment page again (although considerably fewer than in the past — see Appendix) and working on an essay called "Daniel Webster, the Hay Fever, and Me" for the *New Yorker,* a sign that he was still interested in writing longer-form personal nonfiction. He also was beginning the monthly "One Man's Meat" department for *Harper's Magazine.*

His decision to write the column was a compromise. Although it was a return to deadline writing, it reduced the number of deadlines he had to meet from fifty-two to twelve. While it provided him with a regular income, it did not regulate his free time or demand work with little or no gestation period. Finally, while the amount of space he had to fill was longer than it had been at the *New Yorker,* he was given more freedom and flexibility in how he chose to fill it, including the opportunity to make his writing both more personal and more forceful. The ways in which he met the demands of the column had a major impact on how he composed and moved him from someone who saw himself principally as a paragrapher to someone who had reason to see himself as an essayist. The impact was permanent: when he returned to writing Notes and Comment five years later, he was a different kind of paragrapher, and Comment itself changed as a result.

"One Man's Meat" ran monthly for nearly five years, from October 1938 until May 1943; there were fifty-five entries in all, and with one exception all were four pages long. Although its first entry had not yet been published, White had already written three columns for the department when, in a letter to Harold Ross on 16 September 1938, he explained:

> It is not all velvet, this monthly life. I think on the whole they worry more about it than I do — anyway they keep writing me letters, telling me how to go about everything. It seems that the big trick is to fill exactly four pages without any white space on P. 4. This goal is arrived at by a bit of wizardry which I haven't yet mastered but which I study every night before retiring. The deadline they have given me is the tenth of the month for the second month following. Fancy me in a Christmas mood by Columbus day. (*Letters* 180–181)

In another letter to Ross, dated 15 June 1939, White explained that he intended to continue the department but complained that he did not "get the fun out of it" that he had at the *New Yorker*, found it "rather difficult," and disliked "writing an article of a specified length," as he had "disliked writing a comment page of a specified length" for the *New Yorker*. Still, he thought "it was a good thing for me to have done" (*Letters* 197).

Some of the difficulties White had with column writing are alluded to in the opening portion of his column for May 1939 (later deleted from the version of the column reprinted as "Education"). In response to a letter from a schoolteacher from Michigan who envied him his job, White identified its limitations: "The business of making a living by telling what one thinks and sees undoubtedly seems just a step this side of Paradise. There are days when it isn't bad. But the schoolteacher who writes from Michigan obviously knows nothing about the days when the sum of one's thoughts can be expressed in three asterisks, and when the things one sees fail to cohere but spread out in the mind like a drop of gasoline in a wave. There is always the living to be made, asterisks or no asterisks" (664). The asterisk references clearly imply that he was thinking of "One Man's Meat" as the equivalent of a Don Marquis or F. P. A. column. He went on to compare his job to that of a drama critic: "The next time my Michigan correspondent is visited by a Thought, or stands in the presence of a Sight, she should give thanks that she can stay right there and doesn't have to grab her hat and sneak up life's dark aisle to a waiting typewriter" (664).

White suspected that his *Harper's* editors were "a little surprised that the stuff hasn't turned out to be in a comment vein" (*Letters* 198), but the remark really applied to only a limited number of columns. Although the topics that he wrote on were more personal, and the individual items were somewhat more developed than the Comment paragraphs had been, White's initial formatting of the department often resembled Notes and Comment at the *New Yorker*. That is, the monthly columns tended to be made up of several small items rather than one extended essay.

Readers of the first column in October 1938, for example, would have discovered four pages made up of six clearly separated items. The first is a five paragraph commentary on the development of television; the second is a vignette of similar length about trying to get rid of half his possessions in order to remove himself from the city; the third item is a single paragraph about a woman who bought some chairs from him, comparing her condition to that of some chairs. The fourth item, composed of three paragraphs, is a light item about setting his belongings in order: "This life I lead, setting pictures straight, squaring rugs up with the room — it suggests an ultimate symmetry toward which I strive and strain" (554). The fifth item is his discussion of the reasons for leaving the city ("What did it? What was it?"), mentioned above. The sixth and final item is a brief editorial paragraph, commenting that "lightning seems to have lost its menace. Compared to what is going on on earth to-day, heaven's firebrands are penny fireworks with wet fuses" (557). The variety of items in this column, the tenuousness of their connections to one another, would be familiar to readers of Notes and Comment as well as to readers of a number of other newspaper and magazine columnists.

In the months following that debut, the column seemed to promise a similar potpourri. The second and third columns also had six items; the fourth was subdivided into two (both on children's books); the fifth, sixth, and eighth, into three. Only the seventh column, about the "Sabbath morn," lacked a clear marker for separate items. Of the fifty-five magazine columns White published, only fifteen columns are entirely made up of a single item (one of them is a long poem, another a short story). Thus, a little under four-fifths of the columns are actually multiple-item entries, containing as few as two items or as many as nineteen. In some cases, such as the January 1939 column eventually reprinted in full as "Children's Books," the later book version eliminates the paragraph break to make a single item out of a column that had been — at least typographically — divided into two pieces on children's literature. Although there is a clear difference between the two divisions, it is possible to see that particular column as merely an essay in two distinct parts. However, when White came to publish a clipbook of the *Harper's* material, he reprinted only seventeen columns in their entirety as single pieces. Two more columns were used completely, but they were broken up into separate, titled entries in the book; seven columns were deleted entirely. The remaining thirty-one columns were reprinted only in part, most often with independent items deleted, occasionally with an originally unseparated section removed and a minor revision made.

In the foreword to the 1942 and 1944 editions of the book collection, *One Man's Meat*, White explained that "for the sake of clarity, the pieces now carry the date when they were written, rather than the date when they appeared in print." They were also given titles. The decision to print the items by date of composition rather than date of original publication changes the chronology of the columns significantly enough that a comparison of magazine and book versions offers some insight into how they were written.

Some items were written and held in reserve to be published when needed to fill the space in the magazine. For example, the November 1938 column was divided into six items. One item was reprinted as part of "Incoming Basket" and four others as "Security"; a sixth item was deleted. Both "Incoming Basket" and "Security" are identified in the book as having been written in August 1938, but "Incoming Basket" includes as a separate item a paragraph on the retirement of a railroad conductor that is not in the November 1938 column; instead, it appears as "Last Trip" in the magazine's June 1940 department, one in which six items are individually titled. Similarly, although the final column in the book, "Cold Weather," dated January 1943, is drawn from the March 1943 column, it includes one item on geese that does not appear until the following issue, in April 1943; it is likely that White wrote it in January, but it was cut for length and used in the subsequent issue. A similar example would be the first part of "Report," published in January 1940, and the second part, published in February 1940, which were reprinted together as one piece and credited with having been written in December 1939.

We cannot know how insistent White was in the accuracy of his attribution of composing dates. Certainly, in the last example, the two parts, both year-end reports, go together better with each other than they fit with the other material in the columns in which they appeared; thus, there are aesthetic reasons for ignoring strict chronology. In other cases, White might easily have linked related items published only a month or so apart but did not bother to do so, suggesting that the chronological order of the material accomplished his ends better than any thematic arrangement.

As he had, then, for the Notes and Comment page of the *New Yorker*, White sometimes saved extra items for use at another time; he also sometimes added last-minute items to fill out the space requirements of the column. There is evidence of this both in his complaint to Ross about "mastering the wizardry" of writing four pages (about 2,500 words) exactly and also in Elledge's citation of a letter from his *Harper's* editor, Lee Hartman, suggesting changes in the first column.

According to Elledge, White had intended to lead with the item that begins, "This life I lead, setting pictures straight, squaring rugs up with the room — it suggests an ultimate symmetry toward which I strive and strain." Hartman requested a more "robust" opening, which led White to compose the section musing on his observation of a demonstration of television. As Elledge observes, the television item was much closer in spirit to a *New Yorker* Comment than to the kind of personal and individual writing White's original opening exemplifies (Elledge 217). In the book, under the title "Removal," the television item comes after the item on getting rid of furniture and other worldly goods. The rug-straightening item follows the television item, and the three-sentence item that concluded the original column ends the selection in the book. Two additional items are deleted in transition.

Although most of White's columns are made up of more than one item, for the most part he seems not to have relied as heavily on a bank of items for the *Harper's* department as he had for Notes and Comment. Yet, despite his emphasis on the amount of time in between columns, relatively few of the columns give evidence of longer, more thorough gestation and composition than the *New Yorker* Comment had received. Often, it appears, White simply put off composing until the deadline drew near, then had to work feverishly in much the same manner as he had when writing Comment.

Some columns that indicate more speed of composition than others are those seemingly written at the moment of the event, those written in diary or journal form, and those written as a collection of random notes. The column reprinted as "Sabbath Morn" is an example of the first type, the column with a sense of immediacy; so too is the column reprinted as "Memorandum." Both are reminiscent of the Comment page White had reprinted in its entirety as "Chair Car" in *Every Day Is Saturday*; they seem to record thoughts as they come, spontaneously, almost as a stream of consciousness.

In "Sabbath Morn" White records a Sunday morning in his living room, with the radio playing, his son and dogs traipsing through, himself investigating news items collected in his folder that he hopes will trigger a column. Throughout, White quotes sermons, hymns, commercials, readings from the radio, conversations with the boy, as well as summarizing some of the news items. This section of the column generates a sense of immediacy, of being in the room at the time the events are both taking place and being recorded. A page break is followed by the transitional sentences — "Thus the Sabbath morn. Not a wholesome report" — and then musings on religion, religiosity, and the radio.

"Memorandum" is a series of paragraphs recording farm and household chores that need to be done, each chore leading to related ones, again recorded in a stream of consciousness, ending with the paragraph: "I've been spending a lot of time here typing, and I see it is four o'clock already and almost dark, so I had better get going. Specially since I ought to get a haircut while I am at it." The ending pulls the piece together by hinting that all the chores on this list will not get done because of the time spent listing them. In one way, the column details the unending busyness of the homeowner-farmer at the same time that it amusingly hints at procrastination; in another way, it seems to complain that the need to turn out the column keeps White from answering the demands of his daily life.

In any case, in both these columns White seems to be writing rather immediate, even spur-of-the-moment pieces, drawing from immediate observation and spontaneous generation. A similar piece is the column reprinted as "My Day," which simply follows White through the events of a single day from waking to retiring. Although the piece refers in its opening to Eleanor Roosevelt's column about the activities of the First Lady, also called "My Day" (the allusion White intended in his reference to his "sabbatical" as "My Year"), and although it alludes in the conclusion to broadcaster Elmer Davies's routine closing of his newscast ("That is the news to this moment"), the column connects only tangentially to either of these then-familiar media events and reads rather like a record of a day in the life of a common man, its resonances more particular than expansive.

In addition to this kind of immediate column, White had recourse to a related type, the diary or journal ("My Day" bridges the gap between the diary type and the "Chair Car" type). The columns collected as "A Week in April," "A Week in November," "A Winter Diary," and "The Wave of the Future" all use the premise of recording thoughts from different days as a way of arranging a series of separate, sometimes widely unrelated items (although "The Wave of the Future" ends up being an extensive review and response to a book by Anne Morrow Lindbergh). Particularly in "A Winter Diary" — in which one section begins: "The roads are solid ice. Up at 5:15 and after breakfast to the doctor's, the country seeming very beautiful and cheerful after a light fall of snow" — it seems evident that White was modeling his column on Franklin P. Adams's recurring feature, "The Diary of Our Own Samuel Pepys."

In *A Subtreasury of American Humor*, the book he and Katharine edited during the period of the *Harper's* column, White reprinted segments of F. P. A.'s Pepysian diary. A typical entry read:

> Early up and to my office, and read how M. Alonso beat Will Tilden yesterday at indoor tennis, and read some matters about the taxes, but I have the feeling that the taxes are built on such political foundations, and more destined to placate voters than to be equable. To Beatrice Kaufman's for dinner, and she asked me questions about H. Ross's tobogganing, the noise of it having been bruited about for a radius of thirty miles. And did he look funny tobogganing? she asked. Well, quoth I, you know how he looks *not* tobogganing, which seems to answer her. (White, *Subtreasury* 276)

F. P. A.'s diary attempts to imitate the rhythms and syntax of Pepys's and dwells far more often on the bon mot and the gossipy allusion to a specific circle of acquaintance (such as the twitting of Harold Ross in the example quoted), all in ways in which White had rarely indulged himself, and then only in his earliest days writing humor for the *New Yorker*. Nonetheless, F. P. A., whose column White read and contributed to until its demise, whose obituary White composed for the *New Yorker*, and whose influence is evidenced in White's early identification of himself as E. B. W., was the leading exponent of the diary column.

He was also the leading practitioner of the kind of multiple-item column that Notes and Comment itself had been modeled on. For example, a typical column contained items like these:

> "If you want to get rich from writing," counsels the astute Mr. Don Marquis, "write the sort of thing that is read by persons who move their lips when they are reading to themselves." No. Write the kind of stuff about which everybody says, "Of course it's terrible stuff, but it must be popular or they wouldn't print it."

> Her father says that Peggy Joyce, as a little girl, was always trying to please everybody; and our astonishment is great that she didn't grow up to be an unsuccessful journalist.

There are seventy stanzas in the Uruguay national anthem, which fact may account for the Uruguay standing army. (Adams, *Column* 116–117)

These items appear in succession and resemble the kind of comment that dominated the early Notes and Comment feature of the *New Yorker*; indeed, the Comment page echoed the format of Adams's paragraph columns until World War II. White's multiple-item columns (which we will examine more thoroughly in the next chapter) drew upon the models F. P. A., Don Marquis, and Christopher Morley provided, but none of them were quite as randomly assembled as the example from F. P. A.

For *Harper's* White began writing more sustained pieces for multiple-item columns — unlike some other columnists for the magazine, he did not see his task as writing a single essay per month. His only published essay in the early period of the column was "Daniel Webster, the Hay Fever, and Me," a longer piece drawn from his reading and his own experience, which appeared in the *New Yorker*. It was later reprinted as "The Summer Catarrh," the first full-length essay in the book version of *One Man's Meat* and one of three essays in the collection written during the same period and published in the *New Yorker* rather than in the "One Man's Meat" column. The focus of the essay is the relationship between White and American orator and politician Daniel Webster as allergy sufferers. Drawing on a paper in the *Yale Journal of Biology and Medicine* that he had filed in his work folder, White alternates between an account of the influence of hay fever on Webster and its effect on him. The essay informs the reader about the past at the same time that it draws upon White's own experiences and memories; it is significant for taking an item of his reading as a launching point for a reminiscence of his childhood, just as he had done to some degree in "Farewell, My Lovely!" In spite of having written and published the hay fever essay in July 1938, just as he was beginning the magazine column, he did not write another such essay until February 1939, the seventh column, reprinted as "Sabbath Morn," which was also the first single-item column.

When White later complained about the difficulty of writing the "One Man's Meat" column, he was partly frustrated by the openness of the format. To a great degree the ability to be prolific with paragraphs (or any other form) depends on familiarity with the form, the automaticity that arises from repetition. White could not draw on familiar knowledge of his topics the way he had with Comment — on the farm he was not into the currents of city affairs, had no folder of options demanding immediate response, no easy sources of material readily at hand. Because the monthly magazine made him submit the column two months ahead of time, the topics had to be more timeless, less attached to immediate events, less topical. Unlike "Farewell, My Lovely!" — which had been gestating for years — there were not only few opportunities to be prompted to draw on long-standing reserves of memory but also a deadline that encouraged faster incubation of ideas than an essay like that might need. So White tended to fall back on the habits formed at the *New Yorker*: he tended to write close to the deadline rather than to use the full month to work on the piece, and he tended to use a range of items to fill the four pages rather than a single item. When the column was a single item, it tended to be based on a new trip or new experience, on his reactions to his reading, or, less frequently, as in the case of "Once More to the Lake," on materials that were long stored and long gestated.

The column reprinted as "First World War" is based on White's reading, although the source is personal. He uses the formal start of World War II as an occasion to return to his 1918 journal and explore his earlier feelings as a combat-aged youth. Immediate events obviously spur the writing, but the availability of long-stored parallel material gives him an occasion to respond in a way that makes the column less topical (England and France declared war on Germany on 3 September 1939, and White's column, written in October, was not published until December) but still relevant. It also allows him to take up some of the space in the column with material copied more or less verbatim from his twenty-year-old journal. Similar essays include "Aunt Poo," reflecting on the life of Katharine's aunt in Japan and drawing upon her memoirs; "Children's Books," whose two linked sections reflect on the array of books Katharine has been reviewing for the *New Yorker*; "Practical Farmer," a response to a new book on farming in terms of White's own practical experience on his farm; and the long third section of "The Wave of the Future," essentially a critical essay analyzing Anne Morrow Lindbergh's *The Wave of the Future*.

Related to this kind of essay are those in which the author injects himself into a situation and comments on what he observes. The earliest example in this period was again originally printed in the *New Yorker* and later included in the column collection. "The World of To-morrow" (originally "A Reporter at Large/They Come With Joyous Song") takes White to the New York World's Fair and lets him remark upon what he encounters there. Similarly, "Camp Meeting" places him in the audience at a Methodist gathering to hear Dr. Francis Townsend discuss his economic plan for the country; "Trailer Park" sets White to querying residents at a Florida trailer park about world government. White also used this approach in sections of columns that he reprinted as separate essays in the collection: "Bond Rally," originally printed as one section of a three-section column, locates him in the crowd during an appearance by Dorothy Lamour in his local community; "Coon Hunt," a long segment of a multiple-item column, links White as a raccoon hunt novice to a hound pup also on his first outing. Although the range of possibility is broad, from the light-hearted to the serious, from the local to the global, in every case the narrator is not so much a reporter as an observer recording what interests him and commenting on it at random — or at least White represents himself that way. Connected to this group are two columns made up of now-classic essays, "Walden," in which White wanders around Concord, and "Once More to the Lake," in which White revisits a childhood vacation spot with his son. Even the column reprinted as "On a Florida Key" relates to this kind of essay, with its premise of a northerner responding to what he reads and observes in a southern community.

A few of the single-essay columns emphasize immediacy. As we will observe in the next chapter the segmented columns sometimes took the tack that hot weather or war news or spring made consecutive thought so impossible that the writer could only string together a series of related and unrelated items. Immediacy seems to develop into more unified writing in such columns as "My Day" and "Memorandum," which have the unity of spontaneous stream of consciousness, or in a column like "Sabbath Morn," which first records events as they occur and then comments on them, or in mood pieces like "The Flocks We Watch by Night" (originally published in the *New Yorker*, perhaps because White wanted more immediacy of publication) and "Morningtime and Eveningtime," both narrative pieces telling about the day's events and linking them to the menace of the war.

Two pieces that fit none of these subcategories of essay but relate to many of the short items randomly discussing farm activities are "A Shepherd's Life" and "Getting Ready for a Cow," two outright rural narratives easily at home in the bucolic books White recalled when he went to Maine, *My Farm of Edgewood* by Ik Marvel (Donald Grant Mitchell) and David Grayson's *Adventures in Contentment*. Although throughout the columns there are a number of paragraphs or short items referring to the farm (for example, "Book Learning," comparing book knowledge to experiential farm knowledge, is a section of a multiple-item column reprinted as a short essay; "The Practical Farmer" is essentially a book review), these two single-item columns suggest that, in spite of its setting, the farm component of the book is not nearly as important as is the juxtaposition of farm life with city life or with global affairs. The long tradition of farming belles lettres — which antedates Mitchell (who wrote for *Atlantic Monthly* and also *Harper's* in the middle of the nineteenth century) and extends through such contemporary works as Henry Beston's *Northern Farm* and Noel Perrin's *First Person Rural* — includes *One Man's Meat* only tangentially.

In addition to these approaches, White reprints in the collection a few short essays originating as part of multiple-item columns that are chiefly extended commentary. "Motorcars," "Maine Speech," "A Boston Terrier," "Dog Training," and "Movies" comment wryly on items picked out of the newspaper or collected in conversation. Only one essay, "Freedom," is a flatly argumentative piece that does not draw upon narrative, memory, or reportorial distance but is instead a direct piece of impassioned advocacy.

In 1942 Harper and Brothers published an edition of *One Man's Meat* culled from columns published between October 1938 and February 1942, to which were added three essays originally published in the *New Yorker*: "The Summer Catarrh," "The World of Tomorrow," and "The Flocks We Watch by Night." In 1944, after White had quit the column, the publisher destroyed the original plates and printed an enlarged edition, adding material taken from columns published between February 1942 and March 1943. Seven columns were never reprinted in any book edition of *One Man's Meat*; the only column that was entirely a long poem was subsequently broadcast as "Radio in the Rain" but never reprinted; the only one that was actually a short story, "The Hotel of the Total Stranger," was later collected in *The Second Tree from the Corner* and *Poems and Sketches of E. B. White*.

White never refers to the *Harper's* writing as essays in his letters to Ross and others. In the 16 September 1938 letter to Ross he refers to it as "2500 words a month," "a signed department," "a monthly department," "my November department," and "four pages without any white space on P. 4" (*Letters* 180–181); in his later letter the distinction between "a comment page of a specified length" and "an article of a specified length" seems to imply a difference in kind between the departments for the two magazines (197). Generally, he refers to the

Harper's writing as "pieces" or "departments," as when he writes his editor, Eugene Saxton, that the first book edition of *One Man's Meat* would be "made up of about a 75% selection of my total *Harper's Magazine* output, plus two pieces from the *New Yorker* which seemed to fit the scheme. . . . Both pieces were written within the period of my *Harper* department, and both are written in the first person singular" (*Letters* 220). His intentions for the book were somewhat different than for the column; he saw the book as "a sort of informal journal of the three years before the war. It is arranged chronologically. Each piece will have a date and a title" (220). He insisted that it was "a book of essays on a wide variety of subjects, both urban and rural" (220), and, indeed, the scheme of titling and dating pieces tended to make them more separate and individual works than they had been in the magazine. However, the ways in which he composed the columns suggest, as we will see in the next chapter, that the columnist was not exclusively — or perhaps not even primarily — an essayist during the period of "One Man's Meat."

5

"IN SEARCH OF THE FIRST PERSON SINGULAR"

Composing the Column

If we understand that the preponderance of White's writing in the prolific ten years up to his sabbatical from the *New Yorker* was composed
of Comment pages, and if we recognize the elements of the Comment
pages that White drew upon for the *Harper's* column, we are better able
to comprehend the ways in which White saw "One Man's Meat" as a
department, a column, even an ongoing public journal, rather than as a
series of essays. White's own perception of the column in general
and the anthology or clipbook that emerged from it are made plain in
printed comments about the book.

That his concept of the project changed over time is clear from the
original foreword to the book. Although he was concerned about the
impending war in Europe when he began the department in 1938,
the monthly columns weren't initially dominated by the war. But by the
time the selection of pieces was published as *One Man's Meat* in 1942,
international affairs were very much on White's mind. The foreword is
in part an apology: "A book concerned with the routine pleasures and
troubles of a peaceable life is almost embarrassing. To a publisher it
seems a bit of effrontery, or unawareness" (vii). Throughout the foreword White strains to connect his enterprise to the war. After declaring
that "the first person singular is the only grammatical implement I am
able to use without cutting myself," he claims that "this quality . . . gives
it some relation to the war. It is a book of, for, and by an individual. . . .
Individualism and the first person singular are closely related to freedom, and are what the fight is all about" (vii–viii). He presents the
collection as "a book in a time of swords, a thought or two in a time of
deeds, a celebration of life in a period of violent death. Here is a record of an individual pursuing the sort of peaceable and indulgent exis-
tence which may not soon again be ours in the same measure. I offer
'One Man's Meat' not with any idea that it is meaty but with the sure

knowledge that it is one man — one individual unlimited, with the hope of liberty and justice for all" (ix). White follows this passage with three paragraphs that are the opening section of the June 1942 department, later reprinted as "Songbirds," which updates the May entry about events in which the war imposes itself on the routines of daily life: "The field behind the barn has been top-dressed and the upper piece across the road sowed to grass. Each afternoon three patrol planes go over and are mistaken for hawks by the young chickens" (ix); "Blackout curtains are up at the kitchen window, wild cucumber up at the kitchen door" (x); "And in the east beyond the lilac and beyond the barn and beyond the bay and behind the deepening hills, in slow and splendid surprise, rises the bomber's moon" (xi). Such intrusive preoccupation with the war, with the United States into it for only five months at the time of the foreword (30 April 1942), was not the focus of the column when it began. White's sense of the work he was doing had shifted over the three and a half years since he started it.

When the revised edition of *One Man's Meat* was published in 1944, the original foreword was dropped and its final section republished in "Songbirds." In the new foreword he explained that he had "continued to write a monthly piece" for about a year after the first edition was published and that the book was "being re-issued to include this additional material." He claimed to be grateful to his publishers for allowing him this opportunity rather than asking him to hold the pieces for a different, future anthology, because "it seemed to me that these extra pieces, winding up the journal, belonged here, not in some other book." Then he describes the book: "'One Man's Meat' is, as the title suggests, a personal record. It is a collection of essays which I wrote from a salt water farm in Maine while engaged in trivial, peaceable pursuits, knowing all the time that the world hadn't arranged any true peace or granted anyone the privilege of indulging himself for long in trivialities" (*Meat* vii). Later he explained that the reasons "a man quits writing in his journal" did not seem to apply to him. Although White uses the terms "record," "journal," "collection of essays," "monthly pieces" interchangeably in the new foreword, they are surely not interchangeable in practice. Later, in the foreword to *The Essays of E. B. White*, White explained that he had extracted only three "chapters" from *One Man's Meat* for the retrospective anthology, "since it is a sustained report of about five years of country living — a report I prefer not to tamper with" (*Essays* ix).

But *One Man's Meat* is really none of these things exclusively. Certainly the nature of its composition over a four-and-a-half-year period gives it a progressive, sustained quality, but it has nothing of the summary nature of a report; equally the personal items and random responses to local and world events sometimes give it the tone of a journal, but only occasionally do pieces approximate anything like the formlessness and spontaneity of journal entries; finally, while some of the pieces clearly are essays, the term is used so loosely in describing the entire book as to make the entries in *Every Day Is Saturday* or each of White's Notes and Comment pages qualify as essays as well.

The issue is not merely one of terminology but rather gets at the heart of what an essay is and what an essayist attempts to accomplish in writing one. White's goal each month was to compose a column, a new installment of a magazine department. Sometimes he accomplished that goal by writing columns composed of a single item — unified, sustained, unsegmented, a thematic whole, a "conjunctive" essay. Sometimes he accomplished it by writing multiple-item columns, compiled as clusters of paragraphs, notes, and comments; these columns were usually "nonjunctive," a nonsequential series of essentially unrelated items, but often they were composed of items that resonated off one another, related in tenuous or tangential or sympathetic ways that made the column seem like one fragmented or segmented or "disjunctive" whole. Sometimes the column included longer items that could be separated from the other items because of their development and unity into entities in themselves. These items, essentially short conjunctive essays, were joined by other disparate, unrelated items to make up a nonjunctive department. White's conjunctive essays for the department were not always coterminous with the column itself.

The column in the magazine, then, was composed in ways that are not evident from the selective and compartmentalized version of it most readers are familiar with — the clipbook editions of *One Man's Meat*. Both the multiple-item columns and the single-item columns were generated in a number of different ways.

The multiple-item columns reflect in particular White's debt to, and affection for, the colyum conductor, Don Marquis. White had written with his ear cocked to Marquis's voice before — his jaunty Comment from 26 February 1927 beginning "Our report is now ready on why people are so delighted to ask and answer questions that a book full of them has been published" echoes a passage in Marquis's *The Almost Perfect State* beginning "Our inquiry with regard to the bean and its influence upon civilization is fairly complete . . ." (30). His *Harper's* department gave White considerably more room to play with the multiple-item form.

In the "One Man's Meat" column published September 1939 he used the form to comment not only on the effects of hot weather but also on Marquis himself and by implication the very format in which that column was written. After an opening paragraph about a summer morning he writes:

* * *

Asterisks? So soon?

* * *

It is a hot weather sign, the asterisk. The cicada of the typewriter, telling the long steaming noons. Don Marquis was one of the great exponents of the asterisk. The heavy pauses between his paragraphs, could they find a translator, would make a book for the ages.

* * *

Don knew how lonely everybody is. "Always the struggle of the human soul is to break through the barriers of silence and distance into companionship. Friendship, lust, love, art, religion — we rush into them pleading, fighting clamoring for the touch of spirit laid against our spirit." Why else would you be reading this fragmentary page — you with the magazine in your lap? You're not out to learn anything, certainly. You just want the healing action of some chance corroboration, the soporific of spirit laid against spirit. Even if you read only to crab about everything I say, your letter of complaint is a dead giveaway: you are unutterably lonely or you wouldn't have taken the trouble to write it.

* * *

Editor: "Take off your hat when you address a reader!"

* * *

I didn't intend to get off on Don Marquis. But I might as well be there as anywhere, between asterisks. His sickness and death always seemed to me bitterly ironical. He wrote once that he looked forward to a disreputable, vigorous, unhonored, and disorderly old age, when he would sit with a decanter of whisky at hand and shoot out the lights with a pistol when he got sleepy. His last years had none of those lusty attributes, and he departed this life amid all the prosy and disagreeable embarrassments of prolonged ill health. He didn't even die unhonored — merely lonely and broken. I never met Don Marquis, but I always wanted to go out to where he was invalided, taking a pistol and some light bulbs, so he could let 'em have it.

* * *

Perhaps I feel as I do about Don Marquis because of an acute sympathy with anybody who writes short. He wound himself up at the beginning of a paragraph, leaped high into the air, and dissolved in pyrotechnical delight. In the next paragraph he was very likely talking about something else. His works were neither long nor connected. The critics tearfully praised his posthumous novel, but I suspect it was the only laboriously mediocre thing he ever wrote. Don was no novelist — he just felt he ought to be one, like everyone else who has ever lunched with a publisher. (441–442)

* * *

The last three paragraphs above were cut when the column was reprinted in the book. White had informed Thurber of Marquis's death in much the same terms in a personal letter the previous year (*Letters* 171–172). White's comments on Marquis and the asterisk identify the source of this format, and the format may have inspired White to write about Marquis. Certainly, without reference to Marquis, he had used and would continue to use randomly connected paragraphs to fill a column.

In this passage we can follow the development of a thought: "It is a hot weather sign, the asterisk. The cicada of the typewriter, telling the long steaming noons. Don Marquis was one of the great exponents of the asterisk." The cicada, a hot weather insect, is reminiscent in White's phrase of Don Marquis's Archy, the typing cockroach; an asterisk may even look like an insect on the page. White may be thinking partly of Archy as well when he says of Marquis that "he wound himself up at the beginning of a paragraph, leaped high into the air, and dissolved in pyrotechnical delight." Ten years later, in the introduction to a new edition of *the life and times of archy and mehitabel*, White describes the book as having been "hammered out at such awful cost by the bug hurling himself at the keys" and quoted Marquis's description of Archy's composing: "After about an hour of this frightfully difficult literary labor he fell to the floor exhausted." White claimed this as Marquis's own obituary notice, saying of Marquis himself that "after about a lifetime of frightfully difficult literary labor . . . he fell exhausted" (*Second Tree* 182). White's "acute sympathy with anyone who writes short," whose works are "neither long nor connected," who writes a brilliant paragraph and then in the next paragraph is "very likely talking about something else" all connect Marquis with White himself, particularly in this column.

Further evidence of White's association of this kind of column with the writing of Don Marquis comes from a later column, published August 1940 and reprinted, with four of its original twenty-seven sections deleted, as "Compost." The piece opens:

> To-day joined a society called Friends of the Land, as at my time of life a man should belong to a club so that he will have somewhere to sit in the afternoon. I am going to put an old chair out by my compost heap, and shall go there whenever I feel sociable and friendly toward the land. Membership cost me five dollars, which is the first time my high regard for earth has ever cost me a nickel; but these are expensive times.
>
>   *   *   *
>
> Am writing this on the fourth day of the Battle of France, as the announcer calls it, so there will probably be no continuous thought from one paragraph to the next. I am not able to write on a single harmonious theme while jumping up frequently to hear whether freedom is still alive. I don't think I would lose my nerve if I were directly engaged in war; but this radio warfare makes me edgy. I suspect I joined my club only because I was rattled. When I am composed I feel no need of affiliating myself with anybody. There is a lot of the cat in me, and cats are not joiners.
>
>   *   *   *
>
> So great is the importance attached to news from abroad, even my club intends to have foreign correspondents. I should imagine to-day would be a discouraging day for the northern France correspondent of the Friends of the Land. The organic matter now being added to French soil is of a most embarrassing nature. Until we quit composting our young men we shall not get far with a program of conservation.

In these paragraphs White establishes a justification for the disjointedness of this column but also creates a link between the items on the Friends of the Land and the war news with the composting image. The column itself may also be seen as compost, in the sense of an aggregation of random items fermenting together.

As the "Compost" column progresses White turns unexpectedly to the following subject: "I have given up planning an almost perfect state for America, as it is too small a field. Henceforth I shall design only world societies, which will include everybody and everything. Don Marquis began work on the almost perfect state but died before it came into being. I should let that be a lesson to me." This item follows several items on fashion, reprinted in the book, and one item on the arrival of a coal-laden schooner, deleted for the collection. It contains a link back to the beginning with the idea of including everyone, another allusion to joining. Since this is the ninth item separated by asterisks, Don Marquis was no doubt on his mind from the beginning. Marquis's *The Almost Perfect State* was made up of material on that subject from both his columns, "The Sun Dial" (1912–1922 in the *New York Sun*) and "The Lantern" (1922–1925 in the *New York Herald Tribune*), and White alluded to the book frequently in his writing.

From this point on the column develops a series of paragraphs on the state of the world and the need to develop some sort of world society. Many of them include deliberate shifts of direction signaled by "Note," "Parenthesis," "Thought," and "Proposition" (a technique used in early Comment, such as in "Chair Car"), and short items are frequently couched as dialogue or as aphorisms: "The duty of a democracy is to know then what it knows now"; "A seer a day keeps Armageddon away." The next item following this last aphorism reads:

> Impudent interruption: You're trying to sound like Don Marquis, aren't you?
>
> Soft answer: Yes. I have not given up loving his almost perfect state, and will continue to discuss it any time I see fit.

The subject of this particular column was one White associated with Marquis, but it is apparent that the format itself is one he drew from Marquis even when the subject matter was radically different from the kind of thing Marquis wrote.

The fragmented column is a way of composing under pressures of time and length and quantity that discourage more sustained and more holistic pieces. White is often adept at making a virtue of necessity, turning the fragmented column back on itself to make it seem an experiment in, or a comment on, form while using the form as an expedient way of meeting his deadline.

But there are drawbacks to the system, particularly in the quantity of disposable writing produced. In the "Hot Weather" column nineteen sections are separated by asterisks. We can cluster them in this way: one item on summer mornings; six items (recorded above) on Don Marquis and the asterisk; six items loosely connected by comments on world events; two items on chickens; two items about becoming provincial; one item about a baby seagull (introduced with an irrelevant transition sentence about becoming provincial); and one item about marking the seasons by changing crankcase oil. It is difficult to cluster these items in any larger groups than these. When White reprinted the column as "Hot Weather" in *One Man's Meat*, he used only ten of the nineteen sections, eliminating the final three sections on Don Marquis and the entire six sections on world events and also combining the two sections on provinciality into one. White deleted a great deal of the column material from the book manuscript in this fashion because he thought that it no longer measured up to the rest of the material or had grown irrelevant, erroneous, or stale, or that it presented the subject or the author in a no-longer-desirable light. Significantly, nothing was deleted from any of the unsegmented columns — they were either cut in their entirety or reprinted whole. The deletions come only from the multiple-item columns. Since it was perfectly possible to reprint columns in their entirety, White's decision to delete so much material suggests that he did not see these columns as unified wholes but more as variations on the kind of paragraphing he had been doing at the *New Yorker*.

This point is critical to understanding White's development as an essayist. The columns of "One Man's Meat" contain a number of what Carl Klaus has referred to as "traditionally structured and tightly connected narrative essays," such as "First World War," "The Flocks We Watch by Night," and "Once More to the Lake" ("Excursions" 39). The month before "Hot Weather," White published the column reprinted as "Walden," an account of his visit to Concord, and a month later he published the column reprinted as "Camp Meeting," about the Townsend Plan — both are single-essay columns. Even the column of July 1939, two months before "Hot Weather," contains only two sections, one reprinted as "Movies" and the other reprinted as "A Boston Terrier," each of them a short essay independent of the other. The shorter sustained essays tend to grow out of paragraphs, to develop paragraphs further; the longer essays tend to have greater depth and complexity and to be composed under different circumstances. Not all the single-item columns, as we have seen, can really be called sustained essays; that is, in spite of being single items, they may not necessarily develop a single sustained idea but rather invent an occasion for wide-ranging rambles.

Of course, there is a tradition in the essay of great flexibility of form. One of the pleasures of reading some essays is the opportunity to track a mind following a path of associations rather than mapping an argument. In some columns in which the connections between sections are tenuous, although ostensibly working from a single theme, the reader may have some uncertainty about whether a path to follow exists. Take for example the column reprinted as "Spring," originally published untitled in *Harper's* in June 1941. In the original, asterisks divide the column into fifteen sections; in the book the sections are divided by unmarked paragraph breaks. Three sections of the magazine column, one in the middle and two at the end, are deleted for the book. The column begins by announcing its format in the first section: "Notes on springtime and on anything else that comes to mind of an intoxicating nature." As we have already seen, spring was a subject that White never tired of writing about. The opening takes us back to the kind of Notes and Comment page exemplified by "Grace Notes" in *Every Day Is Saturday*, and the column proceeds to offer a series of notes circling around the themes of spring and intoxication.

After the opening, the second section is on the question of his pig's pregnancy; the third, on a visit by a representative of Superman, Inc., to the public library; the fourth, on reading Louisa May Alcott and thinking of Europe in terms of its characters — as Scholes and Klaus suggest, the idea of Superman may have linked White to the Nazi concept of the *Übermensch* and made his joke at the end of the section about Alcott's books (*Little Supermen* and *Little Superwomen*) double-edged, leading to the connection in the third section (59). The fifth, sixth, and seventh sections, on the intoxication of lambs, not finding a snake, and starlings building a nest, all return to springtime farm images. The eighth talks at length about spring weather; the ninth, about his son's sugaring operations; the tenth, linked to the others tangentially by the phrase "Whenever I tell about spring," about a friend's remark to "spare the reading public your little adventures in contentment" (a reference to a series of farm books by Ray Stannard Baker writing under the name David Grayson). The eleventh section contains two small paragraphs making fun of a promotion letter from a New York hotel that obviously does not apply to White as a customer; it is one of the sections deleted from the book. The twelfth section tells at length about the problems of maintaining a brooder stove. The thirteenth recounts the struggle to keep the stove burning at a time when the news from Europe was particularly disturbing, a section linked to the fourth. It ends with a paragraph defending the publication of White's column: "Countries are ransacked, valleys drenched with blood. Though it seems untimely I still publish my belief in the egg, the contents of the egg, the warm coal, and the necessity for pursuing whatever fire delights and sustains you." This is the concluding passage of the piece in the book, but in the magazine two more sections follow, the fifteenth quoting a letter about the care of chickens, the sixteenth discussing the planting of grass in the field across the road.

Focusing on the statement about his "belief in the egg," Scholes and Klaus "see this essay as a kind of dialogue," a "meditation" in response to the request to "spare the reading public your little adventures in contentment." White, they continue, "closes not with an appeal to us but with an assertion on behalf of himself: 'I still publish.' In this meditation he persuades not us but himself, and we overhear the associative pattern of his meditative process. We see the subject *through* the meditator, and what we perceive of *it* is always in relation to *him*" (63). In their analysis Scholes and Klaus have presented "Spring" as a meditative or "poetic" essay, in which the author "connects ideas by an associative rhythm, with no worry about an organized outline leading from assumptions to conclusions" (47); for them "the meditative writer is a kind of explorer, examining himself and his environment in search of truth. He is, in a sense, thinking on paper, trying things out" (46). They see the prose in such an essay as "rich in images which are not exploited . . . but played with and encouraged to produce other images through the mysterious generative powers of the mind" (48).

In columns like "My Day" and "Memorandum" and the opening half of "Sabbath Morn," White did indeed connect ideas by an associative rhythm, generating the writing virtually spontaneously, as he had in the Notes and Comment piece, "Chair Car." Certainly one of his goals in writing Comment earlier in his career had been to arrange disparate items into some kind of associative pattern when possible, although the patterns that emerged tended to be vague, either because of the tenuousness of the associations or because of random, disassociative insertions of other paragraphs by other contributors. However, as demonstrated by the deletions and restructuring performed to make up the book version of *One Man's Meat*, in relatively few columns can we take the magazine originals to be thematic entities rather than multiple-item pastiches constructed chiefly for purposes of space and timeliness. In the book versions some of the restructuring is done chiefly to group items chronologically, not for thematic or aesthetic motives (or rather, to meet the thematic or aesthetic goal of making the book seem more of "a sort of informal journal" or "a sustained report"). Moreover, White's practice in the *New Yorker* and his remarks about Don Marquis's practice together suggest that thematic, if not structural, unity was not necessarily requisite in White's work.

In recent years, as writers have more frequently published segmented essays, composition and nonfiction scholars have come to refer to them as "collage essays" or "disjunctive essays." Like most terms for work in this genre, these are not entirely adequate. As Klaus has observed, terms like "collage" or "montage," taken from art or film, actually describe quite different processes of creation; verbal works are not very exact equivalents of visual works ("Excursions" 40–43). The term "disjunctive" is also problematic, since it suggests a deficiency — a failure to connect — rather than a deliberate, artistic choice. Nonetheless, the terms are likely to stay in use, and I have been circling around acceptance of "disjunctive" as a positive and descriptive label, rather than an evaluative label, particularly in discussing White's "One Man's Meat" columns. But such a term raises the question of how we determine when a disjunctive column is an essay arranged disjunctively and when it is simply a series of independent items with no discernible connections. Is any random sequence of short items, like work in the Notes and Comment format, a disjunctive essay?

A suggestion of an answer to that question may be found in Klaus's assertion that "the segmental, incremental, form of the disjunctive essay tacitly invites one to consider each individual piece of the composition in and of itself, in relation to every other piece, and in relation to the entire set of pieces, resulting in a complex network of understandings gradually arrived at rather than a whole work immediately perceived" (42). These "abrupt shifts and 'odd juxtapositions'" make for a "strange reading experience." Klaus explains:

Each segment, by virtue of its separateness and distinctiveness, calls upon me to read it and respond to it in and of itself. Yet each segment, by virtue of being only one in a series of other segments, compels me to read it and respond to it in connection with the others, and not just those that immediately precede and follow it, but also those that come much earlier or later in the set. Thus in reading a disjunctive essay, I inevitably find myself experiencing at some point an irresolvable tension between two different ways of reading and responding. Early on in my reading of such an essay, I can easily do justice to each segment as a discrete entity as well as to each segment in connection with its immediate neighbor. But as I move further on in the text, my accumulating sense of recurrent or contrastive words, phrases, images, metaphors, ideas, topics, or themes makes it increasingly difficult for me to perceive the later segments in and of themselves. Indeed, the further I read into the piece the more often I find myself intuitively making connections or distinctions between and among the segments, almost as if I were experiencing some of the very same associative leaps that might have provoked the essayist to write a piece in disjunctive form. (48)

The reading of a disjunctive essay, then, is a rich and challenging experience that calls upon different ways of making connections with the essay and among its parts than does the experience of reading "traditionally structured," "conjunctive" essays. On some level the design of the disjunctive essay is a path to lead the reader associatively rather than systematically through the reading. Certainly in the contemporary disjunctive essay the reader expects to find interwoven strands and suggestive markers as clues not only to meaning of the essay but also to the way it should be read. Yet, because contemporary essayists essentially set out to write disjunctive essays, they compose from an overall design or set of thematic parameters. That certainly was not the starting place for the colyums of Marquis, Morley, and F. P. A., or for the Notes and Comment page of the *New Yorker*. Nor is it for all of the multiple-item columns of "One Man's Meat."

The three unreprinted paragraphs in the magazine version of "Spring" suggest that at the time of its original publication White did not see the column as a single entity; moreover, the deleted material in its original context makes some of the undeleted items seem much more random and nonessential. When those paragraphs are deleted for the book version, the ending of the column becomes stronger and more conclusive, and the connections between items, while no less tenuous, seem more viable. Still, the structure of a column like "Spring" is not significantly different from those of a typical Comment page. Although White may not have had a bank of prewritten paragraphs to draw on, he did have a folder of likely topics to consult and a habit of seeing composing as a process of getting together multiple items. If "Spring" is an essay, it is a particularly amorphous kind, a cross between a personalized comment page and a fully developed single entity.

However, "Spring" may be suggestive of the ways such columns were composed. Comparing magazine and book versions of some of the more disassociative multiple-item columns, as well as the evidence of dates, we notice that the items published in the same issue may have been composed at quite different times — for example, the "Last Trip" item seems to have been written in August 1938 but was unpublished until June 1940. In such columns there may be a rhythm or a balance that is sought in the arrangement of items — long ones adjacent to short ones, serious ones tempered by comic ones, decisions of placement decided by abruptness of shift or determination of opening or closing tone. The arrangement may demand composing new items to separate existing ones or simply to fill out the column so that there is very little white space on the fourth page. Such columns do take on the feel of Comment pages and are composed under similar conditions.

But such columns as "Spring" and the two that explicitly cite Don Marquis read more associatively and may have been composed more deliberately in imitation of his columns. This means that while items written before or after the composition of the major portion of the column may have been included, it is more likely that the disjunctiveness of that particular column is a necessary component of its format — in other words, in such instances, the column has been composed rather than assembled. The typical Comment page is disjunctive (in the usual meaning of the word) because it is assembled from random parts — the randomness and the variety are desirable attributes that readers have been trained to expect. The lack of development is a defining characteristic of the Comment paragraph as a literary form. Clearly, in the "One Man's Meat" column White feels free to be disjunctive in exactly that way — in the very first column, in fact, he revises in accordance with his editor's desire to establish that disjunctive, Comment page–like stance.

However, in the Marquisesque multiple-item columns the disjunctiveness is far more likely to be a rhetorical device or a composing strategy. Marquis's goal as a daily colyumist had been to reduce the amount of space that needed to be filled with words by employing asterisks and white spaces strategically throughout the column. (One of White's unreprinted columns was simply a collection of letters from readers, a device Marquis, Morley, and Adams resorted to frequently.) White may have had the same goal as Marquis when the deadline of the column was drawing near, and it may have been the nearness of the deadline that made him think of Marquis and his strategies for dealing with it. Yet, because White was consciously imitating Marquis, there tends to be a greater associative unity to these columns. It arises from a specific voice or tone of impersonation running through the piece as well as from the consistent intertextuality of imitation.

The multiple-item columns, then, can be placed along a disjunctiveness continuum, stretching in one direction toward disassociative, isolated fragmentation and in the other direction toward associative, segmented unity. In the first instance White was extending the tradition of the paragraph, the Comment page; in the second, he was pushing his column intuitively toward the contemporary disjunctive essay.

❧ The length of the "One Man's Meat" column prompted White to produce more extended copy than he had done on the Notes and Comment page. As we have seen, the Notes and Comment approach to such a column can result in a plethora of sections, paragraphs, and snippets of wildly varying lengths. But the single deadline each month, as well as the practice of a number of other columnists, invited a single, unified column, or at least one with fewer, longer sections. From the beginning the *Harper's* department encouraged more developed commentary, although throughout its run White often had difficulty "writing long."

One way of writing more developed commentary is to take a more leisurely or a more thorough approach to the same kind of material that might have served as Comment. Frequently, when the column contains a short essay among its multiple sections, that essay reads like an extended paragraph. For example, the July 1939 column is divided neatly into two segments, reprinted in the book as the independent but consecutive pieces titled "Movies" and "A Boston Terrier." The opening paragraph of the column explains that the author lives in a town with no movie house and has to rely on magazines and newspapers to learn about the lives of the stars. The second paragraph reads:

> The newspapers of course keep one informed of the marriages, births, deaths, separations, divorces, and salaries of the stars. If Gable weds Lombard, I know about it. When Tone and Crawford reach the end of the road, I am informed. Separations and divorces are scented with the same delicate orange blossoms as marriages and elopements, the same romantic good fellowship. One of the most interesting accomplishments of the film community, it seems to me, is that it has made real for America the exquisite beauty of incompatibility. Divorce among the gods possesses the sweet, holy sadness

which has been long associated with marriage among the mortals. There is something infinitely tender about the inability of an actor to get along with an actress. (*Meat* 56)

The third paragraph elaborates on this theme by discussing a specific instance of relationships documented in the fan magazines, and the fourth paragraph suggests that this Hollywood trend is affecting the general culture, making marriage "a sort of stepping-stone to the idyllic life which lies ahead for graduates of the course."

The fifth paragraph begins, "There is something else which Hollywood has done and is doing," and goes on to explain that by habitually living above the standards of its audience Hollywood has communicated to them "a conviction that the standards of this world are the norm," as a film called *Dark Victory* illustrates. Paragraph six explains the situation in the movie that leads Bette Davis's character, Judith, to say of her Vermont home, "Here I have nothing and am happy." The next six paragraphs, to the end of the essay, examine that statement by comparing the estimated expenses of a Vermont life as lived in the film with contemporary prices, fees, and New England property values; White includes an itemized budget (an idea from Thoreau that he used in several different pieces). It concludes with the comment, "It is disturbing to realize that even after we have been reduced to Hollywood's low, we are still rolling in the sort of luxury which eventually destroyed Rome" (59).

In the typical Notes and Comment paragraph observations of this kind were made all the time. The second paragraph, quoted above, could easily be an isolated *New Yorker* comment, if we change "of course" to "continue to," "I" to "we," "me" to "us," and "am" to "are." Most of White's *New Yorker* writing demanded an ability to make a quick observation rounded off with an adept quip; in fact, the newsbreaks were nothing but quips. But the *Harper's* column allowed White the latitude to develop the observation, to flesh out the idea. In consequence, the details of the observation become as important as — perhaps more important than — the summary comment, and the character of the observer is more developed, more integral to an appreciation of the piece. The aptness of the concluding remark in "Movies" is thoroughly reinforced by the detail of the itemized budget. Moreover, the persona of the writer emerges as one who is perhaps quirky, but sensible, observant, down to earth, companionable.

If the format of "One Man's Meat" allowed development, it also allowed greater expansion of the personal dimension of White's comments. The second half of that column, reprinted as "A Boston Terrier," is again the kind of short essay that could easily have been a comment. In fact, it is markedly similar to a paragraph reprinted in *Every Day Is Saturday* as "Terrier":

> *October 17 [1931].* In the interests of honesty-in-advertising we feel we should speak to the B. F. Goodrich Footwear Corporation about an ad of theirs in the *New Yorker* a week or so ago. It showed a pair of galoshes and a Scottish terrier, and it said that the galoshes could "stand any amount of bad weather — like the Scottie." It happens that this department supports (at what cost!) a female Scottish terrier; and if there ever was a fair-weather bitch, she is it. One drop of rain unnerves her, two drops convince her, and at the third drop she is in full cry, headed for the nearest doorway — any doorway at all. We wish a representative of the footwear company could stand with us, some dour morning before breakfast, at the street door of our apartment and watch Daisy when she discovers that it is raining. We wish he could hear her say: "What! Go out in *that*?" (*Every Day* 90–91)

About half of the comment sets up the situation and the second half delivers an account that comments on it, concluding with an anthropomorphic punch line. It is merely a vignette that provides an alternative take on the situation in the Goodrich advertisement.

All of those same elements are present in "A Boston Terrier," which begins: "I would like to hand down a dissenting opinion in the case of the Camel ad which shows a Boston terrier relaxing. I can string along with cigarette manufacturers to a certain degree, but when it comes to the temperament and habits of terriers, I shall stand my ground" (*Meat* 60). In the next two paragraphs White cites and comments on quotations from the ad about Boston terriers, and then he begins a five-paragraph account of the keyed-up nerves of a Boston terrier who "gave a mighty clever excuse . . . 'I'm in love and I'm going *crazy.*'" White then returns to the Camel ad, spends three paragraphs citing another example of a terrier with an obsession, and then gives two paragraphs to a study of his dachshund, concluding: "I'll be glad to have the Camel people study this animal in one of his relaxed moods, but they will have to bring their own seismograph. Even curled up cozily in a chair, dreaming of his cat, he quivers like an aspen" (62).

The principal difference between "Terrier" and "A Boston Terrier" is that in the longer piece White has the leisure to develop his argument and to draw more fully on his own past observations of dogs. The vignette of the paragraph has expanded into the multiple illustration of the essay, not only developing the idea more fully but also changing focus: the original uses the comparison to tweak advertising as well as to evoke an image of dogs, while the latter piece makes the comment on advertising seem virtually incidental, a loose connection to contemporary events with little influence on the actual evidence — some other lead might just as well have started things off; the advertising lead does not seem integral to the body of the essay.

Such short essays, to which could be added a dozen others from *One Man's Meat*, are an intermediate form between the paragraph and the full-length essay. The *Harper's* department and the resultant book are chiefly made up of brief comment and short essays; the memorable full-length essays make up a relatively small part of the column and are augmented in the book by three originally published independently in the *New Yorker*.

The most repeated technique is one in which White wanders, observes, and responds. For example, in "The World of Tomorrow," one of the *New Yorker* essays, he is a reporter at large wandering around the World's Fair. The piece foreshadows the similar techniques of later "new journalists" who focus their reportage through the prism of their individual experience. The essay is impressionistic, filtered through White's discomfort over his hay fever, describing the exhibits and experiences to which he reacted and voicing skepticism with "progress" throughout. "Camp Meeting" and the shorter "Bond Rally" also place White as a bystander at public events.

In "Walden" White ambles around Concord, Massachusetts, and out to Walden Pond, reacting to what he observes and contrasting the world of Thoreau with his own. His reading of Thoreau affected the flavor of his language at various times in the column. Often his remarks in "Walden" deliberately echo or parody Thoreau: "It was a delicious evening, Henry, when the whole body is one sense, and imbibes delight through every pore, if I may coin a phrase" (72); "a man sat listening to Amos and Andy on the radio (it is a drama of many scenes and without an end)" (74). A relaxed essay following the chronology of the visit, it takes the tone of a familiar letter — it begins, "Miss Nims, take a letter to Henry David Thoreau. Dear Henry:" — and notices changes in the town and the pond without drawing much of a larger or more explicit conclusion about them. In the end he totes up the cost of his visit (hotel, meals, baseball equipment for his son) and tells Thoreau, "You must remember that the house where you practiced the sort of economy which I respect was haunted only by mice and squirrels. You never had to cope with a shortstop" (77–78). Despite the opportunity to comment at greater length on Thoreau and *Walden* or to analyze modern society in Thoreauvian terms, White opts for a casual description of the contemporary Concord scene and a light contrasting of his own foibles and obligations with Thoreau's integrity and freedom.

In such columns White's process resembles another of his approaches to Comment writing. As he later wrote to Ross, "in New York I could always dig up a department, by looking around in an old folder or a new barroom" (*Letters* 241). The Comment page demanded constant vigilance for likely subjects, clipping items from the newspaper, recording items in the mail, storing anecdotes and vignettes, or wandering around the city. Many of the items in Notes and Comment grew out of something White spotted on the way to or from work or during a lunch-hour stroll (for example, the item contrasting the chauffeured limousine outside a bank with the underwear on a clothesline). The ambulatory entries in the column arose from a similar tactic, although North Brooklin, Maine, triggered fewer such items than New York City did. Instead, White had to set out with more of a reporter's eye for the location or event, intending to take more in than necessary for a brief snapshot, to develop more of the scene, and to foreground his own consciousness of the dynamics of the setting. From a writer's standpoint these kind of pieces are appealing because they provide a series of immediate notes and observations to draw from and a chronology to follow as an obvious structure. It is less difficult to find a structure for this kind of column or content to fill it with than for more argumentative or abstract topics.

Similarly, White takes an observer's role in regard to commonplace events in his personal life, experiences that are less colorful than the World's Fair or the town of Concord. Three pieces that particularly stress the immediacy of an experience include "Sabbath Morn," "The Flocks We Watch by Night" (originally run in the *New Yorker* but very much in the voice of the column), and "Morningtime and Eveningtime," the only column originally run with a title in *Harper's*. In "Sabbath Morn," discussed earlier as a piece drawing on events as they take place, the first half reads as if the events on the radio, the events in the home, the dialogue, are recorded as they occur, and the second half meditates on the experience of the first half. White sometimes let himself go in bursts of stream-of-consciousness torrents: the odd fantasy at the end of the column entitled "Poetry" is continually interrupted by parenthetical statements — "In the cities (but the cities are to be destroyed) the lights continue to burn on into the morning . . ." (106) — and the sentences are long, phrase piled on phrase, often without a verb. The unreprinted verse column from the July 1940 *Harper's*, read on the radio as "Radio in the Rain," also emphasizes parentheses and repetition:

> Sit here, my soul, and disregard the rain
> That is not falling yet appears to fall
> (We are bringing you the rain as a transcribed feature)
> On every field, in every ditch and gully,
> In the swamps (extra in the swamps)
> In the grass, where the step falls, where the bird is, rain.
> Sit here, my soul, and take your medicine.

The unreprinted final column of the department is couched in terms of a monologue delivered on a walk through Central Park. But "Sabbath Morn," by seeming to record the actual events in the order they spontaneously occur, has less of a sense of urgency than the seemingly breathless pieces just mentioned do, and more of a sense of immediacy.

From a writer's point of view the "Sabbath Morn" piece grows like a journal or diary entry, as it happens, holding off reflection to concentrate on recording, preserving the flavor and feel of the moment. It counts on the description of the experience to trigger discoveries and associations that can be developed later on. In "Sabbath Morn" the clear division into two parts suggests exactly this kind of composing experience — the detailed observation followed by the reflective response to what has been observed.

In the same way "Flocks" and "Morningtime" seem to be simple narratives of events. "Flocks" tells of the physical difficulties of a neighbor's coming to take a sheep from White's pasture and the mundane conversation they share; only the photographs of the man's children and the questions of White's boy later about the men's European war conversation (the piece was written in November 1939, a full two years before the United States's entry) suggest that the essay is something more than a farm narrative, that it is about the intrusiveness of world events into daily life and the fear of war's destructiveness among those (parents and farmers) whose business is life. As in "Sabbath Morn" and "Once More to the Lake," father and son stand for eternal and enduring values. "Morningtime" is a moody piece, written in July 1942, contrasting the serenity of a New England summer and farmwork with the disturbing duties of a civilian spotter and blackout-patrol member, watchful for war but also vigilant for beauty; it reads as if it were being written on those afternoon and midnight watches, rather than during one of the frustrating writing sessions he describes in the piece, when he is unable to produce any usable work. Without any manuscript evidence from this period, we cannot know for certain the processes by which these pieces came into being, but the precision of detail and vividness of setting and action suggest a lived experience, whether recorded at the moment or reconstructed later on.

If we come to "Once More to the Lake," the best known and most widely reprinted essay from *One Man's Meat*, fresh from reading the other single-item columns, we recognize at once that, while it is also built around casual wandering and observation, it is unique in the way it establishes and develops a definite theme. The distinctiveness of the essay arises from the background White brought to it, which altered the circumstances of its composing. Unlike so many of the other columns, which depend upon current events or recent experience, the circumstances recorded in "Once More to the Lake" connect back to years of accumulated knowledge and memory, and thus the essay is one that draws upon a deeper, richer, more intimate reservoir of resources than is true of most other columns.

The triggering event for the essay was the visit White and his son, Joel, made to the Belgrade Lakes in July 1941, but this Maine resort area had been a family vacation site since 1904, and White stayed there from time to time throughout his entire life. Around 1914 he wrote up an imitation travel brochure extolling it to a friend; the pamphlet is reproduced in Elledge's biography. In 1927, according to a letter to Ross, which he wrote in a childlike voice ("Also I have a cricket. I will bet you haven't got a cricket"), he slipped off alone on an unauthorized vacation from the *New Yorker* to Bert Mosher's Bear Springs Camp on one of the lakes (*Letters* 77). He wrote to his brother Stanley from the same place in the mid-thirties and identified it as one of his destinations in his letter to Katharine explaining his sabbatical. It remained important to him throughout his life; as late as September 1983, at the age of eighty-four, he revisited the area with his portable typewriter and canoe in order, as he put it, "to get back in the saddle" after "a six year writer's block" (Elledge, "Coda" xiv). That particular place was to be a haunting, shaping place for him.

Although again we have no manuscript evidence of the composing processes White went through to create "Once More to the Lake," we have an accumulation of circumstantial evidence from his communications to friends and family that suggests that the essay was the result of long incubation and repeated rehearsal of its incidents and themes. For example, his letter to his brother Stanley, probably written in 1936, strikes an elegiac tone and continually repeats the phrase "Things don't change much."

> I returned to Belgrade. Things haven't changed much. There's a train called the Bar Harbor Express, and Portland is foggy early in the morning, and the Pullman blankets are brown and thin and cold. But when you look out of the window in the diner, steam is rising from pastures and the sun is out, and pretty soon the train is skirting a blue lake called Messalonski. Things don't change much. . . . The water in the basin is icy before breakfast, and cuts sharply into your nose and ears and makes your face blue as you wash. But the boards of the dock are already hot in the sun, and there are doughnuts for breakfast and the smell is there, the faintly rancid smell that hangs around Maine kitchens. Sometimes there is little wind all day, and on still hot afternoons the sound of a motorboat comes drifting five miles from the other shore, and the droning lake becomes articulate, like a hot field. . . . You buy a drink of Birch Beer at Bean's tackle store. Big bass swim lazily in the deep water at the end of the wharf, well fed. Long lean guide boats kick white water in the stern till they suck under. There are still one cylinder engines that don't go. Maybe it's the needle valve. (*Letters* 135–136)

White deliberately runs through the letter in a single long paragraph, letting his descriptions pile up and his sentences sometimes stretch out lazily and sometimes announce insignificant and routine events. It ends: "Cow trails lead up slopes through juniper beds and thistles and grey rocks, and below you the lake hangs blue and clear, and you see the islands plain. Somewhere a farm dog barks. Yes, sir, I returned to Belgrade, and things don't change much. I thought somebody ought to know" (137). The letter is rich in observed detail, much of it responding to the familiarity of the place after thirty years of vacationing there. Its theme of immutability (as well as some of its imagery, like the one-cylinder engine and the birch beer) prefigures the theme of "Once More to the Lake," the actual mutability submerged below the apparent immutability of the place.

Belgrade, then, was a familiar place when White and Joel vacationed there in July 1941. White had finished his September 1941 *Harper's* department in New York well before the July 10 deadline; the only fictional column, it was later reprinted (in *The Second Tree from the Corner*) as "The Hotel of the Total Stranger" and drew heavily on White's memories of his life in New York City a dozen years earlier as well as his most recent visit. The title no doubt came from a place called the "Hotel des Etrangers" on Corsica, where he had stayed once with Katharine in 1928 and remembered fondly (Elledge, 156). Although the sketch is presented as fiction, the character of Volente is so clearly White himself that the piece is virtually a lyrical memoir. Perhaps writing that column put him in the mood to return to Belgrade Lake and earlier memories.

White went to the lake intending to work as well as relax, taking with him materials for his preface to *A Subtreasury of American Humor*, the anthology that he and Katharine would publish later that year. Given his experience writing to deadline, he was no doubt aware of the need to have another column done before August 10th. On July 24th he wrote to Katharine from Bear Springs Camp:

> Very hot here today, and everyone is in the lake, lying in the shallows like so many frogs. Joe has been in for more than an hour without showing the slightest tendency to come out. He is a devotee of fresh water swimming at the moment, and it really does seem good to have warm bathing for a change. Very relaxing. . . . Joe and I went fishing last night after supper and caught 5 white perch. We have been eating fish steadily — of our own catching. We now have a perfectly enormous outboard motor on our rowboat, which I am unable to start, except semi-occasionally. This is deeply disappointing to Joe. When the motor does choose to start, it leaps into a frightful speed, usually knocking us both down in the boat. Negotiations are under way to exchange it for a smaller pet. I must say I miss the old one-cylinder gas engine of yesteryear which made a fine peaceful sound across the water. This is too much like living on the edge of an airfield. . . . This place is as American as a drink of Coca Cola. The white collar family having its annual liberty. (*Letters* 214–215)

Many of the items in the letter find echoes in the column, which would have been submitted within the following two weeks. In the essay White speaks of himself as having "become a salt-water man" sometimes driven by "the restlessness of the tides and the fearful cold of the sea water and the incessant wind" to "wish for the placidity of a lake in the woods" (*One Man's Meat* 198) and mentions his son as one who "had never had any fresh water up his nose" (198). One lengthy passage compares the "sedative," "sleepy sound" of one-cylinder and two-cylinder inboard engines of the past with the "petulant, irritable sound" of outboard motors (201). He notes of the general store that "inside, it was all just as it had always been, except that there was more Coca-Cola and not as much Moxie and root beer and birch beer and sarsaparilla" (202) and describes the campers as "the American family at play, escaping the city heat" (201). The recurring phrase to Stanley, "Things don't change much," is echoed in "Over the years there had been this person with the cake of soap, this cultist, and here he was. There had been no years" (200). In neither the letter nor the essay does White make the distinction that he has not come with his family, only with his son, perhaps because, even in the letter, White is thinking about the family vacations he took there with his parents and siblings.

Of course, not all of "Once More to the Lake" is rehearsed in the letters and other writing White did prior to the essay. The essay itself undoubtedly provided him an opportunity to discover the depths of his feeling not merely about the location but also about his relationships with his father and his son. The central premise of the essay is the narrator's confusion of his present role as father of a young son with his past role as son of his own father:

> I began to sustain the illusion that he was I, and therefore, by simple transposition, that I was my father. This sensation persisted, kept cropping up all the time we were there. It was not an entirely new feeling, but in this setting it grew much stronger. I seemed to be living a dual existence. I would be in the middle of some simple act, I would be picking up a bait box or laying down a table fork, or I would be saying something, and suddenly it would be not I but my father who was saying the words or making the gesture. It gave me a creepy sensation. (199)

The interaction between memory and the immediate moment runs through the essay, culminating in the afternoon thunderstorm ("The whole thing was so familiar"), the predictable behavior of bathers in the lake ("the joke about getting drenched linking the generations in a strong indestructible chain"), and the final discovery that ends the piece:

When the others went swimming my son said he was going in too. He pulled his dripping trunks from the line where they had hung all through the shower, and wrung them out. Languidly, and with no thought of going in, I watched him, his hard little body, skinny and bare, saw him wince slightly as he pulled up around his vitals the small, soggy, icy garment. As he buckled the swollen belt, suddenly my groin felt the chill of death. (203)

It is this final moment of epiphany that explodes the illusion that there had been no time and makes the confusion of identities a coming to terms with time. The essay has been as much about what has been and what will be lost as it is about what has stayed the same. It may have taken White the whole process of composing the essay to arrive at this discovery; certainly readers are led associatively through the experience until they too arrive with a jolt in the same place.

Whether White himself recognized it as such, "Once More to the Lake" was a more sustained, more incubated work than virtually anything else he had previously published. It drew on deeper, more personal reserves of material and more complex feelings about the subject. The description of the place, the evocation of memories, the recurring motif of the narrator's confusion of this trip with his childhood trips, of himself with his father, of his son with himself, all work together to produce an elegiac, lyrical essay that is both deeply personal and profoundly universal. But it was created under circumstances much different from those that produced the majority of the columns and it remains as exceptional as it is brilliant.

The idea of collecting and publishing the "One Man's Meat" columns as a book was proposed to White by his Harper and Brothers editor, Eugene Saxton, in 1940. White felt at the time that there had not been enough good columns to make up a book; he was also reluctant because "my last two books have been clipbooks, and I have been hoping that before publishing another such I could produce an Original Work" (*Letters* 205). When he finally put together a manuscript of publishable columns, consisting of "about a 75% selection" from the *Harper's* department, he included the *New Yorker* pieces on Daniel Webster and the World's Fair because they "seemed to fit into the scheme," having been "written within the period of my *Harper* department, and . . . in the first person singular" (*Letters* 220). Hearkening back to the snide association of his Maine life with the self-congratulatory writing of the "David Grayson" series of books by Ray Stannard Baker

(*Adventures in Contentment, Adventures in Friendship, The Friendly Road*) and also to the plethora of back-to-the land books published in those years (some of which he commented on in his column), he was particularly insistent that it not be marketed as a country book. He wrote Eugene Saxton:

> Although the majority of the pieces were written from my home in Maine, I think it would be a mistake to put the book out as another one of those Adventures in Contentment, or as an Escape from the City, or How to Farm with a Portable Corona. This is a book of essays on a wide variety of subjects, both urban and rural; it is not a tract on subsistence farming, and it is not a handbook of retreat. It is, as you know, intensely personal, but not designed to prove anything. It is colored by my New England surroundings, but it is not dedicated to them. In short, it is a book about me-and-life, and should not be tagged with a country label. (*Letters* 220)

Later, sending Saxton material for the front jacket flap, he explained that "that crack about my being 'one of our leading essayists' was put in by my wife, who was whistling to keep her courage up. For 'one of our leading' read 'only remaining.' She's just scared" (*Letters* 230). The remark suggests that White was shifting in his view of his role as a writer, brought on by the emphasis in the *Harper's* columns on personal observation and by a flexible format that metamorphosed itself to match the shape of his thinking. Even those columns that most resembled the paragraph-writing of Don Marquis or the *New Yorker*'s Notes and Comment page were transformed by White's opportunities to develop ideas and infuse more of his personality. "Essayist" may have seemed a vague enough term to cover the range of writing White produced for the department. Although clearly many of the columns are too fragmented and disconnected to qualify as essays in anyone's definition, White also had produced a number of memorable, fully developed essays, some of which, like "Walden" and "Once More to the Lake," stand on their own as independent works.

Reviewers of the book may have taken their cue from the jacket copy and the reference to essays in the foreword. Irwin Edman in particular made the case for White as an essayist, claiming that he "fulfills almost uniquely in our generation the function of a first-rate or (in the Luce language of Time) top-flight essayist," and later declaring him to be "our finest essayist, perhaps our only one" (2). Other reviewers tended to identify the material as essays and loosely refer to White as an essayist, although comparisons with such widely varying figures as Thoreau and Montaigne (Edman, Trilling, Canby), De Quincey and Lamb (Weeks), Addison and Steele (Adams), and Cowper and Gray (DeVane) suggest that the identification was not entirely clear cut. References to the writing as "rural sketches" (*Catholic* 627) "narrative essays" (Canby), and "like no genre at all save that amiable Mr. White creates" (Edman), and to White as "humorist" (*Time* 61), "among the best writers of the familiar essay in English" (DeVane 165), and one of "our cracker-box tree-stump philosophers" (Canby 7) all suggest similar uncertainty about the persona and the genre of the clipbook.

Nonetheless, White was surely correct to take the view that *One Man's Meat*, as he distilled that book out of the fragments of the magazine columns, is "a sustained report of about five years of country living" (*Essays* ix). For his selected essays he reprinted from the book only "The World of Tomorrow," "On a Florida Key," and "Once More to the Lake." Certainly, as we read the book, we have a sense of time and place, of development and change, that we feel in no other of White's collections. The whole is greater than the sum of its parts; it almost reads like a journal and seems locked in time, connected to the mood swings inspired by the events of the period, not just a book of country living but a book of the homefront as well. And yet it is not merely a period book, in part because the spirit that runs through it is one that understands the domestic side of human nature and gives us a thousand things to connect to that are not time bound. In this regard the book is dated only in the same sense that *Walden* is dated: reference points may have grown obscure, but the spirit that underlies the book speaks to us still.

6

"OUT ON THE HIGH WIRE"
White as Editorialist

For the book version of *One Man's Meat*, E. B. White omitted from the very first column the long section explaining why he left the city — "What was it? What did it? What finally was too much to bear?" (*Harper's*, October 1938, 555). One of the harshest sections of any "One Man's Meat" column, it may have seemed to White too hard edged, too negative, too angry to include in the book. However accurately it represented White's state of mind at the time, it couched his retreat to the farm too much in terms of city depravity versus country virtue, a simplistic dichotomy that overlooked his constant attraction to both places.

By August 1942 White's columns had begun to express dissatisfaction with his writing and to foreshadow his eventual return to the city. "Morningtime and Eveningtime," which ran as a titled column in the October 1942 *Harper's*, finds him serving as a civilian spotter, barely able to write:

> Stonily I sit at the machine, refusing, as a jumping horse refuses the hurdle. All that comes forth I drop without regret into the wastebasket; nothing seems to make sense, no matter how you spell it or arrange the words. You write something that sounds informative, throwing the words around in the usual manner, then you put your head out the door, or somebody puts his head in, a knob is turned, somebody says something to you, or your eye is caught by something in the news, a dog barks, and no longer is what you have said informative, or even sensible. At the mere barking of a dog the thing explodes in your hands, and you look down at your hands. As though you had crushed a light bulb and were bleeding slightly. And after lunch the thunder in the north. (*One Man's Meat* 274)

In the context of the column White's inability to write arises from preoccupation with his civilian military service against the background of his daily life on the farm and with his family, but in the context of his imminent abandonment of the column, it also betrays an undercurrent of frustration with the nature and direction of his writing.

Not surprisingly, then, six months and six columns later — in what would be the penultimate column — he returned to the theme of his inability to write. The April 1943 department was unusual in being made up of eight short items, each of them with a brief title, collectively reading very much like a *New Yorker* Notes and Comment page. In an item titled "Interruptions" White writes:

> Worked myself into a high state of indignation this afternoon because I had been interrupted every ten minutes since early morning, by somebody or something, and had made no progress in writing. And I decided that no one in my household, or in my county, had any respect for or appreciation of the enormous difficulties of writing (which is not true) and that I am the most walked-upon person on the place (which is true but which is my own fault, since I habitually allow myself to be taken advantage of by boys, dogs, friends, relatives, domestics, and strangers, and have chosen as a "retreat" a room which has the essential qualities of the Astor lobby). But in the midst of my fit I recalled that I hadn't anything to write anyway, and that to interrupt a writer who has nothing to write is a public service.
>
> If a man does not choose to hang a DO NOT DISTURB sign on his door, the whole world finds its way there, to poke at his books and borrow his desk scissors and read over his shoulder. But if he *does* hang out a sign, then he is in even a tighter spot, with nothing to explain his inability to produce — which can be just as notable in seclusion as in confusion and fifty times as embarrassing. (*Harper's*, April 1943, 500–501)

It is impossible to avoid noticing the tone of discouragement in this passage and its similarity in tone to the passage on writing in "Morningtime and Eveningtime."

The item also relates to the final section of the same column, titled "Goose's Return," in which White compares himself to a goose of his that had wandered off and, when she finally returned, was shunned by other geese. White observes: "I imagine something of this sort would happen if I were to return to the city. . . . I'm not sure you can ever go back even if you want to" (501). He quotes at length Ik Marvel's remark in *My Farm of Edgewood* about how disconnected the self-made rustic discovers himself when he returns to the city ("In a dozen quarters a boy sets you right; and some girl tells you newnesses you never suspected"). White agrees: "The last time I went to town I had a dozen small reminders that my membership has lapsed" (501). Tellingly, the next column, White's last, is made up entirely of a political monologue delivered while strolling through Central Park. When White enlarged the book version of *One Man's Meat*, he omitted the last two monthly columns except for the goose–Ik Marvel item, which he attached to the end of a condensed version of the March 1943 column. Thus, the collection ends with an image of the writer in the country unable to return to the city. The Central Park column, which would have made "Goose's Return" seem an expression of nervous longing rather than contented resignation, was never reprinted. Yet it is evident that White wanted to return to New York and the *New Yorker*.

In March 1943, shortly after sending in the Central Park column, White wrote to his editor at *Harper's*, Frederick Lewis Allen, that he had been "trying to figure out what I had better do about my life" and was "reluctantly reporting" that he had to quit the column. He explained that "the truth is I have had great difficulty, all along, writing essays of this sort, as they do not seem to come naturally to me and I have to go through the devil to get them written. Several times I have sent off a department which didn't satisfy me and which I sent only because it was to fulfill a promise, or continuing obligation, or whatever you call a monthly deadline" (*Letters* 238). Certainly the recent confessions of difficulty and the evidence of rushed and spontaneous pieces throughout the life of the department support White's explanation. But White also told Allen that "the desire is very strong in me to rid myself of any writing commitment. . . . I want to change my state of mind. . . . I want to write when and if I feel like it. A department hanging over a man's head is, as you say, very good discipline — but at the moment discipline is not the sort of medicine I need" (*Letters* 238). Nonetheless, while he may have wanted to change his state of mind, he really was not trying to get himself in a position where he had no writing commitments. In the same period as the column he had also compiled with Katharine *A Subtreasury of American Humor*, worked on his first children's book, *Stuart Little*, and served as editor of *Four Freedoms*, a political pamphlet; in addition he had continued to contribute Comment, poetry, and newsbreaks to the *New Yorker*.

White had also maintained his correspondence with Harold Ross. His letters show that Ross repeatedly tried to encourage White to return full time to the *New Yorker*. Other than his loyalty to the *Harper's* column, White's reluctance to take up Comment again had chiefly to do with the nature of the Comment page and his own sense of what he hoped to accomplish with his writing. When, in mid-1939, Ross — probably in an attempt to get White to offer to return — wondered in a letter whether the magazine ought to simply drop the Comment page altogether, White approved of the idea and recommended that if it stayed it would be better off with more people writing it, more thought to its contents, more "elasticity (mechanically)" to its page, and less attention to its structure and problems (*Letters* 196–197). But by June 1941 White's ideas about the page had hardened in the direction of making it more of an outright editorial and less of an entertaining commentary:

> I think the comment page, as presently managed, is discouraging for a writer. (I have thought this for a long time, maybe ten years.) I believe that an editorial page should be one of two things: either a signed page, for which one man would take the responsibility, or an unsigned page designed to express a sort of group opinion and which would be considered sufficiently important to warrant the managerial staff's meeting and discussing it each week, to give aid and counsel and ideas, and where opinions would generalize in group fashion. (*Letters* 211)

The problems of tone for which he had been criticized while writing Comment bothered him more as he found himself increasingly disturbed by world affairs. In the same letter he told Ross that he was sometimes annoyed by some of the things the *New Yorker* said, "usually not because of what they are but because of the way they are said. And other times it fails to say things that seem to need saying. The war is so damn near that it is no longer possible to use printer's ink in place of blood in a man's circulatory system, and Tilley's hat and butterfly return to plague us all. I couldn't bounce off a paragraph a week on the subject of the war, full of 'we's' and 'us's,' when I wasn't sure what key we were all trying to play in" (212). Clearly, White saw a need to use the Comment page to address world affairs and the inevitable American involvement in the war but found the supercilious persona of the page too slight to serve that need.

While these aspects of Comment discouraged him, White was nonetheless attracted to the *New Yorker* because of the shortness of the span between composing and publishing. Throughout the "One Man's Meat" column he was troubled by its lack of immediacy; at *Harper's* two months passed between writing and publication, rather than the couple of days possible at the *New Yorker*. His forewords to both editions of *One Man's Meat* contain apologetic remarks for the lightness of some of the entries, and his insistence on putting in the date of composition instead of the date of publication may have been a nod toward justifying the lack of currency in many of the columns and locating events closer to the time they happened.

The Second World War changed White's sense of his duty as a writer, which five years earlier, at the start of his sabbatical, had been so much centered on his duty to his own talents and interests. Shortly after the United States joined the war, he wrote to a friend from college:

> I'm in a quandary about the war — or, as Bert Lahr says, I'm in a quarry. Maine suddenly seems too remote to satisfy my nervous desire to help in a bad situation. My reason tells me that I can contribute most effectively by staying right here and continuing to produce large quantities of hens' eggs and to write my stuff every month; but the human system seems to demand something which has more of the air of bustle and confusion. I may try for a job in Washington, in the high realms of propaganda. (*Letters* 218)

That urge to get back to the center of things and join the "bustle and confusion" led to the dissatisfying, even frustrating experience of working on the *Four Freedoms* project.

White went to Washington to work with a team of writers under Archibald MacLeish's direction. They were to expand upon Franklin Roosevelt's reference to the four freedoms to which everyone ought to be entitled. White initially was to write the "Freedom of Speech" section but was reassigned to the task of rewriting the drafts of the other authors, Max Lerner, Malcolm Cowley, and Reinhold Niebuhr. He reconciled himself to that role by claiming, "I am determined that there will be no pretty writing, and an absolute minimum of statements which I do not fully understand myself" (*Letters* 224). Preliminaries delayed the writing on the project; once he was relegated to an editorial role, White had little to do.

His complaints in a letter to Katharine reflect on his attitude not only about the project but also about the *Harper's* column as well.

What I fear will happen to this writing job is what always happens to anything that I don't get going on right away, but let hang around to cool for a week or two. I have never been able to revive anything. But I haven't written a word on this, largely because of the way MacLeish arranged the whole thing. I always write a thing first and think about it afterward, which is not a bad procedure, because the easiest way to have consecutive thoughts is to start putting them down. But with this project there have been mountains and oceans of talk, and dozens of people and shades of opinion. (*Letters* 225)

White found the research-heavy manuscripts from experts "pretty forbidding and dreary." He suggested that Cowley's piece on freedom from want should be copied, circulated, and commented upon by the others. "This seemed like a bright idea to the rewrite man in me, as I was hoping to get other people into my own predicament, the necessity of saying the words on paper" (225). White's best instincts as a writer led him to discover his subject through his writing. He depended on the spontaneous generation of ideas and words over a relatively short period to create the shape of the piece. Distancing himself from a project through inactivity or through an inability to sustain immediacy tended to reduce his commitment to the piece and to dampen its liveliness when completed.

In September 1942, a month after complaining in "Morningtime and Eveningtime" about his inability to write, White promised Ross to write "a little comment each week." He then asserted, "I would like to do a great deal of comment, as it appears to be the way I am best fitted to earn a living," but added that writing Comment in Maine was nearly impossible. His concern for accuracy and currency reveal an increasingly serious perspective toward the Comment writing he expected to do. He worried that "the war tends to make me (and everybody) lose my perspective, or grip" and claimed that "writing any sort of editorial stuff about this universal jam that everyone is in, is for me a gruelling and rather frightening job" (*Letters* 232). Nonetheless, White's sense of responsibility toward the *New Yorker* and Katharine's continued editorial involvement with it tended to keep him more committed to it than he had ever been to *Harper's.* By the end of 1942 he wrote his brother Stanley that "K and I have both taken back some of the *New Yorker* work which we chucked when we came here, because the staff has been so depleted and the magazine is very short handed and they keep pestering us to do the work!" (*Letters* 235).

Still, when he finally left *Harper's*, his explanation to Ross that he had quit "for no particular reason, other than what seemed to me an inability to write any more pieces of that nature and that length" did not include the excuse that he had given Allen, that he wanted to avoid deadlines. Instead, he shied away from accepting Ross's offer to be the "principal contributor" to Notes and Comment (although he left the possibility still open) by claiming again that he could not accept any weekly income arrangement because it would only be "sensible if a person is doing the whole department, and accepts that as his basic responsibility" and because he did not want to commit himself to "a specified amount of comment as long as I am living 500 miles from first base" (*Letters* 241). His attempt to keep some distance from Comment writing lasted only a few more months. By October 1943 he was writing to a friend that he and his family would be spending the winter in New York: "We'll be working for the *New Yorker* as usual. My theory about myself and the war is that I can contribute most from my old editorial perch, where my screams and flappings are not supervised by any agency" (*Letters* 247).

As Elledge has observed, White's decision to abandon the *Harper's* column and write editorials for the *New Yorker* "was one of the most critical of his professional career" because "he chose to give up the freedom to write the kind of meditative essays" that had earned him "a reputation as a man of letters"; in taking up the Notes and Comment editorials, principally to discuss his ideas on world government and the aftermath of the war, White entered a period in which he denied himself "the leisure and confidence he needed for writing anything as substantial as the best of the essays in *One Man's Meat*" (239).

From even before White's full-time return to Notes and Comment, the department had begun its transition into a more forthright editorial page. By the twentieth-anniversary issue, 17 February 1945, White "acknowledged the obvious change that had taken place in the tone of 'Notes and Comment,'" asserting that "we feel like a man who left his house to go to a Punch-and-Judy show and, by some error in direction, wandered into *Hamlet*" (Elledge 247). For the most part the editorializing in Notes and Comment was White's principal work throughout this period of his career. In some sense he had become reconciled to this role, as if he had decided that writing as a profession should entail this kind of work. When he had longings for more personal writing, he turned to entirely separate projects and generally published them elsewhere. This was the period of his children's books, *Stuart Little* (first mentioned to his publisher in 1939 but not published until 1945) and *Charlotte's Web*, published in 1952. In spite of having been acclaimed as an essayist for *One Man's Meat*, he did not return to the personal essay until "Afternoon of an American Boy" for the *New Yorker* in November 1947 and "Death of a Pig" for *Atlantic Monthly* in January 1948.

Some understanding of the divisions of labor White gave his writing can be gained by examining his productivity in each of several categories over the years (see Appendix). For example, as we noted earlier, in 1937, the year he started his leave from the *New Yorker*, he wrote all of thirty-two weeks' worth of Notes and Comment and bits of other pieces; the humor he turned out included two Talk of the Town pieces and several light contributions to other departments, and the fiction consisted of three "Preposterous Parables," two of which were collected in *Quo Vadimus?* the next year. But from 1938 through 1941 his contributions to Notes and Comment were much more infrequent, all of only four, part of only thirty-eight in four years, the lowest number coming in the middle of the "One Man's Meat" column's run. The humor in those years consisted largely of contributions to the Answers to Hard Questions department in the *New Yorker*.

However, in 1942 White's contributions to Notes and Comment began to increase, and, when he quit *Harper's* after three columns in 1943, he had a role in Notes and Comment in forty different weeks, eleven of them producing segments of the material collected later in *The Wild Flag*. In 1944 he increased to forty-four weeks, and in 1945 not only did he contribute to Notes and Comment forty-six weeks of the year (thirteen of them composing the whole department), but the articles he wrote that year were related pieces about the formation of the United Nations. In 1946 the last twelve segments of *The Wild Flag* appeared in the first six months of the year, but he was a contributor for a total of thirty-one weeks. Throughout these four years the sixty-one pieces that were collected in *The Wild Flag* made up a substantial share of the contributions to Comment, although only rarely taking up an entire Notes and Comment page or even serving as the entirety of White's partial contribution.

In 1947 two of his three articles were segments of his "Turtle Bay Diary," an attempt to start a new series on the United Nations, and the third was the essay, "Afternoon of an American Boy," a reminiscence. Essays continued to appear intermittently over the next several years ("Death of a Pig" in 1948, "Here Is New York" in 1949, "Two Letters, Both Open" in 1951), but after the war most of White's considerably less prolific output was concentrated on "Notes and Comment" (forty-three weeks in 1948, twenty-three in 1949, thirty-one in 1951 and 1952, thirty in 1953, twenty-seven in 1954). Even when White began to contribute the essays that would be collected in *The Points of My Compass*, his output was much more random and widely spaced than it had been for *One Man's Meat* and *The Wild Flag*.

With only the exception of a few random years when White's writing output overall was not particularly high, White was principally an editorialist from 1943 until 1955. We have already noted the shift in reference to the Notes and Comment section from "comment" to "editorial" in White's correspondence; the Comment pieces themselves demonstrate the shift in White's approach. In the 4 March 1944 Notes and Comment he responded to a remark by Gilbert Seldes in the *Saturday Review* that he had "never known of an editorial writer who wrote as he pleased." White observed: "An editorial page is a fuzzy performance, any way you look at it, since it affects a composite personality with an editorial 'we' for a front. Once in a while we think of ourself as 'we,' but not often. The word 'ourself' is the giveaway — the plural 'our,' the singular 'self,' united in a common cause" (*Writings* 27). He went on to explain the system under which he wrote editorials for the *New Yorker*:

> The system is this: We write as we please, and the magazine publishes as *it* pleases. When the two pleasures coincide, something gets into print. When they don't, the reader draws a blank. It is a system we recommend — the only one, in fact, under which we are willing to be kept. . . . The more devious the motives of his employer, the more difficult for a writer to write as he pleases. As far as we have been able to discover, the keepers of this house have two aims: the first is to make money, the second is to make sense. We have watched for other motives, but we have never turned up any. That makes for good working conditions, and we write this as a sort of small, delayed tribute to our house. (27–28)

The editorial suggests that White had reconciled himself to the role of editorial writer and settled into it without the ambivalence that had characterized so much of his Comment writing in the previous decade.

White's late Comment has a pointedness and argumentativeness not usually found in his paragraphs written before the war. This is generally the case with most of the postwar Comment, especially in the articles eventually collected as *The Wild Flag*, which are bound together by the common thread of world government. For example, the editorial that gives *The Wild Flag* its title, published in the *New Yorker* on 25 December 1943, opens this way: "This is the dream we had, asleep in our chair, thinking of Christmas in lands of the fir tree and pine, Christmas in lands of the palm tree and vine, and of how the one great sky does for all places and all people" (*Flag* 20). The dream describes a time "after the third war was over," when the survivors send delegates to a peace convention; each delegate has his or her country's flag, except for the Chinese delegate, who brings instead a flower, "a wild flag, *Iris tectorum*," proposing that all countries adopt it as their symbol. Objections are raised and countered, and the Chinese delegate distributes irises to the rest of the delegates: "Next day the convention broke up and the delegates returned to their homes, marveling at what they had accomplished in so short a time. And that is the end of our dream" (23). The piece has sprightliness and energy, even whimsy, but it urges those considering a peace convention after World War II to "act in a sensible, rather than a popular, manner" and directs itself at a fairly specific political goal rather than a fairly general striking of attitude.

Few of the pieces in *The Wild Flag* are as light in tone as this. Many are straightforward pieces of argumentation, such as two (dated 15 September and 20 October 1945) arguing that the Nuremberg trials have no foundation in international law: "Nobody, not even victors, should forget that when a man hangs from a tree it doesn't spell justice unless he helped write the law that hanged him" (121). One article is simply a list of quotations from various sources, including Albert Einstein, Robert Oppenheimer, and Harold Stassen, endorsing the idea of world government or emphasizing the dangers of national sovereignty; others quote Stassen, Thomas Dewey, and H. G. Wells. When White's favorite writers are quoted, they are cited in service of the persuasive point. Thoreau is called on to set the tone for the opening United Nations conference: "It was one of the most thrilling discords I ever heard. And yet, if you had a discriminating ear, there were in it the elements of a concord such as these plains never saw nor heard" (84). The quotation is not merely descriptive or allusive but also persuasive, urging concord to arise from discord.

Similarly, the imminent explosion of atomic bombs at Bikini Atoll reminds White of a passage on cockroaches in a book by Edwin Way Teale confirming the likelihood that the cockroach is the creature best equipped to survive nuclear holocaust; this in turn reminds him of

Archy, Don Marquis's typing cockroach, and gives him an opportunity to quote a passage on Warty Bliggens, the egocentric toad. He "considers himself to be / the center of the said / universe" for whose sake all things were created and whose response to the question of how he merited these favors is, "ask rather . . . / what the universe / has done to deserve me" (163–164). The allusions to Don Marquis serve White's polemical ends far more than they had in *One Man's Meat*, where the personal dimension of White's writing was dominant.

The allusions also suggest that White was identifying with specific aspects of Thoreau and Marquis, in particular with Thoreau the observer and Marquis the political philosopher of *The Almost Perfect State*. Despite the inclusion of political pieces in *One Man's Meat*, White was not wholly comfortable with this aspect of himself, especially as it manifested itself in the world government editorials. Elledge is surely right to ascribe to White himself the *Wild Flag* dust-jacket description of the author as someone who, "when the war came on," felt "his editorial propensities again get the better of him," but who nonetheless "does not regard himself as a Thinker and says he feels ill-at-ease writing editorials on massive themes. He regards himself as a clown of average ability whose signals got crossed and who found himself out on the wire with the Wallendas" (*Flag* back cover). The self-deprecating tone of this, so modest for dust-jacket puffery, suggests White's own hand, as does the "Thinker" reference, complete with capitalization, which seems to stem from a letter White wrote referring to the book as "a collection of *New Yorker* paragraphs on tremendous themes, . . . my debut as a THINKER" (*Letters* 277).

The paragraphs reprinted in *The Wild Flag* date from the 10 April 1943 issue of the *New Yorker* to the 1 June 1946 issue; they appeared intermittently, sometimes twice or more a month, sometimes once, sometimes skipping a month. They would be only a portion of a week's Notes and Comment, with a variety of other Comment accompanying them. For example, in the 1 May 1943 issue, the piece about the D.A.R.'s resolution against American union with other nations, reprinted as the second entry in the book, leads off the Comment page, followed by segments on the writing of presidential aspirants and a policeman's remarks about the day the war ends. In the 8 May issue the reprinted section is on Japanese execution of American officers; unreprinted are pieces on counterfeiting, the ineffectiveness of a Disney film as propaganda, and voting for alumni trustees. In the 15 May issue the piece on Gallup's poll on an international police force is followed by pieces on British political parties, the mugging of a divinity student, and the impracticality of Victory garden publicity. In such examples, it is notable that the segments making up Notes and Comment are generally fewer, longer, and more sober than they were before the war.

All but one of the editorials in *The Wild Flag* written between 10 April 1943 and 27 May 1944 were first reprinted in a pamphlet titled *World Government and Peace* and distributed by the magazine (Hall 92–94). The subtitle of *The Wild Flag* identifies the contents as "Editorials from the *New Yorker* on Federal World Government and Other Matters," as do the acknowledgments and the preface. In the preface White calls attention to his use of the first person plural again: "An editorial writer refers to himself as 'we,' but is never sure who the other half of the 'we' is. I have yet to encounter the other half of 'we,' but expect to nail him in an alley some day and beat his brains out, to see what sort of stuffing is behind such omniscience" (*Flag* vii). Yet the argumentative nature of the entries and the impersonal subject matter make the first person plural less of a problem for White than it had been before *One Man's Meat*. It clashes less with the subject matter and the implied persona in the authorial voice; instead, the collective pronoun seems inclusive of the reader as a concerned citizen of the world, and more often than not the editorial "we" is altogether missing from the argument presented.

Once again, the writing that White engaged in was immediate journalism. Although *The Wild Flag* seems to me to be in many ways a prophetic book — I write this at a time when superpowers have all but lost their relevance and atrocities are committed daily around the world in the name of national and even tribal sovereignty (Bosnia, Somalia, Rwanda, Israel, Northern Ireland, Serbia — the list has changed several times in the writing of the book) — many of its references are now dated and its specific issues seem time bound. That is the nature of editorial writing. Although the book has a unity of purpose, if not design, imposed by its very limitations, it is nonetheless a clipbook rather than a cohesive book-length argument for world government. Its reception by reviewers was generally favorable, although the political subject of the book tended to draw out the political slant of the publication reviewing it. For example, *Time* typically pigeonholed him as a writer — "Author White made his reputation as a humorist" — and accused him of "practiced glibness" and "whimsy"; the anonymous reviewer wrote that White "plugs federal world government with the dazed urgency of an Esperanto salesman. He has the same high purpose, the same rosy vision, the same conviction that all it needs is a try" (48). Isaac Rosenfeld in the *Nation* questioned the "bourgeois sophistication" and middle-class "fear of dispossession" of the *New Yorker* as a whole, and scorned the motives of the editorials: "it is *bon ton* to mention fascism and racism and come out against them" (763). Robert Warshow in *Partisan Review* suggested that despite White's "good will and intelligence," the book was merely intended "to arouse certain familiar responses in the liberal middle-class reader" and likewise issued a blanket condemnation of the magazine as the premise for his dismissal of the argument of White's editorials (105–108).

Other critics were more receptive to the book's ideas. Charles Poore in the *New York Times Book Review* wrote that "Mr. White advances his ideas with a singularly forceful diffidence" and urged a reading of the book by "both statesman and skeptic" (58). Mark Watson in the *Saturday Review* spent most of his review encapsulating the argument of the book before repeating White's assertion — "The only condition more appalling, less practical, than a world government is the lack of it in this atomic age" — and then asking: "Who, at the coming meeting of the General Assembly, will say anything so truthfully voicing the yearnings of a dismayed world?" (15). Warren Beck in the *Chicago Sun Book Week* was even more forceful in his advocacy of the book, praising "White's foresight and impressive consistency," claiming his "logic is mobile and incisive," and crediting him with "speak[ing] the luminous vernacular of common sense, rather than the inbred jargon of social science or the office-seeker's vote-jerking generalities." In sum, he wrote: "This book answers Plato's call for philosophy, a love of truth, in politics; it bespeaks government of, by, and for all people with a humorously illuminated profundity not unlike Lincoln's; it offers the incomparable stimulation of a broad and scrupulous wisdom genially and imaginatively expressed" (3). Such comments suggest that, in some circles at least, White's debut as a Thinker was taken quite seriously, and a change in the identity of the magazine was recognized.

Irwin Edman, who had earlier extolled *One Man's Meat*, was a constant reader of White's work. His review in the *New York Herald Tribune Weekly Book Review* credited White with bringing "freshness and lucidity to the theme" of one world.

Ever since the beginning of the war it has been plain to the most casual reader of "Talk of the Town" that Mr. White's editorials have been concerned with the more urgent and the most central of contemporary themes. Mr. White has written comment about the war and about our easy peace that is more moving and more sensible than that of many more pretentious and pundit-like analyses. Time and again he has written a paragraph or a page that in its combination of the casual and the poetic has spoken out with simplicity and quiet intensity what has been agitating the hearts and perplexing the minds of people all over the globe. (5)

Edman's attempt to define the character of White's reflections in the editorial writing of Notes and Comment reinforces a view of White by Clifton Fadiman the previous year.

Prompted by the editorials collected in *World Government and Peace* and drawing on years of familiarity with White's work, Fadiman wrote an article "not as a critical essay but as a longish advertisement constructed to induce you to buy a few of Mr. White's ideas" (105–106). It appeared on the front page of the *New York Times Book Review*. Drawing on paragraphs going back to White's earliest days at the *New Yorker*, Fadiman asserts that "Mr. White is a very useful writer because he is an abstract thinker who does not write abstractly. His base is always a generalization, which is what makes him more than a journalist; but the development is always concrete" (107). He also shrewdly observes what the *Time* reviewer hoped to deny, that White was a writer who "insist[ed] on developing whether [his] readers like it or not"; he considers White "one of the most useful political thinkers" and "one of the finest living writers of prose in this country." He further declares: "E. B. White is a major writer. He is a major writer because his ideas and sentiments are large and basic and because, within the limitations of his chosen style and form, he writes about them perfectly" (105). White's attitude, he claims, "is not the attitude of an amiable, educated young man with high ideals. It is the attitude of a realist. His whimsical remarks are not sweet, though they are sweetly put; each one grasps a truth, holds it fast, exhibits it for all to see. That is why I have called this advertisement, 'E. B. White, Realist.' His wit is realistic, his humor is realistic and of course, his fantasy is realistic" (109). Fadiman's remarks pinpoint many of the most salient features of E. B. White's prose, particularly the development of his thought within the constants of his literary forms. While *The Wild Flag* has not been an enduring book in terms of republication, it remains a milestone achievement among White's works, a turning point that largely lays to rest, as *One*

Man's Meat had not done, his identification as simply or principally a humorist.

White's return to the *New Yorker* was in part an attempt to achieve an immediate editorial outlet, to have a place to comment on current issues while they retained their currency. The cost was a loss of the opportunity for the more intimate and personal writing of so much of the "One Man's Meat" column, which necessitated his willingness to look elsewhere for the satisfactions of noneditorial writing. At the *New Yorker* his Comment after the war continued to be chiefly editorial, expressing concern over the development of atomic weapons, the pollution of the environment, the demagoguery of anticommunist legislators and officials, and the progress of the United Nations, among other subjects. The tenor of the Comment page, having changed so much from the brief drolleries of the early days, continued to develop as an editorial page, its sections fewer and more developed, until, by the early 1950s, it bore almost no resemblance to the page White had dominated two decades earlier. The final multiple-section Notes and Comment page appeared 2 March 1957, consisting of a paragraph on a printing error and five paragraphs on the decline of the railroad, all by White.

In his biography of E. B. White, Scott Elledge has noted that the "number of White's readers increased enormously during the period from 1938 to 1946" (249). He cites the circulation of *Harper's* and the *New Yorker* and the availability of Armed Services Editions of *A Subtreasury of American Humor*, *Quo Vadimus?* and *One Man's Meat*. The *New Yorker* was given the Newspaper Guild's 1946 Page One Award for editorial excellence, "especially as exemplified in . . . the editorials of E. B. White," and *One Man's Meat* was awarded the Limited Editions Club's Gold Medal, "given every three years to the American author of a book considered most likely to attain the status of a classic" (249). It is notable that the momentum of White's editorial work at the end of the war carried him through the dozen years following, and that he returned so seldom to the kind of writing that had distinguished the "One Man's Meat" column and that had given the book version such prestige. It is notable too that two of his most successful postwar essays, "Death of a Pig" and "Here Is New York," were published elsewhere than in the *New Yorker*, and that as a pair they perfectly capture the duality of White's authorial persona.

When Morris Bishop suggested that White "spare the reading public your little adventures in contentment," he may have been thinking of the way the "David Grayson" series of books had been rife with self-satisfaction and smug superiority. White was too modest to think himself superior, too self-deprecating to be self-satisfied, and too much aware of his allegiances to the city as well as to the country. *One Man's Meat* was much more wide ranging in subject matter than the typical farm book, such as the Ik Marvel books about a Connecticut farm familiar to White from childhood. It is fairer to say that the book was written on a farm rather than about a farm, and that it does not so much advocate the author's lifestyle (the way, say, a book like Peter Mayle's *A Year in Provence* does) as record it.

One Man's Meat certainly is White's Maine book. Set as it is on a saltwater farm, drawing on such experiences as buying a cow, herding runaway sheep, raising chickens, and collecting eggs, it has a pastoral charm that is continually offset by brooding over world affairs and the author's constant self-consciousness about his ability to play the role of farmer. In "Clear Days" he writes, "My routine is that of a husband-man, but my demeanor is that of a high school boy in a soft-drink parlor" (18). The author's rural routine — the way the boy gets to school, the way neighbors note each other's comings and goings, the community events such as the town meeting and the coon hunt, the complications of raising chickens and looking after newborn lambs, the observation of the weather and the recording of daily events — anchors the entries in an immediate, localized context, while his persistent concern with the world outside his community broadens it into something more than a regional book. Given the intensity of his immersion in that place, it is all the more remarkable that Maine and the farm are so seldom the focus of his writing between the "One Man's Meat" period and the period of his "Letters from the East" features in the late 1950s and early 1960s.

The prominent exceptions to that rule are the essay "Death of a Pig" and the children's novel *Charlotte's Web*, both set in the barn. The children's book falls outside the scope of this study of White's nonfiction, but it is indicative of the way he compartmentalized his interests in writing that his most personal work and greatest artistic achievement of this period was in a form so radically different from the editorial form in which he wrote every week. The essay is among White's best work in that form and fits the scheme of *One Man's Meat* even better than the Belgrade Lakes and World's Fair essays do. "Death of a Pig" is a narrative about an incident on the farm that would be unexceptional except for the way White gets the reader involved in the struggle to save the pig and the suggestion he makes that there is an intimacy between farmer and pig that transcends the expedient purposes for which the pig is raised in the first place. The incident is clearly the origin of the concern with farmyard mortality that led to *Charlotte's Web*.

The only other piece that draws at all on Maine experience is "Two Letters, Both Open," which purports to be White's response to two letters he received from official agencies, one about the licensing of his dog, the other about his taxes. The situation in both letters turns on White's having two residences, one in New York, where he worked, and one in Maine. The piece is a satire on bureaucratic officiousness, in which White contrasts his chatty, casual, personal voice with the imperious, formal, impersonal voice of the official notices he receives. By exaggerating his personal response with a simple, human explanation, White heightens the aloofness and imperiousness of the governmental voices. The piece is not only funny but sharply ironic.

The political satire implicit in "Two Letters, Both Open" suggests the way that public circumstances continually intruded upon the explicitly private situations at the center of White's writing. The only other personal essay of the period, "Afternoon of an American Boy," originally published in the *New Yorker* (29 November 1947), seemingly recalls a youthful folly in the manner of such a memoir as "Farewell, My Lovely!" but is spurred by current political events. The essay recounts a quirky date White had as a teenager with Eileen Thomas, sister of J. Parnell Thomas, chairman of the House Committee on Un-American Activities, and concludes with a fantasy in which Thomas interrogates White for "un-American activities," exposing him as someone who dated his sister thirty-five years earlier under the pretext that he knew how to dance. As a satire on the efforts of such a House Committee, the piece is very slight, but as a memoir of adolescence, it is amusing and charming. Yet it is an essay that would not likely have been written except for the connection to current events.

The piece that serves as the antithesis to "Death of a Pig" is "Here Is New York." It was originally published in *Holiday* in April 1949 and then published by Harper and Brothers as a fifty-five-page book the same year. It is simply a personal celebration of the city. In it White recalls his excitement in being on the same island as his writing heroes in poetry and prose, and his exhilaration over its pace, scope, and variety. It displays the part of White that seems contradictory in regard to the love of country life that his Maine writing reveals, but it is really part of a comfortable duality that stayed with him most of his life. He was as much at home on the streets of Manhattan as he was on a salt-water farm on the Maine coast.

That White was comfortable with this duality is made clear by the contents of his major clipbook from this period, *The Second Tree from the Corner* (1954). Perhaps because he had presented more unified work, at least thematically, in *The Wild Flag* as well as in his first two children's books, for this collection White was willing to gather a potpourri of his uncollected writing — short stories and sketches such as might have appeared in *Quo Vadimus?*; poetry published after *The Fox of Peapack*; introductions to other people's writing, as in *A Subtreasury of American Humor* and a collection of Don Marquis's work; a few essays, including "Farewell, My Lovely!" "Afternoon of an American Boy," and "Death of a Pig," and Comment such as had appeared in *Every Day Is Saturday*. Except for the children's books, the whole range of his writing is rep-resented in *The Second Tree from the Corner*. "It is a mere collection, and a very miscellaneous one at that," Joseph Wood Krutch observed in the *Saturday Review*. "A mere scrapbook if there ever was one and com-posed of nothing except 'fugitive' pieces. As any publisher would say to almost any other writer, the thing has no unity either external or internal — except perhaps the unity of personality which is not a thing anybody now cares about" (15). Like Krutch, most reviewers seemed either implicitly or explicitly to identify the author's personality as the connecting thread of the collection.

For example, Robert E. Sherwood in the *New York Herald Tribune Book Review* observed of the variety of material in the book: "It would be idle to contend that all of them represent Mr. White at his wonderful best. His work (like that of every other important writer the world has ever known) is 'uneven'; but so are the coastline of New England and the skyline of New York, the two contrasted localities which have be-come his chosen breeding ground" (1). But Sherwood emphasized not the forms of the work (although he admired the essays over the stories) but the attitude with which White approached the material:

> The sense of melancholy which has always been evident in his writings, even the funniest ones, increases as the world in which he lives becomes more and more exasperating (as he says, he cultivates "a disconsolate attitude which has some slight literary value"). But

there is nothing passive about his melancholy, as has been the case with other gentle writers who have been content to take it lying down. The answer to E. B. White's occasional tendencies toward despair is E. B. White's persistent and zestful capacity for indignation. (1)

To some extent Sherwood seems to be answering the earlier objections of liberal reviewers of *The Wild Flag* to the *New Yorker*'s refusal to take a strident editorial stance.

Like Sherwood, most reviewers of *The Second Tree from the Corner* were admiring, although they disagreed, as usual, about the nature of its author's personality. *Time* persisted in identifying him as "Humorist White" and in praising the wit of his satires and "tales" (118). The *Nation* titled its review "The New Yorker's Addison" (although the anonymous reviewer never mentioned the connection). Harvey Curtis Webster in the *New Republic* insisted: "To find Mr. White's peer one has to go back to the eighteenth century. He is no austere Addison, no savage Swift; rather he is a gentle, sometimes sentimental Steele prodded to severity by what should be and isn't hated by all of us" (19). Krutch and Irwin Edman in the *New York Times Book Review* compared White to Thoreau.

Krutch made much of White's connection to the *New Yorker* and the ways in which he seemed both to epitomize the magazine and to operate continually against its conventions:

His manner is debonaire, so that even when discussing World Government or country life he manages to suggest that he is, nevertheless, a man who knows his way about town. When he lapses from "smartness" the lapse is deliberate and of course he writes with that almost finicky awareness of "good usage" which it is said Mr. Ross, otherwise a rough diamond, paradoxically insisted upon. But once all this has proved that he "belongs" he can be permitted to indulge in what would otherwise seem the wildest eccentricity. (16)

White was, he insisted, "highly personal, persistently oblique, and generally concerned less with the Queen than with the little mouse under her chair" (15), and, in the sophisticated magazine where one would not expect it, "Mr. White manages to get in not only quotations from Thoreau but also sentiments of his own which are decidedly Thoreauish" (16).

Irwin Edman's front page review in the *New York Times Book Review* emphasized the connection to Thoreau all the way through, making relatively few distinctions among the kinds of material in the book and focusing instead on the persona of the author projected throughout the collection.

It is high time to declare roundly what a good many people have long suspected, that E. B. White is the finest essayist in the United States. He says wise things gracefully; he is the master of an idiom at once exact and suggestive, distinguished yet familiar. His style is crisp and tender, and incomparably his own. A city-dwelling Thoreau holed up very frequently on the first page of the New Yorker, but from that Tower of Irony remembering Maine, where he lives part of the time, and Walden Pond, where Thoreau lived briefly.

Edman identifies White's subject —"that of any first-rate essayist" — as "mankind, its follies, its humor, its passions, its predicaments" and takes his theme to be "contemporary man as he lives." White's writing "is often ablaze with deep feeling about important matters, about freedom which, it is clear, is in Mr. White's scale of values the most important of all. One feels the heat, too, of his passion for life, however troubled, for mankind, however foolish, and for New York, however maddening." Trying "to analyze the secret of these telling and economical effects" Edman decides that "this writer's style . . . is one with his substance. The wit is marked at once by penetration and by compassion, the nobility is without affectation, and the homespunness is unaffected, too."

Perhaps in tune with White's observations on freedom of expression and his editorial resistance to repressive trends in Cold War politics, Edman concludes: "Here is the Thoreau of our day, the play of mind, the uncorrupted seriousness, the dry unquenchable humor, all in danger now of coming to be regarded as and eventually perhaps coming to be un-American activities. This book is American prose and, one is tempted to say, Americanism at its best."

When we remember that no one identifies more than two or three of the pieces in this collection as essays, the identification of White as an essayist in Edman's review ("the finest essayist in the United States") and in Krutch's review as well ("Mr. White breaks all the rules. He doesn't even know that the familiar essay is dead") pinpoints his approach to writing rather than the product of his writing. As we have observed, in spite of the variety of forms in which he wrote and from which he selected the material in *The Second Tree from the Corner*, the principal work of this period of White's writing life was his editorials for the *New Yorker*. That work is really the measure of his development as an essayist.

7

"WHOEVER SETS PEN TO PAPER WRITES OF HIMSELF" *Composing Late Comment*

The best evidence for the changes in White's writing of the Notes and Comment page can be found in a chronological reading of the Comment selections reprinted in *The Second Tree from the Corner*. As in his other collections, the work was selected by White himself as representing his most accessible, pertinent, or successful magazine writing. The majority of his weekly contributions to Notes and Comment went uncollected in White's lifetime. The anthologies are made up of the material that is least time bound, least ephemeral, least flat and formulaic. The changes in White's composing were incremental and virtually immeasurable from week to week. But the range of selections in *The Second Tree from the Corner* makes clear the contrast between early and late Comment, and the manuscript evidence documents a concomitant change in composing strategies.

In his study of E. B. White's prose styles John Wesley Fuller made the following distinctions between early and late Comment: "The Notes collected in *Second Tree* differ slightly in structure from those in *Every Day*. A higher proportion of the *Second Tree* Notes (61% against 25% for the *Every Day* Notes) are more than one paragraph long. They have space enough to be somewhat digressive and to examine differing aspects of their subjects" (180). Calling attention to the three-paragraph Comment titled "Mrs. Wienckus" in *Second Tree*, Fuller observes that the "shorter notes of *Every Day* rarely expand that much upon a topic." In his view, the "longer Notes in *Second Tree* approach the traditional essay and represent a mid-point between the short notes of *Every Day* and the full-length essays included in *One Man's Meat*" (180).

The Comment pieces in *The Second Tree from the Corner* include items written between 1935 and 1953, the largest number coming from the late 1940s and early 1950s. They are always presented not as individual pieces but as subtopics under a more encompassing general heading — "Notes on Our Times" (the longest grouping), "Shop Talk," "Notes on the City." In response to Fuller's remarks, it should also be observed that almost all the Comment pieces that are three or more paragraphs long were written after 1948, with the very longest written from 1950 to 1953; of twenty-three "Notes" in the book written before 1948, only four are more than two paragraphs long and two of them are sectioned off, indicating that originally separate Comments have been combined because of similar subject matter. Rather than traditional essays (with a few possible exceptions like "The Age of Dust"), most of the longer notes come closer to traditional editorials.

The three pieces that are the earliest in the book, "Transient," "Quietude," and "Sadness of Parting," all from 1935, are typical White Comments of that period. They could easily have been included in *Every Day Is Saturday*. In "Transient," for example, White takes five sentences to note "the special satisfaction to a city person" of the visit of a thrush to the "patchy little gardens of Turtle Bay" (where the Whites had rented an apartment), and concludes: "The city is the place for people who like life in tablet form, concentrated: a forest resolved into a single tree, a lake distilled into a fountain, and all the birds of the air embodied in one transient thrush in a small garden" (207). White manages to celebrate nature and society simultaneously and demonstrates his ability to find something worth attending to in the simplest, ostensibly least noteworthy event.

In "Sadness at Parting" the narrator, sitting in a barber's chair with his eyes closed, "deep in a world of our own," hears an unseen customer exchange farewells with the barbers and involuntarily joins in: "'Goodbye,' we said, before we could catch ourself. Then, all at once, the sadness of the occasion struck us, the awful dolor of bidding farewell to someone we had never seen. We have since wondered what he looked like, and whether it was really goodbye" (*Second Tree* 210). Again, the daily, trivial event inspires the note, and the incident strikes a tone of whimsy. The editorial "we" seems too elevated for the occasion and the exaggeration of "the awful dolor of bidding farewell" and the self-dramatizing of "whether it was really goodbye" make the piece tread the line between genuine sentiment and self-mockery.

"Quietude" takes a detached, ironic tone as it examines New York City's antinoise campaign, first identifying the campaign itself as a contributor to the volume, then making distinctions about the quality and intensity of the sounds one hears. For the Commentator, New York's noise is too angry rather than too loud, while the noise of Paris is gay, and that of a country sawmill is undisturbing. He then imagines that the honking he hears as he writes comes from the horn of someone on his way to a committee meeting to reduce noise. The tone is that of someone aloof, amused, and wry, someone mildly disdainful of bureaucracy and bustle but still discriminating about mundane subjects.

Because the nature of constant written production inevitably leads writers back to the same or similar subjects again and again — for example, we might trace White's development as a writer solely in terms of his output on television or on railroading or on spring — these three Comments have their parallels in pieces from the end of the period represented in *The Second Tree from the Corner*. For example, the topic of noise surfaces again in the book in a Comment titled "Sound." The selection is actually made up of two Notes and Comment items, one from 19 June 1948 ("The sound truck . . .") and the other from 6 May 1944 ("In radio . . ."). In the second item White's attention is focused on the tendency in radio to avoid silence at any cost — "The rule seems to be: make sense if you can, but if you can't make sense say something anyway" (*Second Tree* 112). The tone is scornful but not particularly playful, and the paragraph is only tangentially related to the other section by being about sound.

The first "Sound" item is more closely linked to the issue raised in "Quietude." Its two paragraphs are provoked by a Supreme Court ruling in favor of the use of sound trucks in political campaigns. In the first paragraph White identifies the problem as a confusion of "free speech" with "free extension-of-speech" and predicts it will arise again; in the second he doubts the necessity for additional decibels — quality communication can get through without it — and worries that those who want to stifle free expression will have the ammunition to do so if free speech is too freely identified with electronic amplification, since it will be more tempting to legislate against amplification. Such an aphoristic remark as "Loud speaking is not the same thing as plain speaking" reveals a straightforward editorial voice. In the whole of the two sections he uses the editorial "we" three times, in "We have a feeling that," "We have an idea that," and "We doubt that"; it is here a truly impersonal use of the first person plural, quite different from the "We have never regarded," "We are not fooled," "We have been all through," "beneath our window," and "Even now, on our pointed ears" in "Quietude," a truly personal use of the first person plural.

The more editorial tone is sounded in the majority of the later Comments reprinted in the book. "Air Raid Drill," "Life in Bomb Shadow," and "The Age of Dust" are all on preparations for nuclear war; "Little Green Shebang," on the United Nations; "Remembrance of Things Past," on artificial methods of raising pigs; "The Distant Music of the Hounds," on the mechanization of Christmas. They are essentially editorials, often witty and usually direct, taking a more pronounced stand on the issues raised than the arch and humorous Comment of the 1930s had.

Even a Comment like "Twins" — ostensibly in the tradition of the "Transient" paragraph as a celebration of the natural world in the unnatural setting of the city — has a more sober tone than its earlier counterpart. Discovering newborn twin fawns at the Bronx Zoo, the narrator describes a "scene of rare sylvan splendor" set in "the deep fastnesses of the Mittel Bronx" (*Second Tree* 228) and conveys a sense of wonder and delight. The scene is developed in three paragraphs of detailed description that does not merely comment on the scene but instead evokes it in a way that draws the reader into its mood and ambiance. Although the editorial "we" is given its familiar personal use, the voice that we hear is not aloof, whimsical, merry, detached, or gay.

Thus, even in the more personal paragraphs, the persona of the anonymous New Yorker of the Notes and Comment page is far different from the one who appeared on its pages before World War II. Throughout the period of the "One Man's Meat" column and the *Wild Flag* items, White's character on the Notes and Comment page changes from that of the detached, ironic, and whimsical Eustace Tilley into a more purposeful, more serious, more philosophical editorialist.

In the Comment that White produced after *One Man's Meat*, not only was the flippant, whimsical voice of the detached observer replaced by the concerned, sensible voice of the committed commentator, but the size and scope of the Comment changed as well from the single paragraph dependent on an arch comparison to a sustained, multiple-paragraph development of an idea or a miniature essay. These changes in tone and scope also meant a change in the importance of individual items in the context of a single Notes and Comment page. Both "Quietude" (from 24 August 1935) and "Transient" (from 26 October 1935) are short single items in multiple-item pages, neither carrying any more weight than the other items nor being any less or more ephemeral. In contrast, "Twins" and the first paragraph of "Sound," both from the 19 June 1948 issue, together make up almost all of that week's Comment (except for two trivial notes about ad language separated from them by a bullet and an all-caps heading), suggesting the direction the page was taking, with glacial slowness, toward a single-item editorial page.

But the change in Comment also meant a change in composing. If the example discussed earlier of "the News from Lake Placid in-the-Adirondacks" is indicative of the kind of composing White did in the 1930s, the manuscript evidence of the composition of "Twins" and "Sound" (1948), available in the Cornell collection, demonstrates White's composing in the 1940s and the ways it was affected by changes in Comment format, White's decreased output, and his altered attitude. If we examine the composing of these two Comments closely, we discover that the kind of Comment they were made different demands on White's composing strategies.

The opening piece of the 19 June 1948 Notes and Comment page was "Twins," followed by "Sound," but the pieces were composed separately, and the order in which they were printed is not necessarily the order in which they were written. If both were written the same week, they may have been composed sequentially, with either Comment first, or they may have been composed simultaneously, with White shifting his attention between them over the course of several days. Both pieces went through several stages of composing.

"Twins" is based on personal experience; it is the kind of Comment White so often generated in the past simply by wandering the city with an expectant and observant eye. The manuscripts begin with a hand-written single-page series of notes on the behavior of a doe and her newborn fawns:

> She has just finished twinning — under an oak. Old ~~oa~~ dry leaves
> The first lamb ~~had~~ was on his feet, was dry & had nursed. The
> 2nd was wet. She got to her feet, began thoughtfully chewing
> the afterbirth — dangled as a beet top —
> The 12 o'clock whistle — The hooting from the monkey house —
> The first lamb crossing the stream, ~~lip adds~~ pausing
>   midstream & adds a little to it — stimulated by the
>   feel of cool water. Lay down behind rock — /under
>   cabbage leaf.

The cow moose & her calf—
"Here comes the papa" "Looka that wobbly old thing
The beech, carved with so many initials —
Black button of a nose. Quiet trustful eyes.
The sunlight
She licked against the grain
Crossing the brook — the cold water affected
   him the way it water always affects young bathers —
& he paused to add a slight contribution to the
   brook

We cannot know whether these are notes White took at the zoo or listed as he recalled them when he decided to write about them, but we can see that the detail involves the deer and especially the behavior of her fawns. We also cannot tell whether the two references to the fawn crossing the brook are to the same fawn or to two different fawns — the evidence of the drafts is that it is the same fawn, but White could have conflated the two. The other items tend to be quick references to visual and aural details — clearly they are meant to serve as stimuli for memory later on, not as perfect records of observed events.

This record of White's notes on the incident is as significant for what it does not reveal as for what it does. White apparently felt the need to record images and sounds for detail but did not need to record much of his own behavior — for example, why he was there and what he did, in particular the scratching of the fawn's head (which may have occurred after he wrote the notes). Nor does he record the only comment he attributes to the child quoted in the drafts, the remark about kangaroos. These omissions suggest priorities in the note taking and the possibility that, as White himself has observed, it was important to him to write things up before he decided what they were about. In this case, the discovery of the newborn twins is the initial instigation for the piece, but White has yet to figure out the twist or the perspective he wants to bring to it. On the basis of what he has recorded he seems most interested in the fact of the newborn fawns and the experience of seeing the first fawn urinate in the brook, an occurrence that he analyzes both physiologically and metaphorically.

White apparently began typing his first draft at the office and, for whatever reason, completed it in handwriting. In the following representation of the draft italics indicate handwriting.

white

comment   *we had things to ourself — a*

                    miserable   *good*

On a warm, ~~sultry~~ morning last week we
went up to the Bronx zoo to see the moose calf: and to break in a
new pair of black shoes. ~~The deer park was~~ We had ~~far~~ better luck

          bargained for.   and her young one were   of the deer park
than we expected. The ~~moose~~ ~~w~~ cow moose ~~was~~ near the wall, on the
          sope below the monkey house, and in order to get a better view
                              so that we could look up at them.
we strolled down the lower end of the ~~deer~~ park by the stream. ~~As~~
The path there is not much traveled, and ~~nobody was about.~~
As we approached the corner near where the steam runs under the

                                                                                        initials

          They stood   under a beech carved with dozens of hearts & ~~letters~~
wire fence, we noticed a red deer ~~just~~ getting to her feet. ~~She had~~
~~With her~~ A fawn ~~stagg~~ ~~spotted lamb staggered~~ Beside her, looking
stood a fawn, ~~his~~ on legs that were just learning their business ~~(he~~

                                        in the ~~wet~~ *leaves*

~~had on black shoes, too).~~ ~~On~~ Stretched on the ground was another
     & we then realized   *fawn*
fawn ~~:~~, ^ The doe had just finished twinning, and the second ~~lamb~~ was
          Here   rare
still wet. ~~It~~ was a scene of ^ sylvan splendor, in one of our five
favorite boroughs, and we couldn't have asked for more. Even our shoes
          be working out   *pinching*
seemed to ~~fit~~ all right, and weren't hurting much.
                              With
                                        The doe sniffed the second lamb, and the
when he ~~sto~~ boosted himself up on his feet she
                              The d oe was only a couple of feet from
                    quietly   ~~a few~~ nearby and kept still
the wire, and we ~~stopped~~ sat down on a rock, with only the path
between us, to see what sort of start young fawns get in the fastness
                    mildly unhappy
of ~~the~~ Mittel-Bronx. The mother, ~~was a trifle miffed~~ at our presence,
occasionally raised one forefoot, and stamped in protest conscientiously
                                        without relish but with
but not much. She stood ~~doggedly~~ eating the after-birth, with
          in a long d   *looking*
which swung from her mouth crazily, ~~like so man~~ as though she had

found some beettops. ~~As she~~ From the monkey house came the insane

a   *woodland*

hooting of some captious ~~ape~~ primate, filling the whole ~~woods~~ with

~~*horrid*~~   *came*

a terrible hooroar. ~~*The*~~ *As we watched, the sun* ~~*broke*~~ *through* ~~*the*~~ *& brightened*
the rich red of the fawns, & kindled their white spots. ~~*The cow moose*~~

                                           in driblets

~~*wandered down, her calf Som*~~ *Occasionally people appeared on*
the path & wandered past, but none ~~*with*~~ *was aware that*

                       "Looka the   *s*

anything had happened. ~~*"Is that a*~~ *kangaroo?" a child*   *cried*
~~*demanded of*~~ *He &*   *inspected the kangaroos*
~~*asked*~~ *his mother* ~~*;*~~ *.* ~~*They looked*~~ *for a moment,* ~~*seem*~~ *and went on*
In a few moments the ~~*new*~~ *second twin gathered all his four lengths*
and all his ~~*wi*~~ *ingenuity & arose,* ~~*for the*~~ *to stand for the first*
time and survey the wonders of ~~*the*~~ *Bronx life. the doe*
~~*unintel*~~. *quit*   *drying*
~~*dropped*~~ *her other work,* ~~*went*~~ *began* ~~*licking*~~ *him — running her*
her tongue against the grain, & paying particular attention to the
   Meanwhile
~~*rear.*~~ *The first fawn* ~~*doing what so many newborn*~~ *approach the*
                   ~~*unintel.*~~   *that had just a*
brook erratically on little hopeful steps, and started across
pausing midway to ~~*contri*~~ *make a slight contribution, as*
youngsters always do in bathing. He continued across, ~~*to*~~
gained
the other side, ~~*and*~~ *selected a hiding place, &*
           by a rock   *skunk*
settled himself^ beneath a ~~*large*~~ *cabbage leaf,* ~~*between a*~~
Without actually going out of sight he managed
                  ~~*from view*~~
completely to disappear & remained there, apparent
only to someone who ~~*knew*~~ *happened to know where to look.*

In this draft White seems chiefly concerned with getting the events in sequence, and we recognize items from his page of notes rearranged into chronological order. The details about the dryness of the first fawn, the wetness of the second, the direction of the mother's licking, the behavior of the first fawn crossing the stream and hiding, the appearance of the beech, the hooting from the monkey house — all these are worked into the draft; so are the comparisons of the afterbirth to beet tops and the fawn to a young bather. Only a few details are omitted — the 12 o'clock whistle will return in a later draft — and more important new details emerge, such as the effect of the sunlight on the fawn's coat and the confusion and indifference of other passersby. Two phrases from the notes — "just finished twinning" and "slight contribution" — recur verbatim in the draft, phrases that will survive through to publication.

But clearly White has yet to determine what the point of this vignette will be, although the decision to delete the parenthetical comparison "he had on black shoes too" suggests that he does not intend to treat the event humorously and the decision to ignore the notes about "black button nose" and "trustful eyes" suggest as well that he does not intend to sentimentalize it either. In the next draft he adds details that are new to both the notes and the text he has produced so far; he also plays with a thesis, a kind of editorial position about the difference between country kids and city kids.

white

comment   *trinket*

On a warm, miserable morning last week we went
went up to the Bronx zoo to see the moose calf and to break in a new pair

encountered   *had*

of black shoes. We ~~had~~ better luck than we ^ bargained for. The cow

[uninte]

and her ~~calf were~~ young one were standing near the ^ wall of the
deer park below the monkey house, and in order to get a better view

brook.

we strolled down the lower end of the deer park by the ~~stream~~. The path

slipped

there is not much traveled, and ~~we could slip our arm around Nature's waist without anybody seeing~~. As we approached the corner near where the

\ *trickles*

brook ~~runs~~ under the wire fence, we noticed a red deer getting to her

as small and perfect as an object seen

feet. Beside her was a fawn, on legs that were just learning their

through a reducing glass.

(business.) They stood under a grey beech ~~carved~~ with dozens of hearts

whose trunk was engraved

and initials. Stretched on the ground was another fawn, and we
realized that the doe had just finished twinning. The second fawn was

promise

still wet, still unrisen. Here was a scene of rare sylvan splendor, in one of our five favorite boroughs, and we couldn't have asked for more.

~~black~~ new

Even our ^ shoes seemed to be working out all right, and weren't hurting much.

The doe was only a couple of feet from the wire, and we sat down on a rock nearby, with only the path between us, to see what sort of start young fawns get in the deep fastnesses of Mittel

and dazed from her labor,

Bronx. The mother, mildly unhappy at our presence, raised one forefoot,

primly.   lowered her head ~~*picking*~~ *and began doggedly to eat*

and stamped daintily. Then she doggedly ~~chewed up~~ the after-birth,

bunch

allowing it to swing crazily from her lips as though it were a ~~wisp~~ of

withered   loud

beetgreens. From the monkey house came the ^ insane hooting of some captious

~~ill-tempered~~ primate, filling the whole woodland with a wild hooroar.
As we watched, the sun came through weakly, brightening the rich red of

K   ing   ir

the fawns and ~~Lindled~~ them white spots. ~~A family of human beings~~

Now & then   *straggled along*

Occasionally a passerby would appear, and wander aimless by; but of all those who passed, none ~~noticed~~ was aware that anything had

and the ~~little kangaroo~~ baby

occurred. "Looka the kangaroos!" a child cried, and he and his

gazed briefly   & ~~*incuriously*~~ *sullenly at the deer & her 2 lambs*

mother examined the deer ~~park for a moment~~ and then passed on,
~~brooding on kangaroos. It was the sort of occasion that many a farm boy would, in the hunting country, would have given his right arm to have witnessed — the birth of twin fawns.~~

under him   *courage*

In a few moments the ~~new~~ second twin gathered ^ all his legs and all his

mysteries

ingenuity and arose, to stand for the first time sniffing the wonders

for captive   ~~*nervously fretfully*~~   *methodically*   *her youngest*

of a ~~deer~~ park. The doe quit her other work and started drying him. running her tongue against the grain and paying particular attention to the key ~~spots~~ points. Meanwhile the first fawn ~~wobbl~~ tiptoed

shallow

toward the ^ brook, in little stops and goes, and started across. He paused midstream to make a slight contribution, as a child does in bathing. Then he continued across, gained the other side, while his mother watched, selected a hiding place, and lay down beside a rock

and under a skunk cabbage leaf, in perfect concealment. Without *actually*
in the shifting light and shade
going out of sight, he managed to disappear completely. We hung around
From somewhere a long ways away a 12 o'clock whistle sounded.
for ~~about~~ a long while, but he never budged. Before we left, we ~~walked~~
crossed the brook ourself, just outside the fence, knelt, reached
can scratch a new wild
through the wire, and tested whether you ~~could scratch~~ a young fawn
starting
between the ears without distrbing him. You can indeed.
enchanting
Many a farm boy would give his right arm for so ennobling a
experience, but city children seem to care less — and even when they
get there, don't know what they're looking at.
~~what~~ the truth of what we had once
heard

In the final paragraph of the second draft, circled by White for deletion, he attempts to draw a moral from the experience in the comparison of the reaction of the city child with the hypothetical reaction of a country child, perhaps thinking of his own son, Joel, by then seventeen. But the editorial position he strikes actually diverts attention from the events he describes. As in "Transient," where White simply hopes to celebrate something he has observed, so here he finally elects to celebrate the moment without suggesting any larger significance to the occasion, and the final copy retyped and sent to the typesetter shows only minimal revision. In the final draft the concluding emphasis is on the delight of the experience of having scratched the head of a newborn fawn.

white
comment

On a warm, miserable morning last week we went up
to the Bronx zoo to see the moose calf and to break in a new pair of
black shoes. We encountered better luck than we had bargained for. The
cow moose and her young one were standing near the wall of the deer
park below the monkey house, and in order to get a better view we strolled
down to the lower end of the park by the brook. The path there is not
l
much traveled. As we approached the corner where the brook trickles

under

the wire fence, we noticed a red deer getting to her feet. Beside her,
on legs that were just learning their business, was a spotted fawn, as
small and perfect as a trinket seen through a reducing glass. They

a

stood there, mother and child, under a grey beech whose trunk was
engraved with dozens of hearts and initials. Stretched on the ground
was another fawn, and we realized that the doe had just finished twinning.
The second fawn was still wet, still unrisen. Here was a scene of rare
sylvan splendor, in one of our five favorite boroughs, and we couldn't
have asked for more. Even our ~~shiny~~ new shoes seemed to be working out
all right, and weren't hurting much.

    The doe was only a couple of feet from the wire, and

at the edge of

we sat down on a rock ~~nearby, with only~~ the footpath ~~between us~~ to see
what sort of start young fawns get in the deep fastness of Mittel
Bronx. The mother, mildly resentful of our presence and dazed from her
labor, raised one forefoot and stamped primly. Then she lowered her

dutifully

head, picked up the afterbirth, and began ~~doggedly~~ to eat it, allowing
it to swing crazily from her mouth as though it were a bunch of withered
beetgreens. From the monkey house came the loud, insane hooting of
some captious primate, filling the whole woodland with a wild hooroar.

ed

As we watched, the sun came weakly through, brighten~~ing~~ the rich red of
the fawns, and kindled their white spots. Occasionally a sightseer
would appear and wander aimlessly by, but of all who passed none was
aware that anything extraordinary had occurred. "Looka the kangaroos!"
a child cried. And he and his mother stared sullenly at the deer and
then walked on.

    In a few moments the second twin gathered all his legs
and all his ingenuity and arose, to stand for the first time sniffing
the mysteries of a park for captive deer. The doe, in recognition of
his achievement, quit her other work and began to dry him, running her
tongue against the grain and paying particular attention to the key
points. Meanwhile the first fawn tiptoed toward the shallow brook, in
little stops and goes, and started across. He paused midstream to make
a slight contribution, as a child does in bathing. Then, while his
mother watched, he continued across, gained the other side, selected a
hiding place, and lay down under a skunk cabbage leaf next to the fence,
in perfect concealment, his legs folded neatly under him. Without actually
going out of sight, he managed to disappear completely in the shift-

ing light and shade. From somewhere a long way off a 12 o'clock
whistle sounded. We hung around a while, but he never budged. Before we
left, we crossed the brook ourself, just outside the fence, knelt, reached
through the wire, and tested the truth of what we had once heard:
that you can scratch a new fawn between the ears without starting him.
You can indeed.

Like a good many of the whimsical pieces of the 1930s, White draws
for the Comment on personal experience, the random wanderings
around New York City, and his observations of "tiny capsules of truth,"
but unlike most of the Comment of a decade earlier, White has drawn
this out to a fuller depiction of the surroundings and the events, given
a fuller sense of his own feelings about what he has observed, and
has refused to settle for a quick snapshot of a bemused personality
in ironical circumstance. The wonder of witnessing the moment after
birth of twin fawns is sufficient unto itself; earlier, the irony of witnessing such an event in the middle of what was then the world's most
inhabited city would have been the focus of the event, but now White
mentions the irony only in passing references to the "Mittel Bronx"
and the "park for captive deer" and avoids an easy criticism of the
urban child's lack of appreciation for natural events. The added detail,
the more developed picture, serves the subject observed, not the author's persona, not the author's politics.

Part of White's willingness to step back from the potential editorializing of earlier drafts of "Twins" may have grown out of his willingness to editorialize in its companion piece. That piece was reprinted as
the first section of "Sound" in *The Second Tree from the Corner*. (We will
simply refer to it by that title and for the moment disregard the second
section, separated from it in the anthology by a page break and originally written in 1944.) "Sound" sets out to comment on the quality of
modern life and to make a specific point, but it is evident from the
drafts he goes through that the point is not clear to White at the outset.
Unlike the zoo Comment, this piece is grounded not in personal
experience but in exposure to public affairs and political news. It is
centered not in specific observation but in general speculation. The
first draft consisted of a page and a half of typing with some revision:

white
comment

The sound truck won its first round

in the Supreme Court the other day, in a close decision ~~which~~. We

theme of

predict the question of amplification will recur in many forms. The

and di rather badly, we thought.

Court found itself in a curious snarl, in which free speech was all

The decision seemed to us to ~~mix~~ confuse

mixed up with free ~~noise and in which~~ extension of speech. More and

objectionable

more, the right of a citizen to make himself obnoxious because of

the wonders of science. One wonders how far the human race will

private   public

abide amplicati n can tolerate. — the radio in the train, the private

press agents

radio in the public park, the aurplane shouting down from the air,

through ~~amplified~~

super-voice

and accepted a loud and artificial voice ~~or its~~ without

questioning its origin. or its meaning. A ~~l~~sou d truck is not

a man, expressing himself. — it is superman, on a ~~binge~~ political

or moral ~~oige~~ binge. It invades ~~the~~ privacy ~~of,~~   O r

constitution provides that we shall not muzzle any man; what we

don't know yet is whether it provides that we shall also provide him

stirr up

with an electric megaphone on wheels, to disturb not only our ideas

but our   Sound is already a weapon, divorced from meaning

It ~~has been used in war~~ could be used in war, to drive people ~~out~~

~~of their sens~~ mad

As for free speech,

We have a feeling that only through severe sound

restrictions, can the principle   rself be preserved, ~~and we~~ We'rve long

been in favor of far greater restrictions on the use of radios in publi

places — such as in club cars, taxis, etc. We regard it as outragesou

to hire a cah, and be subjected ~~to~~ not only to the terrors of traffic

but to the ~~results of a ball gave every so~~

We would be for a federal safety law prohibiting the installation of

a radio in any vehicle except a police car or ~~some such public co~~ ambulanc

army cars, and the like.

The number of typing errors, the incomplete sentences, the dangling ideas, all suggest that in the first rough draft White is searching for the main idea. Unlike the "Twins" piece, he has no chronology of events to help with the structure and no clear-cut thesis he wants to espouse. The issue of extending the protection of freedom of speech to the operation of sound trucks, whose job is to drive slowly up and down the streets blaring political messages, is obviously one that disturbs him — the conflict instigates the Comment, in effect — but in the first draft he has yet to determine how to describe what disturbs him about it, because it is not clear in his own mind.

The typed draft serves as a foundation for the further development of his ideas. To this page and a half he adds a number of items in pencil. At the very top of the first page, in the space above the first typed sentence, he writes:

> *We shall soon come squarely up*
> *against the question of whether the right of a*
> *speaker to get heard includes the right*
> *to get heard at a great distance.*
> *Already a too great tolerance has been developed by*
> *the race, & we submit meekly to indignities which our*
> *irrascible forebears would ~~have~~ never have put up with.*

Opposite that addition he writes in longhand: "*if we know our decibels.*" He adds the phrase "*in many courts*" to "in many forms" in the second line and in the space under "shouting down from the air" adds "*flying through the public sky.*" He scribbles in the phrase "*word binge*" over the earlier strikeover "binge" and the replacement "political or moral binge," still struggling with the appropriate description. At the bottom of the first page, where the piece divides formally into two paragraphs, he writes: "*Our song says let freedom ring. What we have to work at is whether it also means 'Let Electrical Freedom ring'*"; he amends that immediately to "*Let Freedom's Enlarged Gland ring.*"

As with "Twins," where the initial typed draft leads to considerable longhand addition at the end, so in the initial draft of "Sound" White struggles in longhand for an additional page and a half following the typed portion, at first rehearsing an idea he immediately revises and expands:

Free speech is in itself considerable of a nusiance
and only those who love it dearly are tolerant of its
 privilege itself does not become
a public nuisance of another sort

            considerable of
    Free speech is ~~unintel.~~ of a nuisance just
                    and
in itself— ~~so much so that~~ only those who
 love it dearly truly tolerate it. If we
confuse
~~subject~~ it to the added nuisance value
                        utterance at a decibel rate
of uninhibited public noise, we may find
it even less popular a principle
~~than it sometimes~~

        There are plenty of people who
                off
always want to shut ~~up~~ an
opinion they don't like; & if the
            ~~becomes identified~~ is packaged
opinion ~~is clothed~~ in a burdensome
volume of sound, the number of people
who will be willing to shut
it up will greatly increase.
Amplification, like alcohol, is neither
                curse
a total blessing nor a total ~~unintel~~
~~It has is in a middle groun~~
    When a sound truck is told to move along,
free speech is not dying— anymore than
when a drunk is told to move along ~~Bacchus is~~
the grape has withered on the vine.

The additions bring in new ideas, perhaps connected to White's own ambivalence about allowing free speech and silencing sound trucks, and they bring him around to the need for a distinction between the two, so that if and when the sound truck is silenced, free speech will not be. In the next draft some of these things begin to come together:

white

comment

swooping   *inner*

~~unintel.~~ *into* ~~the depths~~ *of ear.*

~~enveloped~~

encased

or the ideas ^ *in noise*

    The sound truck, as a vehicle of Freedom, won its
first round the other day in a close decision of the Supreme Court.
~~But~~ if we know our ~~political and~~ soicl decibels, the theme of
amplification will recur in many forms. ~~We~~ The Court found itself
in a curious snarl and ~~mix~~ did rather badly, we thought. Free
speech got all mixed up with free extension of speech, until pretty
soon ~~unintel~~ the judges hardly knew whether they were talking about *noise*
~~unintelligible~~. A sound truck, ~~in our view of t~~ it

opening his trap

seems to us, is not a man expressing himself, it is Superman on ~~a~~
~~word binge, a rubber~~ a word binge. The distinction will eventuall
    ~~unintel.~~ *demanding that your ears be lent.*
have to be drawn. It has never seemed to us that loud-speaking was
essentially the same as speaking; and the electririfcation of the
human voice is a social problem in itself, It bears both   n freedom
of ~~ps~~ speech and on the right of privacy. So far, we have pretty
much accepted, without question, the phenomenon of elctrical *jumboism*
exaggeration, or amplification; and the extension of sound is something
our   was
a baby is born to — and even ~~gets wired~~ the nursery is wired to the
            and the Silent Nurse
living room, so that the mother can hear sounds of strangulati n or
despair, and his first cries are amplified in the ears of his mother
            & political speeches
(along with street noises ^ that drift in through the nursery window.)
One wonders how far the human race will string along with its own
stentorianism
blatancy. We'll soon come squarely up against the question of whether
the right to get heard includes the right to get heard-at-a-distance.
The Constitution provides that no man shall be muzzled; it does not
provide that people who don't want to listen shall hear, anyway. ~~This~~
~~is a fundamental matter.~~

Having typed that page and worked on it some in pencil, White tried
to draft an alternative version of the first section of the piece:

white
comment

        The sound truck, or Freedom on Wheels, won its first
round the other day in a close decision in the Supreme Court. ~~If we
know our social~~ The theme of amplification will probably recur in many
forms ~~in many courts~~. The Court found itself in a curious snarl and
did rather badly, we thought. Free speech got all mized up with free

                    unsure

extension of speech, and the judges seemed ~~doubtful~~ whether they were
talking about noise or the ideas wrapped in noise. A sound truck, it
seems to us, is not a man expressing himself — it is Superman demanding
that your ears be lent. The distinction will eventually have to be

                         loud-speaking

drawn. Loud-speaking is not quite the same thing as speaking, the former

           inconvenience,   speaking

being capable of causing madness and death, whereas the ~~latter chiefly
causes exasperation, irritation, or~~ is a public menace only to the
~~Loud Loud Speaking is the projection of ideas, loudspeaking is
the projection of ideas beyond the natural~~ extent that the ideas
cause exasperation. The distinction will eventually have to be drawn.

speaking infringes on one's privacy only to the extent that the ideas
~~are~~ infirnge; loud speaking infringes not only with ideas, but with
a vlume of sound that can become greater than the The loud speaker

                        Amflified sound

is already known among military men as a ~~potential~~ weapon of relatively
untried ~~dimension~~ potenecy, and we will probably hear more about it
(and hear IT) if there is ever another war.

The changes here seem to be an attempt to clear up the confusion in
the immediately preceding draft and to find clearer expression of ideas.
White gets bogged down with phrasing halfway through, and the bottom section of this page is a reworking of lines in the top section that
had not come out as he wanted.

    Having worked through the first paragraph in this sheet, White be-
gins a new draft from the beginning:

white   *enlarged*

comment   ———— *miracle of its* ^ *vocal chords*

Free Speech

Opinion

The sound truck, or ~~Freedom~~ on Wheels, won its

by

first round the other day ~~in~~ a close decision of the Supreme Court. We

however

have an idea ^ that the theme of amplification is not dead and will recur

in ~~many~~ many variations. The Court found itself in ~~unintel~~ snarl and

did rather badly, we thought. Free speech became confused with free

some of the

extension-of-speech, and ~~the~~ judges were not quite sure whether they

about

were talking about noise or ^ the ideas wrapped in noise. A sound truck,

on a soapbox   ~~on wheels~~

it seems to us, is not a man ~~expressing himself in a free country~~ — it

haranging the world of suds.

is Superman ~~on a soap tower.~~   The distinction will eventually have to

at all   *plain-*

be drawn. Loud-speaking is not the ^ same thing as ^ speaking; the loud

piles   *on*   *disturb the peace,*

speaker ~~adds~~ decibel ~~to~~ decibel and can cause madness and death, whereas

natural

speaking ~~merely causes exasperation~~ is a public menace only to the

annoyance at

extent that causes ~~exasperation and an~~ irritation with the whole

Amplified sound

principle of free speech. The loud speaker is already known among

suffer

military men as a weapon of untried potency, and we will probably ~~hear~~

agonies

from it it there is another war.

meekly

So far ~~we have~~ the human race has ~~pretty~~

~~much~~

the *electification of utterance jumbo sound is* ~~unintel.~~

accepted ~~the jum~~ jumboism; ~~or amplification and the extension of~~

~~and beyond its natural volume~~   *modern*

~~sound beyond its natural bounds~~ is something a ^ baby is born to — even

distress   *earliest*

the nursery is wired for ~~distress~~ and the ~~child's~~ infant's ~~first~~ cries over a Silent nurse syte,

are carried to the living room and amplified in the ears of the mother
(along with street noises that drift in through the nursery window).
One wonders, though, how far the human race will string along with its

and   *speak*

own stentorianism, how long the right-to-~~be heard~~ can remain involved

greater stepped-up ~~*level*~~ *voltage*

with the right-to-be-heard-at-a-distance. We~~x~~ have a feeling that
only through ∉meeting this issue can the principle of free speech
itself be preserved.

private distress system

There are always people who are anxious to shut off opinion they don't

electrified

like; and if the opinion ~~becomes~~ comes packaged in a ~~burdensome~~ volume
of sound, the numner of people who will want to shut it off will increase.

something

Amplification ~~is a bit~~ like alcohol — ~~it can serve or destroy well, or~~

its

~~it can destroy, according to~~ ^ use: *it can heighten meanings &*

also

visions. But it can ^ *also destroy the mind.*

*both the sound
& the fury*

which is in itself intolerable
[unintelligible]

By the time White finished this draft he had found the perspective
he had been searching for. There are two subsequent drafts, but he
never substantially changed this draft. The next draft changes the long-
standing "first round in a close decision" to "first brush with the law
by a close decision"; it tightens up the third sentence, after trying to re-
work commentary on the judges, so that it reads: "Free speech became
confused with free-extension-of-speech, noise with ideas wrapped in
noise." It decides that Superman is "on a tower of suds" and adds
"through excess of volume" to explain how "loud-speaking is capable
not only of disturbing the peace but can cause madness and death,"
whereas first natural speaking, then plain speaking, then the human
voice "is a public nuisance" rather than a menace "to the extent that it
aggravates the normal human resentment against the whole principle
of free speech" instead of causing exasperation, annoyance, or irritation with it. In the second paragraph, after the observation about

sound entering the nursery window, he adds: "(Note to political candidates: always set your sound truck under nursery windows, and your arguments will be picked up by an interior network and carried to uneasy elders.)" "Stentorianism" becomes "stentorian gifts" with the addition of wondering "how long the right-to-speak can pretend to be innocent of wattage." None of these are major revisions.

In the next draft, the draft sent to the printer, White's changes are minimal: he drops the phrase "and did rather badly, we thought," which had been added in the first rough draft; the positions of "is capable" and "not only" are reversed; a "which" is changed to a "that." "Sound" is finished. The version that is finally published is more direct, more restrained, and more polished than the earlier drafts.

> The sound truck, or Free Speech on Wheels, won its first brush with the law by a close decision in the Supreme Court. We have an idea, however, that the theme of amplification is not dead and will recur in many variations. The Court found itself in a snarl; free speech became confused with free extension-of-speech, noise with ideas wrapped in noise. A sound truck, it seems to us is not a man on a soapbox — it is Superman on a tower of suds. The distinction will eventually have to be drawn. Loud speaking is not the same thing as plain speaking; the loudspeaker piles decibel on decibel and not only is capable of disturbing the peace but through excess of volume can cause madness and death, whereas the human voice is a public nuisance only to the extent that it aggravates the normal human resentment against the whole principle of free speech. Amplified sound is already known among military men as a weapon of untried potency, and we will probably suffer from it if there is another war.
>
> Up till now, modern man has meekly accepted the miracle of his enlarged vocal cords. He has acquiesced in jumboism. A modern baby is born amplified, for even the nursery is wired for sound and the infant's earliest cries are carried over a private distress system to the ears of its mother in the living room — along with street noises that drift in through the open nursery window. (Note to political candidates: Always park your sound truck under nursery windows and your remarks will be picked up by an interior network and carried to uneasy elders.) One wonders, though, how much longer the human race will string along with its own electrical gifts, and how

long the right to speak can remain innocent of wattage. We have a feeling that only if this issue is met will the principle of free speech survive. There are always plenty of people who are eager to stifle opinion they don't admire, and if the opinion happens to be expressed in a volume of sound that is in itself insufferable, the number of people who will want to stifle both the sound *and* the fury will greatly increase. Amplification, therefore, is something like alcohol: It can heighten our meanings, but it can also destroy our reason.

Unlike "Twins," this Comment seems to have been a tougher struggle to get under control, to bring to fruition, because the ideas are more abstract and argumentative. Like "Twins," however, "Sound" reaches its final form through a process of exploration, a process of discovery during the composition. At this stage of White's career, with the Comments longer and more complex than they once were, he depended upon a more recursive process to produce the final text than he had a dozen years earlier.

Because the Comment page could now be two or three longer, more developed items, instead of five to ten short items, and because White's experience with the "One Man's Meat" column and the *Wild Flag* editorials had habituated him to producing more thoughtful and more complicated texts, the late Comment makes different demands on his composing. The longer Comment items make it more difficult to rely on format or genre knowledge to carry the weight of the composing, and thus they necessitate multiple revisions. The editorials make demands on his powers of argumentation as well. Rather than simply sharing an experience or making a wry quip about affairs of one kind or another, the editorials demand more careful considerations of language and logic. "Sound," which is trying to take a position and argue a convincing case, may require more fine-tuning than "Twins," which only turns on White's reaction to what he observes, but both demand more laborious composing than the glib, clever, and formulaic early Comment had.

On 2 January 1949, White wrote to his brother Stanley, "I am starting 1949 in a somewhat relaxed and benign condition as the result of a decision to give up the responsibility of the New Yorker's editorial page. I intend to apply myself to more irregular and peaceable pursuits for a while, to work patiently instead of rapidly, and to improve the nick of time" (*Letters* 305–306). The last phrase is an allusion to Thoreau. Although White continued to contribute to the Notes and Comment page, he resigned his role as the chief editorial voice for the *New Yorker* and, as he had ten years earlier, may have felt that he was again simplifying his life.

The editorial writing of the previous half-dozen years had moved White's nonfiction persona away from the town wit–colyumist–commentator role he had had in the previous two decades. It had also tempered the voice of the essayist in his writing. The editorial approach to late Comment allowed more development than early paragraphs had but also demanded more impersonal writing, more seriousness and less whimsy. In the long run that may have been good for the development of White's two children's books, works of imaginative, inventive, and idiosyncratic fiction, but the intimacy and poetry of the "One Man's Meat" columns at their best is missing from the nonfiction. For the most part, this period of White's writing dominated by editorial writing is one in which he steps back from the literary side of his nonfiction and works diligently on the journalistic side. It is significant that the clipbook that summarizes this period is so diverse in genres and that, in spite of the number of editorial comments — literally hundreds — he contributed to the *New Yorker* after the publication of *The Wild Flag*, he finds less than two dozen to include in *The Second Tree from the Corner*. The Comment in the posthumous collection, *Writings from the New Yorker 1927–1976*, are valuable to the degree that they show us how the regular writing of weekly editorial journalism produces so much prose that is both accomplished and ephemeral, serviceable for the short term with little literary staying power. Throughout much of this period White simply seems resigned to the production of workmanlike prose for the *New Yorker*.

Other factors should be noted, however. In 1949 White turned fifty, and he and his wife, Katharine, had been going through periods of ill health that would haunt them for the rest of their lives. Giving up the weekly obligation to the editorial page freed White to begin work on *Charlotte's Web*, which occupied much of his writing time over the next several years. In December 1951 Harold Ross died, ending an era at the magazine, and the Whites were planning for Katharine's retirement through much of the decade. She intended to retire in 1955, but upon the death of Gus Lobrano, the fiction editor, she stayed on two more years, until William Maxwell permanently took over. Even then she continued to work part time from Maine until 1961, when bad health forced her to give up editorial work altogether. By that time the success of *Charlotte's Web* and the freedom to turn back toward the personal writing that had marked the "One Man's Meat" column allowed White himself to enter into a new period of writing.

"A MORE ACCOMMODATING WIND VANE"

White as Correspondent

The final period of E. B. White's emergence as an essayist, like the other periods we have been considering, not only overlaps with the period that preceded it but in some ways is a period of transitions. The Whites did not simply resign from their work at the *New Yorker* but rather withdrew in stages, replacing each abandoned responsibility with new activity. White's article for *Holiday*, "Here Is New York," appeared in April 1949, but he had written it in the summer of 1948, and it followed the publication of "Death of a Pig" in January 1948. The success of these occasional pieces may have been part of the spur to reduce his load with Notes and Comment. Stepping back from responsibility for the editorial page freed him for the significant activity of *Charlotte's Web* and the compilation of *The Second Tree from the Corner*; it also allowed him the space to engage in other forms of writing as well. He contributed a short piece on the Model T Ford, "From Sea to Shining Sea," for *Ford Times* in July 1953, as well as two articles with brief descriptions of birds, illustrated by Charles Harper, in 1954 and 1955. In September 1954 he worked on the script for a brief television documentary called "The Lobsterman," which ran, with his voiceover narration, on the NBC cultural affairs program, *Omnibus*, in December of that year.

These kinds of writing, while producing work of no particular significance, were successful ventures into freelance writing. They did not lure White away from the *New Yorker* entirely, but they gave him room to experiment and to try out other options while he retreated slowly from Comment writing. In 1954, the year that *The Second Tree from the Corner* was published, White contributed all or part of twenty-seven Notes and Comment pages, more than half the pages for the year; the next year he wrote Comment for only fourteen issues; in 1956, for only two. In 1957, when he and Katharine retired, White contributed to only six Comment pages. The following year was the first year since 1926 that he wrote no Notes and Comment items. From this point on White's work appeared only sporadically. Yet the experiments had the effect of creating new possibilities for his writing, possibilities that would draw on the forms of writing in which he had already accomplished so much and would result both in his final new collection of material, *The Points of My Compass* (1962), and most of his retrospective collection, *Essays of E. B. White* (1977). Two pivotal pieces published in 1954 nudged White toward the material that would make up these two books.

To celebrate the hundredth anniversary of the publication of *Walden*, the *Yale Review* solicited White for a commemorative essay. He wrote Gus Lobrano: "I can't think of anything to say about this event. . . . I take on hard stuff like that all the time. Hell, I am just through writing some bird captions for the Ford Times — which turns out to be a bird magazine. If I had known what the last days of a writer were going to be, I would have watched my step, years ago" (*Letters* 396). The resulting essay was published as "Walden — 1954" in the Autumn 1954 issue of the *Yale Review*. It is one of White's rare literary essays, in the intermittent tradition of his critical remarks on Anne Morrow Lindbergh's *The Wave of the Future* in *One Man's Meat*, his introduction to *A Subtreasury of American Humor*, and his essay on Don Marquis. Considered alongside earlier references to Thoreau and to *Walden* in his work, it is a markedly different work in tone and perspective. Earlier, White had spoken of Thoreau as a comrade in arms or evoked him in attacks on veniality in society ("The Deacon's Effects") or crass politicians ("A Visitor at the Pond," a satire on Senator Joseph McCarthy) or played with his language ("The Retort Transcendental"). In "Walden — 1954" White steps back from Thoreau and focuses on the man and the book. White himself appears in the essay, of course, not as the transcendentalist's henchman or herald but rather as a detached admirer, couching Thoreau's effect on the reader in terms of his own example but distancing himself sufficiently to assert that Thoreau's effects are more powerful on the young than on the old. He concludes, "I should hate to be called a Thoreauvian, yet I wince every time I walk into the barn I'm pushing before me, seventy-five feet by forty, and the author of *Walden* has served as my conscience through the long stretches of my trivial days" (22). It is White's best piece of literary writing, and it again raised for him all the issues that had risen before his retreat to Maine in 1938 and the beginning of "One Man's Meat."

The second pivotal piece was written in September 1954, before the essay on Thoreau was published. It is a long essay recounting the period he spent awaiting the arrival of Hurricane Edna in his part of Maine. Published in the *New Yorker* as "Our Windswept Correspondents: The Eye of Edna," it introduces a new note into White's writing, one not unlike the columns in *One Man's Meat* that were couched as reports from the farm. The article is a dispatch from the front, as it were, a report on conditions around him. He wrote it not as an editorialist responding to current affairs but as an involved observer corresponding more casually with readers. Although it was written quickly, it did not demand the immediacy or analysis of the Comment editorials and, as a feature article rather than a Comment or column, it also did not restrain White in terms of format or length. It allowed him the freedom to develop his subject further than the revamped Comment page or even the "One Man's Meat" column had permitted. Eventually, White came to see the possibilities for other pieces that "The Eye of Edna" and "Walden — 1954" presented.

Toward the end of the following year White wrote a piece drawn again from his time in Maine. It served as the basis for an irregular department, inspired by "The Eye of Edna" but nominally modeled on departments already appearing in the *New Yorker*, such as Janet Flanner's "Letter from Paris" (published under the pen name Genêt). White wrote his editor, William Shawn, that he had "tried various heads and now lean to Letter from the East. Seems to me that if I can latch on to the four points of the compass, I can manage anything" (*Letters* 410). White's department would take the form of a dispatch or report on current affairs but with no fixed location and no predictable subject. Later, when he had collected these Letters into *The Points of My Compass*, White explained in the foreword that "having forsworn weekly journalism but wishing to continue writing, I invented a system of orientation that would serve my convenience" and "decided to become a letter writer," even though "unlike other correspondents, I seldom went anywhere or did anything."

> Clearly, if I were to serve as a foreign correspondent to a responsible publication I would have to alter the world itself, and rearrange geography to give me a wider range.
>
> Not wanting to rule out any portion of the globe as my territory, or any subject matter as my concern, I invented a new compass and a more accommodating wind vane. . . . I selected my office in mid-

town Manhattan as a locus — a spot in air between Forty-third and Forty-fourth streets, between Fifth and Sixth. In my new design, anything east of this point was "the East," anything west of it was "the West," and so on. . . . All I had to do was sit down anywhere and I was somewhere. (viii–ix)

The first contribution in this series was published as "Letter from the East" in the 24 December 1955 edition of the *New Yorker*; it was later reprinted as "Homecoming." Together with "The Eye of Edna," the two pieces from Maine established for White his role as "correspondent" for the magazine.

The correspondence article, of course, dates back to the *Tatler* and the *Spectator*, the eighteenth-century precursors of journalistic wit, opinion, and observation upon which the *New Yorker* was loosely modeled. More recently, Christopher Morley had used the premise in his "Bowling Green" column, including both "A Letter to Henry [Seidel Canby, his editor]" and "A Birthday Letter" (to Charles Lamb, possibly a model for White's letter to Thoreau published as "Walden"); both were reprinted in a collection titled *The Romany Stain* (1926). In the *New Yorker* Letters could be either single articles or, more frequently, a collection of short reports. In the three months immediately before White's first "Letter from the East" the magazine printed Letters from Paris, London, Washington, Belize, Bali, Denver, and Vienna — from, as White put it, "far distant or far out places" (*Points* viii).

A representative example of the Letter format is Genêt's "Letter from Paris" in the 10 September 1955 issue. It was divided into several sections by page breaks. The first section was a report on the politics behind the "repressive measures carried out by the military governor of Casablanca" against Moroccan nationals in retaliation for a massacre of Europeans a week earlier. The second item, a piece about the death of the artist Fernand Léger, was completely unrelated, as was the third, a report on the celebrity of diarist Paul Leautaud. A concluding item about summer in Paris talked about the popularity of *les streap teases* and *les snack-bars* and Americanizing influence in general. None of the four items is connected in any way other than in having been collected in Paris by Janet Flanner. In keeping with the "correspondence" motif, the writing gives off a sense of informality as well as a sense of currency: "During the hottest August fortnight in fifty years, crowds have been patronizing the handsome new Deligny swimming pavilion in the Seine" (88).

Another example of the format is Mollie Panter-Downes's "Letter from London" in the 8 October 1955 issue. In her first item she discusses the resurgence of interest in the defection of Donald Maclean and Guy Burgess a few years earlier; in her second, the debut of a commercial television network to compete with the BBC; in her third, performances of the Stuttgart State Opera Company and the Old Vic; in her fourth, Nancy Mitford's article on "The English Aristocracy" in *Encounter*; and in her fifth, the concern among the English over President Eisenhower's health. The letter writer's tone is adopted: "Londoners are talking with either amusement or irritation about the article by Nancy Mitford, . . . who looks like becoming a sort of Mayfair Emily Post" (124).

The point of the Letter series is not to report directly on specific issues and news events but rather to suggest the currents of conversation, the recent topics of discussion in London and Paris, and, by implication, to inform the sophisticated reader of the *New Yorker* of the items of interest in sophisticated circles in those European capitals. Because the Letter could hardly be a news article, the interests and observations of the Letter writers determined the nature of the contents. The joke in White's initial use of the format was that his Letters would not report from the centers of power, glamour, and sophistication but rather from everyday activities and routine places.

Unlike the monthly columns of "One Man's Meat" or the weekly items for Notes and Comment, publication of the "Letters from the East (or wherever)" (*Points* xii) was intermittent, often widely spaced (see Appendix). The first appeared in the 10 December 1955 issue of the *New Yorker*; there were five in 1956, three in 1957, two in 1958, and three in 1960, and the final entry, "Letter (Delayed) from the North," about his youthful adventures on an Alaskan cruise ship, was published in 1961. At this point White began to compile the materials for *The Points of My Compass*.

The series of fifteen Letters White contributed to the *New Yorker* was congenial to him both for the casual tone the correspondence could take and also for the possibility of making up the piece out of several items, as he had done on Comment pages and in the *Harper's* column. Of the Letters written between 1955 and 1961, the Alaskan memoir is a single long narrative, and the Letter reprinted as "Unity" is arguably a single argumentative essay on arms agreements (divided into two sections in the magazine by a page break). Two other Letters, reprinted as "A Report in Spring" and "A Report in Winter," are rambling pieces that fill the reader in on currents of conversation and activity in Maine. Three other Letters have sections that are more or less self-contained but nonetheless are tightly linked thematically: the Letter on the United Nations has three sections: on its membership policy, its definition of aggression, and its police force; the one on the "motorcar" has two: on car buying and car design; and the one on the railroad has three railroading items.

The items in other Letters are closer to the potpourri of Genêt's "Letter from Paris" or Panter-Downes's "Letter from London." The earliest "Letter from the East," reprinted as "Homecoming," has sections on a chimney fire, Bernard DeVoto's opinion of a highway into Maine, deer season and Christmas decorations, and Maine birds — all related by being about Maine, but self-contained and not tightly connected. "Bedfellows," about sharing a sickbed with the ghost of his dog Fred, books by Democrats, and a news article about Eisenhower's linking of democracy and prayer, makes overt but tenuous connections between its items, weaving references to Fred throughout. "Coon Tree" has three sections: on a raccoon's behavior, scientific ideas about energy in rocks, and the difference between modern and old-fashioned kitchens; "Sootfall and Fallout" includes an item on Mary Martin's moving, along with items on sootfall and fallout and political campaigning; "The Ring of Time" has two sections: on a bareback rider in the circus and southern racial attitudes; "The Shape of Television" includes a section on new developments in Maine and one on politics and the farm, as well as a section on the effects of television viewing. The least connected seems to be the "Letter from the East" collected as "Will Strunk." In the magazine it had a section on mosquitoes, a section on William Strunk, Jr., White's Cornell professor, and his textbook, *The Elements of Style*, and a long final section on the dumping of atomic waste at sea; when White revised *The Elements of Style* (1959) he dropped the mosquitoes and atomic waste sections and used only the middle section as the introduction to the book, but in *The Points of My Compass* he kept the mosquito section as well as the Strunk section and deleted only the atomic waste section.

At least half of the pieces originally published as Letters are similarly tentative about the relationship among their various sections. Some sense of the range of looseness in the structure of these essays may be had by examining two of them, "The Shape of Television" and "The Ring of Time."

"The Shape of Television" opens with a chatty epistolary tone, as if updating a distant friend: "All kinds of new, interesting developments are taking place around me, and I always feel behind events. Our new post office, now nearing completion, has two picture windows in the front, and I think this is in preparation for the day when the mail arrives in town by rocket" (*Points* 193). The section on the postal service goes on for three paragraphs, not only musing further on rocket delivery but also, in the second paragraph, describing the Metro System and its workings and, in the third, commenting on the proposed electronic "speed mail" system of the future. Then, in the fourth paragraph, White shifts abruptly to commenting on the use of enforcement frogmen to deter underwater lobster thefts, and in the fifth paragraph he discusses the deer population on Mt. Desert Island, hearkening back one paragraph by suggesting that frogmen could also serve as census takers.

In the magazine these five paragraphs are set off from the rest of the piece by a page break or white space. Although it is standard practice in the magazine to section off articles in this fashion, the page break here is appropriate because in the sixth paragraph White starts a series of four paragraphs on farming. Using the comments on farming by presidential candidates in the 1960 campaign as a springboard (the piece is dated 21 November 1960 in *The Points of My Compass* and was originally published in the 3 December 1960 *New Yorker*), White claims in the sixth paragraph that "the root of the farm problem" is "that the farmer himself has disappeared" (195). The seventh paragraph contrasts the farm of thirty years earlier with the contemporary farm scene: "Thirty years ago, almost every house along the road was hooked up to a family cow. . . . The family cow has gone the way of the ivory-billed woodpecker. Householders no longer plant gardens if they can avoid it; instead, they work hard, earn money, and buy a TV set and a freezer. Then, acting on advice from the TV screen, they harvest the long, bright, weedless rows at the chain store" (196). The remainder of the paragraph discusses the change in the status of the farm hen.

Having introduced television, White raises the subject again in the eighth paragraph. He comments on an article in a farm paper attributing changes in husbandry to television, which keeps farmers up late and changes them from early risers to late risers. In the ninth paragraph White cites a television comedian ridiculing those who would watch educational programming at six in the morning and then describes an episode of "Today on the Farm" — in which a modern farmer delivers a litter of pigs — in order to contrast it with his own old-fashioned experience at animal husbandry. In the magazine this paragraph is followed by another page break, clearly setting off these four paragraphs as a distinct section of the piece.

Thus far, this "Letter from the East" has dealt with television only tangentially; in the third section of the piece, beginning with the tenth paragraph, it deals directly with the subject: "The effect of television on our culture and on our tone are probably even greater than we suspect from the events of the last few years" (198). After this introductory paragraph White begins an extended comparison of "the shape of the audio-visual world" with "the shape of the world of journalism and the world of the stage and music hall" (198) in the eleventh paragraph, and develops it through the next four paragraphs, shifting attention in the last to advertising. In the sixteenth paragraph he editorializes about the exploitation of the viewer's attention and then discusses the effect of advertising's control of the medium on its editorial and entertainment elements through the remaining six paragraphs, concluding: "Any creative person who, as a sideline, engages in promoting the sale of a product subjects his real line of work to certain strains, and fogs the picture of himself in the minds of all. It seems sad that the TV industry, on which ride the country's hopes for entertainment, education, and information, should have felt it necessary, as a first step, to equip its pundits, its clowns, its reporters, and even its children, with something to sell" (203). The tone of those final two sentences is far removed from the tone of the essay's opening; the conclusion is clearly not epistolary but editorial. Often in his "Letters from the ———" series White puts the most serious or complex issue toward the end — in the "Will Strunk" letter, for example, the light topic of mosquitoes comes first, then the gentle reminiscence of Strunk, and finally the discussion of the disposal of atomic waste. As in the Strunk letter, the most serious discussion in the television letter is really detachable from the rest of the piece — the sections on the mail service and the family farm are self-sufficient commentary that do not necessarily preface or lay the groundwork for the television section. Rather, the television comments in the farm section intimate that a more focused discussion of TV and contemporary life might be possible but do not connect to the television section in such a way that the reader reverses that section's relationship to the farm discussion — that is, the farm discussion does not become merely tangential to the television discussion.

The tendency of White to see the Letter pieces as a department, as a more or less loose series of associations, can also be found in "The Ring of Time," one of his most anthologized and admired pieces. First published as a "Letter from the South" and dated 22 March 1956 in *The Points of My Compass*, "The Ring of Time" is always printed with a page break dividing it into two sections. The first section describes a teenage girl practicing her bareback riding in the winter quarters of the Ringling Brothers' circus in Sarasota, Florida. It begins with quite a different tone from most of the Letters: "After the lions had returned to their cages, creeping angrily through the chutes, a little bunch of us drifted away and into an open doorway nearby, where we stood for a while in semidarkness, watching a big brown circus horse go harumphing around the practice ring" (51). It is not a sentence of an amiable letter writer but rather a literary opening, beginning a narrative in medias res and following through with extended and detailed description of the setting and the performers. Unlike the pieces that begin formally as editorials or analysis and also unlike those that, more commonly, begin informally as one-sided conversation, introducing a topic in order to comment on it, White here is attempting a sustained narrative scene in order to evoke both the scene and the feelings it generated in him. The whole segment illustrates the twin themes of illusory and pragmatic understanding of time and the momentarily spellbinding effect of "the exuberance and gravity of youth."

The segment is also a self-conscious performance on White's part. He claims that "as a writing man, or secretary, I have always felt charged with the safekeeping of all unexpected items of worldly or unworldly enchantment, as though I might be held personally responsible if even a small one were to be lost" and that he is "acting as recording secretary for one of the oldest of societies" made up of those who "have surrendered . . . to the bedazzlement of a circus rider." He says of his attempt "to recapture this mild spectacle" that "it is not easy to communicate anything of this nature" (52) and afterwards asserts: "It has been ambitious and plucky of me to attempt to describe what is indescribable, and I have failed, as I knew I would. But I have discharged my duty to my society; and besides, a writer, like an acrobat, must occasionally try a stunt that is too much for him" (55). Such comments suggest that White himself recognized the extent to which the circus piece is a departure from his usual style and pattern of development. It is an attempt not only to describe but to recreate his "trance"; the replication of the event is captured in the rhythms of such a sentence as this: "The rider's gaze, as she peered straight ahead, seemed to be circular, as though bent by the force of circumstance; then time itself began running in circles, and so the beginning was where the end was, and the two were the same, and one thing ran into the next and time went around and around and got nowhere" (54). The idea that time seems to be circular, the escape into the trance inspired by the performance, the recognition that the magic of the performance arises "from internal fires of professional hunger and delight, from the exuberance and gravity of youth," the observation that the difference between the finished show and the rehearsal was the "difference between planetary light and the combustion of stars" — all these elements make the circus piece self-sustained and intensely unified.

The second segment of "The Ring of Time" is closer in tone to the kind of epistolary piece the reader might expect, closer in tone to "On a Florida Key" from *One Man's Meat*, for example, or most of the other Letters. An introductory paragraph sets the scene in Florida; a second paragraph describes the beginning of the day; a third and a fourth treat the character of the sun and the humidity, before White begins to develop the theme of race relations, briefly introduced in the first paragraph through a vague reference to a Tampa Lions Club vote on segregation. The race issue is treated in paragraphs five through eight, mostly through anecdotes like one about how black spectators sit in a "separate but equal section of the left-field bleachers and watch Negro players . . . using the same bases as the white players, instead of separate (but equal) bases" (*Points* 58). The sequence eventually concludes in a way that connects the political situation to the typical southern day he had described earlier: "The Supreme Court decision is like the Southern sun, laggard in its early stages, biding its time. . . . I think the decision is as incontrovertible and as warming as the sun, and, like the sun, will eventually take charge" (59). That paragraph connects all the elements from the paragraph break through to this comparison, and the southern segment would have no connection with the earlier circus segment (except for an off-handed comparison of the bareback rider to a mullet) if it were not for a final paragraph reviving the theme of time: "But there is certainly a great temptation in Florida to duck the passage of time. Lying in warm comfort by the sea, you receive gratefully the gift of the sun, the gift of the South. This is true seduction. After a few days I was clearly enjoying the same delusion as the girl on the horse — that I could ride clear around the ring of day, guarded by wind and sun and sea and sand, and not be a moment older" (59).

This paragraph suggests that the essay has been about the delusions about time inspired by both the climate and the circumstances of White's most recent visit in the South. By implication it suggests that this kind of delusion is characteristic of the South, particularly in matters of race and change. Yet the paragraph focuses on White and explicitly turns away from the musing about politics to close on the author's delusion, not the southerner's; it undercuts the force of the previous paragraph by generalizing delusion and turning the reader away from the political situation. In *The Points of My Compass* White adds a postscript to this piece (as he does to many of the Letters in the book) that talks about the changes in Fiddler's Bayou, where he was vacationing, the closing of the winter circus locale in Sarasota, and the unchanging habits of the fiddler crab. He never mentions the political situation in the South in the postscript.

Thus, although the two parts of this essay are thematically linked, the tone, style, structure, and focus of each suggests that they are essentially two independent pieces juxtaposed to one another by their similar theme and common setting; they are almost two short essays that serve as self-contained verbal variations on a theme rather than two inseparable sections of one whole. This is particularly clear if we compare "The Ring of Time" to the other great White essay on self-delusion and time, "Once More to the Lake," which is a completely unified, single work. "Once More to the Lake" is always reprinted intact in trade and college anthologies, but — particularly in college composition readers — "The Ring of Time" is presented more often as only the bareback rider section than as both sections together and is never presented as only the second section (Root, "Once"). This may be seem less significant if we consider that such textbooks frequently excerpt essays and book chapters and publish only the portion they want to use as an illustration of some element of composition or some idea for discussion. Often such excerpts are presented as if they were entire works, without clear markers that they are portions of the complete original. As lamentable and misleading as this practice often is, it is notable that "Once More to the Lake" is never excerpted and that the circus segment of "The Ring of Time" is always presented in its entirety. These circumstances seem to suggest that, at least on the part of textbook editors, there is some ambivalence about the overall unity of the two sections of "The Ring of Time." This situation seems not to arise in critical discussions of the essay, which tend to treat both sections as an inseparable whole (Haskell; Klaus, "Chameleon"; Smith).

In the Letter series, then, White drew on the form and strategies with which he was familiar from his past work with Notes and Comment and "One Man's Meat." His subjects ranged from the personal and intimate (a fire in his chimney, mosquitoes in his bedroom, his head in traction) to the public and argumentative (the direction of the United Nations, the opinions of politicians, the changes in railroads and automobiles). The forms in which he wrote were varied — memoir, editorial, report, correspondence, profile. The organization of the Letters ranged from tightly structured to rambling, from conjunctive to disjunctive to detachable. The Letter reprinted as "The Years of Wonder" uses a news event (a reference to a Russian proposal about the Bering Strait) as a trigger to explore personal history through references to and quotations from his youthful journal, as he had done in the "First World War" column for "One Man's Meat." The Letter in which "Will Strunk" first appeared places a personal experience with a favorite professor alongside a position piece on dumping atomic waste, as "Twins" and "Sound" had appeared side by side in the same issue of Notes and Comment. The chief differences between the Letter and the "One Man's Meat" column are the degree to which his editorial voice is more visible and more assertive and the virtual absence of the voice of either humorist or colyumist.

Fashioning his anthology *The Points of My Compass* from his previously published articles, White went through a series of tentative tables of contents that suggests something of the difficulty of titling works that essentially are not unified wholes. The collection was organized chronologically, as *Every Day Is Saturday* and *One Man's Meat* had been, rather than thematically, as *Quo Vadimus?* and *The Second Tree from the Corner* had been. It began with the piece that predated but initially suggested the Letter series. Because it had been printed with a title, "Our Windswept Correspondents: The Eye of Edna," and was solely an account of the hurricane, it kept the title "The Eye of Edna" throughout the planning for the book. But, in his initial plans for the book, all the other material he intended to use had been published in the *New Yorker* under the title "Letter from the East" (or other direction). Speculating on the probable contents, White typed twelve items, identifying them by subject. (In the magazine he referred to his home as Wormwood, in imitation of such named farms as Ik Marvel's Edgewood, but in the book reverted to the actual locale, Allen's Cove.)

1. The Eye of Edna
2. Wormwood — Trending into Maine
3. Fred
4. Circus — Sarasota
5. Raccoon and the Stove
6. Sootfall and Fall Out
7. U.N. Charter
8. Taking Puppy to Maine
9. The Elements of Style
10. Leaving Turtle Bay
11. Wormwood — Getting the Fox
12. Motor car design

Only two of these (1 and 6) ended up as titles. Later, in longhand, White added a column of dates of the issues of the *New Yorker* in which the pieces appeared and extended the list:

13. *Railroading*
14. *Unity*
15. *Television*
16. *Alaska*

Still later, in pencil, White created a third column identifying how much of the article should be reprinted, designating most of them as "all," the pieces on unity and television as "all or most," and The Elements of Style as "First 2 sections."

Set apart from these columns were two items not from the "Letters from the ———" series:

17. *Pigeon piece — date?*
18. *Walden piece — (Yale Review)*

The pigeon piece was an exceptionally long "Answers to Hard Questions" humor department on the rock dove; the Walden piece was "Walden — 1954."

White then typed up a new list of contents, placing the "pigeon piece" in its chronological order and including seventeen items from the *New Yorker*; later, in longhand, he added *Item 18. A Slight Sound at Evening (Walden)*, then penciled it in as Item 2 and renumbered the rest. On this list he began to title articles, a process that went through two other lists. Some of the struggles with titles simply indicate the difficulty of capturing the essence of any piece in a title: for example, the piece finally titled "The Motorcar" went through "Motor Car Design," "The Shape of Motor Cars," and Katharine White's choice, "Old Shabby"; "The Years of Wonder," a title proposed by Katharine, was called "A Time of Wandering," "Near the Beginning of Life," "Voyaging," "Messboy," "Alaska," and, very briefly, "My Trip to Alaska."

But White's problems with some of the titles reflect the difficulty of identifying the focus of multiple-item pieces. Titles considered for "Will Strunk," which had the atomic waste section immediately deleted, included "Turtle Bay," "Mosquitoes and Rhetoric," "William Strunk, Jr., Recalled," "Recollections of a Professor," "A Professor Remembered," and "The Late William Strunk, Jr." Alternative titles for "Coon Tree" included "Back Kitchen," "The Coon Tree and the Kitchen," and "The Coon, the Corn, and the Rock" (Katharine's choice). "The Shape of Television" ran through "Farming and Viewing," "The Farmer and Huckster," "The Farmer and the Pitchmen," "The Farmer and the Peddler," and "Something to Sell." In these instances the problem with the choice of a title clearly grew out of the problem of identifying the subject, because there are really two or three subjects in the piece. Even after White early on found the title "The Ring of Time," he still struggled to be more specific, considering "Bareback Rider" and then "Sarasota," before settling on his final choice, one better able to encompass both sections of the Letter.

The Letter premise freed White from the kind of editing and selection process he had followed in earlier collections, particularly *One Man's Meat*. Unlike the more disparate and independent selections in the "One Man's Meat" column, for which White felt the need to separate and title and restructure the material, the selections for *The Points of My Compass* could be loose and occasionally disjointed in the manner of letters, especially in the manner of Letters from the *New Yorker*'s "far-flung correspondents." There is remarkably little difference between the original work as published in the magazine and the reprinted work in the collection.

The pieces in the Letter series were written intermittently and irregularly. The longest gap between contributions extended almost two years. A "Letter from the West" was given 16 March 1958 as its date of composition when it was reprinted as "The Motorcar" in *Points*; the next piece was a "Letter from the East," reprinted as "The Railroad" and dated 28 January 1960. They were published in the *New Yorker* on 5 April 1958 and 20 February 1960, respectively. In the interval White's major project was his revision of William Strunk's textbook, *The Elements of Style.*

The project was initiated by J. G. Case, an editor at Macmillan, immediately after the "Letter from the East" on Will Strunk appeared in the *New Yorker.* Case had simply proposed reprinting the book with a slightly revised version of White's remarks on Strunk as the introduction, but White suggested that he might "even have a bit more to say on the subject of rhetoric, now that I am suddenly faced with this unexpected audience" (*Letters* 443). However, the more White examined Strunk's text, the more he realized that it had dated considerably and needed to be not simply republished but also to be carefully revised. White had been looking at Strunk's 1918 self-published textbook, but Strunk himself had revised and republished it several times in his career, over a roughly twenty-year span.

White's revision took up most of 1958. On 3 November 1958 he wrote to Case about the progress of the revision, claiming, "I have tinkered the Strunk text — have added a bit, subtracted a bit, rearranged it in a few places, and in general have made small alterations that seemed useful and in the spirit of Strunk" (*Letters* 453). As Scott Elledge has pointed out, "Strunk was sometimes too brief to be perfectly clear, and his instructions were too dogmatic and pedantic to encourage young writers to deviate from them occasionally and to trust their ear the way most good writers do" (*E. B. White* 327). White's revisions of Strunk's prose enlivened and clarified the language. He also took pains to eliminate sections that seemed to have grown irrelevant or, in his words, "narrow and bewildering" (*Letters* 453). His most extensive revision was to drop altogether a chapter on spelling and substitute for it a new chapter of his own, entitled "An Approach to Style." He explained to Case that the chapter would "discuss style in its broader meaning — not style in the sense of what is correct but style in the sense of what is distinguished and distinguishing. . . . In short, I shall have a word or two to say about attitudes in writing: the why, the how, the beartraps, the power, and the glory" (453–454).

White's chapter on style is quite different from Strunk's chapters, even though White's revisions have made Strunk sound much more like White than he had originally. White is much more tentative, much less prescriptive than Strunk, and very often critical responses to the book have judged the whole on the basis of one of two quite different sections. Prescriptive grammarians who worry about issues of correctness tend to prefer Strunk's sections of the book and question White's hints of flexibility and personal preferences; working writers tend to prefer White's recognition of the difficulties of writing and his emphasis on letting the sound of a sentence take precedence over rules of usage. Clearly, in his own chapter in the book, White was insistent upon drawing on the example his own writing experiences gave him. He couched his remarks as rules, in keeping with the tenor of Strunk's book, but referred to them more reservedly as "suggestions and cautionary hints." Because they do not apply to every circumstance and may be violated when necessary, White stresses the tentativeness of his suggestions.

Some hints are very practical: "Work from a suitable design"; "Write with nouns and verbs, not with adjectives and adverbs"; "Do not overstate"; "Avoid the use of qualifiers." Some hints seem particularly applicable to White's own composing: "Place yourself in the background"; "Write in a way that comes naturally"; "Revise and rewrite." Beyond the numbered sections of advice, White discusses a writer's experience as only a practicing writer would understand it. For example, at one point he writes: "Writing is, for most, laborious and slow. The mind travels faster than the pen; consequently, writing becomes a question of learning to make occasional wing shots, bring down the bird of thought as it flashes by. A writer is a gunner, sometimes waiting in his blind for something to come in, sometimes roaming the countryside hoping to scare something up. Like other gunners, he must cultivate patience: he may have to work many covers to bring down one partridge" (*Elements* 55–56). Such is surely the advice of someone who has had to scare up something and to make occasional wing shots in his writing.

White also emphasizes the need to develop an "ear" for language: "as in so many matters pertaining to style, one's ear must be one's guide" (63). He believes this to be "vital," adding: "Only the writer whose ear is reliable is in a position to use bad grammar deliberately; only he knows for sure when a colloquialism is better than formal phrasing; only he is able to sustain his work at the level of good taste" (63–64). In the examples we have seen of White's revisions throughout the book, and in the examples we will consider in the next chapters, White's own ear for language is clearly a factor in the choices he makes about syntax and vocabulary. It is a point he himself makes in a postscript to the Will Strunk essay, where he writes of the difficulty of revising the book: "the job, which should have taken about a month's time, took me a year. I discovered that for all my fine talk I was no match for the parts of speech — was, in fact, over my depth and in trouble. Not only that, I felt uneasy at posing as an expert on rhetoric, when the truth is I write by ear, always with difficulty and seldom with any exact notion of what is taking place under the hood" (*Points* 122).

The basis of that assertion is White's sense of how he acquired the literary talents he had. In *The Elements of Style* he advises students: "The use of language begins with imitation. The infant imitates the sounds made by its parents; the child imitates first the spoken language, then the stuff of books. The imitative life continues long after the writer is on his own in the language, for it is almost impossible to avoid imitating what one admires" (56). Certainly we have seen how White drew on the models provided by Thoreau, Marquis, Morley, and F. P. A. throughout his career, and the evidence of his correspondence, as collected in *Letters of E. B. White*, supports the view that White's voice was varied and flexible but nonetheless consistent within a definable range throughout his life.

The advice that White provides in his own chapter of *Elements* has the ring of experience. Unlike Strunk, who always speaks with certainty and authority, White stresses freedom as much as he does conformity. Acknowledging that the "language is always in flux, . . . a living stream, shifting, changing, . . . losing old forms in the backwaters of time," White admits the folly of suggesting "that a young writer not swim in the main stream of this turbulence," yet even when he recommends that the "beginner err of the side of conservatism, on the side of established usage," he insists that there are choices that can be made "between the formal and the informal, the regular and the offbeat, the general and the special, the orthodox and the heretical" (69–70). As much as White declares himself the disciple of Will Strunk, he is still steadfastly the spiritual companion of Thoreau. White concludes his revision of Strunk's book with advice Strunk would have been unlikely to give: "The whole duty of a writer is to please and satisfy himself, and the true writer always plays to an audience of one. Let him start sniffing the air, or glancing at the Trend Machine, and he is as good as dead, although he may make a good living" (70–71). White may have been thinking of his own battles with Macmillan over recommendations by outside reviewers in English departments to be less "prescriptive" or "traditional" and more "descriptive" and (in White's terms) "liberal." In response to such recommendations, White had written Case, "I am used to being edited, I like being edited, and I have had the good luck and the pleasure of being edited by some of the best of them;

but I have never been edited for wind direction, and will not be now." He had flatly stated: "Either Macmillan takes Strunk and me in our bare skins, or I want out" (*Letters* 455). But this belief in marching to the beat of his own drummer had been a consistent stance throughout his career. In recommending it to young writers, it was the acknowledgment of a deep-seated principle underlying the very best of his writing for the past thirty years.

The Elements of Style was published in 1959, and it proved enduringly successful. Elledge notes that it was a Book-of-the-Month Club selection and a trade-book bestseller that year. It was also sold in a college edition. White eventually revised the book twice, in 1972 and in 1979, and by 1982 it had sold more than five and a half million copies. In 1998, forty-one years after the Will Strunk "Letter from the East" set the revision in motion and eighty years after Strunk's own first edition, the book is still used in college composition courses and sold in bookstores. It brought White a large volume of mail over the years, either asking grammatical advice or arguing with his and Strunk's recommendations. White wrote a friend, Howard Cushman, in October 1959: "Life as a textbook editor is not the rosy dream you laymen think it is. I get the gaa damndest letters every day from outraged precisionists and comma snatchers, complaining every inch of the way" (*Letters* 464).

White returned to his Letter series in the beginning of 1960. The pieces that followed, reprinted as "The Railroad," "Unity," and "The Shape of Television," were more editorial than personal. In mid-1960, thanking his editor at Harper and Row, Cass Canfield, for congratulations on winning the Gold Medal for Essays and Criticism of the American Academy of Arts and Letters, White mentioned the possibility of "bund[ling] up a few of my essays and send[ing] them to you to make a book" (*Letters* 469). With the publication in the *New Yorker* of "Letter (Delayed) from the North" on 25 March 1961, White had a fitting final piece for *The Points of My Compass*. Preoccupied with both his own and his wife's ill health, White's writing between 1961 and 1976, the last year he contributed to Notes and Comment, was at best sporadic. He continued to contribute slight humorous pieces to the *New Yorker*, most of them for the Answers to Hard Questions department. His editorials for Notes and Comment often tended to be obituaries for longtime friends and *New Yorker* contributors — Gus Lobrano, Wolcott Gibbs, F. P. A., James Thurber — or public figures — John F. Kennedy and Rachel Carson — or commemorations of events such as the moon landing. A prolific letter writer over the years (as the 1976 collection *Letters of E. B. White* indicates), his publications frequently were letters to the editors of local newspapers. He contributed three commentaries to "Topics" in the *New York Times* (including "Dear Mr. ⑈0 2 ⑈4⑈ ⑈06 3⑈⑈ ⑈0 2⑈ ⑈0 7 30⑈ 8⑈ ") and a handful of essays to *Ford Times* and the *New Yorker*. In 1971 he wrote two "Letters from the East" for the *New Yorker* (later reprinted as "The Winter of the Great Snows" and "The Geese") and a third letter (reprinted as "Riposte"), published in the *New York Times* in 1971 as "Farmer White's Brown Eggs," a response to an article on eggs by J. B. Priestley; in 1975 he wrote one more "Letter from the East" for the *New Yorker* (it was reprinted under that title). The four are linked by their focus on local and farm events and by their casual, epistolary tone. The approach to writing engendered by the Letter format at the time of White's "retirement" in 1957 dominated his writing for the remainder of his life.

9

"THE TRUTH IS, I WRITE BY EAR"

Composing the Letters

As for the early and late Comment and for the *Harper's* department, so E. B. White's processes for composing the Letters were influenced by the circumstances in which he wrote them and by the literary form itself. When he wrote "A Slight Sound at Evening" and "The Eye of Edna," he was still producing a large number of Notes and Comment for the *New Yorker*, contributing all or most of half the department that year. But the next year his involvement was halved again, to only fourteen Comment pages, and he ended the year with the first true entry in the "Letter from the ———" series on December 24. In 1956 he wrote only two Notes and Comment departments but contributed five Letters as well as the article "Strategies for Retirement" for *Holiday*, a clear forecasting of his and Katharine's imminent departure from New York City. His work in 1957 was various and sporadic: four Comment pages in February and March, the long Answers to Hard Questions that was reprinted in *The Points of My Compass* as "The Rock Dove" in May, Letters in May, July, and November, two more Comments, and a few short items. In all, eleven of the Letters were published during the twenty-seven months after White's first deliberate "Letter from the East" ("Homecoming") appeared. After a two-year lapse, he then published the final four Letters at roughly five-month intervals. In the period that these articles were accumulating, from December 1955 to March 1961, White wrote only seventeen Comment pages and contributed to only seven more; after his retirement he contributed to only twenty Comment pages during a twenty-year period.

One of the effects of White's decreased productivity after retirement was an alteration in his approaches to composing. This becomes evident when we examine the notes and drafts for some of the Letters collected in *The Points of My Compass*. The manuscript evidence suggests that White made adjustments to his process not only in subject matter and format but also in regularity of composition.

🎋 "The Eye of Edna," the piece that served as the prelude to the Letter series, was written over several days, 11–15 September 1954. It is not difficult to imagine the circumstances of the initial impulse to write the piece; as White wrote his brother Stanley, "We had two hurricanes hit us right in the teeth" (*Letters* 398). In the aftermath of Hurricane Carol, White learned of the predicted approach of Hurricane Edna and no doubt realized that following the progress of the storm both on the radio and on the homefront would give him a suitable design to work from and result in a promising piece. White had done this kind of piece before, particularly "Sabbath Morn." He tells us in the article that he first heard of Hurricane Edna "on the morning of Friday, September 10th, some thirty-six hours before Edna arrived" (*Points* 4); the date of composition that precedes the piece in the book is 15 September 1954; the final copy for the printer is dated 16 September, and the article was published in the 25 September issue of the *New Yorker*.

White's preliminary writing for the piece consisted of a 16-page handwritten log of the hurricane's progress, complete with times, barometer readings, quotes from radio broadcasts, and notes on activities around his house. The log begins:

(1)

Riverhead, L. I. — "Was the spray from those puddles, dashing
up around the mudguards?"

The Eye of My Hurricane

Weatherby, the B2 weatherman, at 11:12 was preparing
to go on record that Edna would not be a [sic] severe
as Carol

"Unindated" — voice from Providence —

66 lives in Carol
nearly 100 in Worcester tornado —

State of emergency in New London, Conn., Portland, Me.

About to hit Long Island (at 11:15 a m)

"Irving R. Levine, wishing you good news"

New Eng. Mission Study Club
VFW
Piano studio in ~~Blo~~ Brookline, Mass.
2nd shift at the Commercial Filter Corp., at Melrose.

Weatherby:
~~Eye locat~~ "Moving NNE at 50 miles an hour
N Eng as a whole will not have the sustained
force of wind — (this prediction was followed by
a slight blast of inspirational music 21 ½ seconds
after 11 a.m.)

(2)

Providence News man at the weather station = storm is
150 mi south of Block Island

~~Latest description~~

Temp in Providence 68
29.28 barometer

This hurricane (Edna) may have a double center
Total of 6 deaths — one of them a Civil defense man preparing for the blow

---

Sylvia and her eggs
Henpen screen
Barn doors in barn cellar
Brought the geese into the barn — the geese, who adore hurricanes
Propped up the windbreak
Found K in bed curled up with tiny radio, 10 of seven a.m.
tuned to disaster wave length
Walking back from pullet range, measured with my eye the
point on the house roof where the Balm o'Gilead tree would
strike with its full blow, if uprooted.
Mrs. Freethy made a sponge cake

Hennis pineapple ice cream. Time now = 11:30

Henry went for gas.
Kerosene lamp was made ready some 26 hours in
    advance. But it had no wick.
Minnie, unalerted for a number of reasons, slept
    under the stove
Hauled FORENOON

(3)

Rockland — about 1450 on my dial WRKD
Town manger [sic] of Camden — Mr. Gilbert = "We
                        mass
have preparations for ^feeding. Patrolling streets.
Try to keep people off the streets — A Number
of trees have been weakened by the other storm."
Now Andy Anderson — Our phones are
going like mad. Pls don't make unnecessary
calls. (Man thinks of his stomach well in advance)
                                    Can bring own
Grange Hall + Congo parish house   food or food will
                                    be provided

Refrigerator
Clock — get one that runs in the old-fashioned way. before
                            hurricanes carried girls' names
Flush Toilets —

Bulletin : Core would pass to the east of R.I.
~~Maine~~   Bangor — sit tight and wait. Gene
            Autry shows will continue as planned.
            Dow Air Force — personnel restricted to their
                homes (?)

Boston Fire ~~Chief~~ Commissioner = "Keep calm
            and follow instructions."
Ken Mayer — Nantucket — winds of 77 m.p.h.

(4)

        At noon I took a short vacation from the radio
and looked out at the familiar scene. It was about
36 hours since I'd got the first warning bulletin

A light breeze stirred from the S.E., and rain
fell in a drizzle. The pasture pond was
unruffled but had the prickly surface caused
by the drops of rain. The pullets stood about
in beachcombing attitudes. Rose bushes ~~bowe~~
bowed courteously to each other.

South shore — Weatherby. Radar and plane
observations. Storm is not going to western
Long Island or Central Massachusetts. Storm
center still over the open ocean. ~~illeg~~. 11:20 a.m.
Edna's eye was ~~29.53 W~~ etc.
Path bet. Buzzard's Bay + Nantucket Island.

All of New England except Cape Cod will have
                    Down
the weaker part of the storm.   Bar Harbor way,
can be hard hit by Edna late this afternoon
All threat is over for N. Y.
~~Winds in Boston~~ — heavy North Easter
Outer Cape Cod will see Edna in her worst mood

(5)

Everything is
^ Pretty well "battered" down in Westerly.

Rockland low tide 4:23
            barometer 29.88 falling
            Temperature 62 degrees

Tigers and Dragons game — cancelled (?) or not
Chicken Shoot cancelled for tomorrow
All Rockland Stores will close at 3 o'clock
            Suits with new novelty weave — Novel
            button and pocket trim

These pages give an indication of the kind of record keeping White engaged in throughout the period preceding and during the storm. He recorded certain data about times, temperatures, barometer readings, windspeeds, and storm locations in order to have them right and to follow the sequence of events later on. He recorded snippets of announcements, reports, and advertising in order to remember them, although he may have had no real certainty that he would use them in the article to come. He also drafted an occasional passage for his potential text, as he does at the top of page 4, and occasionally uses lines and borders to separate groups of material.

The log continues at intervals throughout the day and at one point records an extended series of items from an 8:00 P.M. newscast about the aftermath of the storm before it has actually reached White's location. He records in his log at the bottom of page 14:

1290 — Somebody promises that at 11 o'clock there'll
be a "wrap-up" on Hurricane Edna —

8:40 pm. 28.72 rising
Between 8 and 8:40 I made my
strange journey to the woods, looking
for the spring.

(15)

Came back from my journey (the night had been
agreeable, moon showing, light rain) to find that
the glass had started to climb, and that the
Bangor station was predicting 90 mi winds in
30 minutes, and that my wife had copied
three emergency numbers:
    Bangor 9437
      7173
      2313

Lights out 8:44
Very strong wind almost immediately
Barometer

9:25 — 28.9

Now the storm grew to its full height —
The round moon showed, clouds raced wildly
across the moon, the woods bowed low,
    the trees prayed for salvation.
fearfully low, as though in prayer.
The house roared with the terrifying

thunder of the wind. During this full
stage of the storm's tide, the radio

(16)

chirped in the most blithe fashion, acted as though
   Up to the westward, the storm had become   of states
~~*it were*~~ ^ *a thing of the past.   Governors* ^ *thanked agencies*
for their cooperation, punchy newscasters found
tired old witticisms, recorded music.

10:05 — 29.1

Fuchsia
Balm o gilead
Old apple
Trip to the spring
Minnie's trip upstairs, lighted by flashlight

10:20 The moon rainbow — ~~*after 10 p.m.*~~

This extended log of the storm serves as a rough outline for the article that White then proceeds to compose between 11 September and 15 September. It contains all the factual items and references in much the order that they appear in the completed article, as well as snatches of descriptive and analytical prose that help White focus the work in progress, such as the passage on page 4, cited earlier, for example. On page 6, in a paragraph boxed off from the rest of the page, White discovers or states for the first time a central theme of the later article:

> *I have never thought of myself as a man*
> *ideally equipped to stand up to a*
> *hurricane, but I'm now convinced that*
> *the radio is even less well* ~~*equip*~~ *endowed*
> *than I am.*

On page 7 he observes:

Nature is largely ignored by her sons and daughters ~~*and suddenly*~~ *in her benign moods, and suddenly, because she turns a bit difficult — she is taken up in a big way.*

Those items are written between noon and two o'clock in the afternoon; between 6:45 and 6:55 P.M. he boxes in another item:

> *Our Windswept Correspondents*
> *Our Windblown Correspondents*

This was an attempt to play with alternative titles to "The Eye of My Hurricane," the tentative title given on page 1 of this prewriting.

By the time White types the first draft of the article he has decided on a title and types on the first page:

OUR WINDSWEPT CORRESPONDENTS
The Eye of Edna

although a circle around "Windswept" suggests that he was still uncertain about that choice. He proceeds through one typed, double-spaced draft, revising all along the way by typing rows of x's through deleted words and new alternatives in between lines. Sometimes, apparently when the revisions become confusing, he retypes the revised section immediately on the same page. Twice in this draft he adds new material by typing passages on separate sheets, labeling them Insert A and Insert B, and identifying insertion points in the draft. Later he returns to the draft and revises in pencil. Still later he uses a red pencil to make further revisions.

An example of a section going through most of these revisions is the following, from the bottom of the first page of the draft through the top of the second page:

> To me, nature is continuously abosrbing, that is, she is ~~interesting~~
> ~~in~~ a twenty-four hour proposition, fifty-two weeks of the year; but
>   *to*   *people*   *an oddity, ~~a sort of freak~~*
> ~~to radio, on the~~ radio ^ Nature is a ~~sometime thing, arresting only in~~
>   *tinged with malevolence*   *worthy etc*
> worthy of note only in her more ~~bizarre or~~ violent +~~difficult~~
>   moments.
>
> 2.
>
> ~~her more bizarre or violent moments~~. The radio either lets nature
>   her the full treatment.,
> ~~severly~~ alone or gives ~~itself over to her lock, stock, and barrel, in~~

~~all wild abandon.~~ as it did at the approach of the hurricane called

illeg.

Edna. The idea, of course, is that the radio shall perform a public

approach   that might kill them,

service, by warhing people of the ~~arrival~~ of a heavy storm, but ~~the~~

and this i̶t̶ the radio certainly does

another effect of the thing, by and large, is to work people up to a n

incredible state of alarm, many hours in advance of ~~the smallest wind.~~

even the mildest zephyr. *One ~~death~~ of the deaths from*

Hurricane Edna was a civil defense worker. whose heart

failed him before the wind hurt him at all.

Most of the changes have to do with tone and rhythm and precision. The opening sentence sets up the contrast between two views of nature, what it is "to me" and what it is, first "to radio," then "on the radio," finally "to radio people." The use of "to" instead of "on" keeps the parallels intact, and the use of "radio people" rather than "radio" keeps the parallel between human beings rather than between a man and an industry or object. In the same sentence White tries out various terms to capture radio people's concept of Nature: first he calls it "a sometime thing" (alluding to a song lyric), "arresting only in her more bizarre or violent moments"; then he crosses that out and substitutes in longhand "an oddity, a sort of freak"; then, keeping the first and deleting the second, he decides to return to part of the first description by adding "worthy etc." at the bottom of the first page and typing in the whole phrase, "worthy of note only in her more" at first "bizarre and violent," then "violent + difficult," finally just "violent moments" at the top of the already completed page 2. At the end of the passage, to illustrate his statement about radio's "working people up," he adds in longhand a sentence about a civil defense worker's heart attack.

This kind of drafting "rehearses" the language of the piece and demonstrates White's tendency to use the work-in-progress as a means of discovery. In this case White gets going on the project immediately after the events have occurred, while his mind is still racing with thoughts about it, and the "consecutive thoughts" arise out of ideas he has been incubating since he decided to write about the hurricane. This section is from White's introductory material; the remainder of the article will be generated consecutively following the material in his notes. White relies heavily on the text produced so far to continue generating the text that follows.

The evidence from the draft also supports a second tendency in White's writing, to follow his instincts about sound and rhythm. As he later asserted in the postscript to "Will Strunk" and urged in his "Approach to Style" chapter, he wrote by ear. The search for the exact word or phrase in this drafting is as much based on an intuitive sense of sound as it is in precision of meaning.

White wrote a final draft of the article to turn into the *New Yorker* printer. It contained proofreader's marks and also a handful of sentence revisions. In the passage we have been examining, other than longhand capitalizations of the "n" in Nature, White's only change was to alter "many hours in advance of even the mildest zephyr" by inserting in longhand substitute, in place of the word "even," "*the blow, while they are still fanned by.*" In the published essay the passage reads:

> To me, Nature is continuously absorbing — that is, she is a twenty-four-hour proposition, fifty-two weeks of the year — but to radio people, Nature is an oddity tinged with malevolence and worthy of note only in her more violent moments. The radio either lets Nature alone or gives her the full treatment, as it did at the approach of the hurricane called Edna. The idea, of course, is that the radio shall perform a public service by warning people of a storm that might prove fatal; and this the radio certainly does. But another effect of the radio is to work people up to an incredible state of alarm many hours in advance of the blow, while they are still fanned by the mildest zephyrs. One of the victims of Hurricane Edna was a civil defense worker whose heart failed him long before the wind threatened him in the least. (*Points* 4)

In the case of "The Eye of Edna" White's composing process is relatively straightforward. He is aided by having a chronological chain of events to describe, one he had compiled a day or two before beginning his first draft, while the events were occurring and while his mind was attuned to prewriting the article — that is, preparing to write by gathering information and ideas and making preliminary remarks. The chief new material in the draft is the introductory matter and some passages of analysis throughout; most of the article has its origins in the notes and quotations of the prewriting. For this reason the composing process is one in which White writes one draft, embedding the revising in the drafting and returning to the completed draft for fine-tuning without significant or major alteration in the existing text. The final draft is little more than copyediting preparation.

White's ability to produce this long a text (thirteen pages in type-script) in this fashion is probably attributable primarily to the circum-stances of its composition and its having been written during a period of considerable productivity, when White was still generating Notes and Comment on a regular basis. Except for length and detail, White's pro-cess is quite similar to his writing of "Twins," another piece arising out of immediate experience and preliminary notes and reactions.

But "The Eye of Edna" is something of an anomalous piece in the Letter series. Although it probably instigated the series, it really did not conform to it. Most of the "Letter from the ———" entries are quite different in tone, topic, and particularly format, and White wrote under different circumstances while composing them. For example, in 1957 White had written only one Comment in March and an Answers to Hard Questions on the rock dove in April before composing the Letter reprinted as "A Report in Spring" in May and the one reprinted as "Will Strunk" in July. For both pieces a number of factors contrib-uted to varying the process of their composing from that of "The Eye of Edna."

"A Report in Spring" is one of the shortest Letters and was appar-ently written in a single longhand draft and then revised during prepa-ration of a single typed draft for the printer. We cannot know whether there was an intermediate draft, now missing, but the changes between the first draft and the final draft are chiefly matters of addition. Only a few changes in the original text occur after the final draft was typed. However, unlike other printer's copies in White's files, further changes were made to this text between the printer's draft and publication.

The piece is more epistolary than essayistic, a factor that may have contributed to its ease of composition. It is low key, chatty, in the man-ner of such seemingly spontaneous *One Man's Meat* pieces as "A Winter Diary," "Fall," and "Spring." "A Report in Spring" reads like a letter bringing a distant correspondent up to date on recent doings in the family. It opens with a section on buying a puppy and realizing that it might outlive its owner, then discusses the run of smelt for a para-graph, the drought for a paragraph, minor problems around the farm and the puppy's developing a farm diet, the fight between raccoons for the coon tree, the stirrings and plantings in the vegetable garden and the arrival of goose eggs, his wife's work in her perennial bor-der, and the image of his grandchildren carrying spring wildflowers.

White's process of "writing a thing first and thinking about it after-

ward" and producing "consecutive thoughts" by "putting them down"
is illustrated by the first draft. The opening of the piece runs:

Quite aside from
the expense of it,

I have provided at
the obsequies of
many a dog

Letter From the East

Turtle Bay 10 May

I bought a puppy last week and drove him
to Maine in a rented Ford that looked like a sculpin.
The adventure gave me a queer feeling [which] I was at
a loss to explain until I realized that this was
the first adoption case, for me, in which there was a

master

strong likelihood that the dog would survive the man.
It had always been the other way round, and I am
not sure I shall enjoy this association as much.
A man can't live forever; I take fine care of dogs,
and they take lousy care of me; and the expectancy
and this puts a new
figures are now in the dog's favor. and I'm
darned if I want a male dachshund helping make
final   interment   burial
the   arrangements for my funeral. and I have been
too lazy (or too busy taking care of dogs)
and have no place to lie.
to make any myself. I regret having brought up
morbid   apologize for
this unseemly subject, at the beginning of — I
feel all right at the moment, but one trouble with
although far behind on my sleep, like all puppy owners
(2)

runs

me is, my mind is either running on ahead, to explore
take in uncomfortable events of an uncertain future, or
retraces its steps, to dwell upon the remembered f
linger among well-loved forms of the recent past.
in the green warmth
This morning, although Turtle Bay is a pleasant

countenance
~~spot, my thoughts~~ I see only the lovely face of spring
in the country. No matter what ~~happens~~ changes
take place in the world, or in me, nothing ever
seems to disturb the face of spring.

This paragraph, with the changes indicated and only one further revision (substituting "lags behind" for "retraces its steps"), survives intact into the printer's draft. It suggests that in the final sentence White has found his theme, turning away from the issue of his mortality to celebrate the "face of spring." Indeed, most of the rest of the piece refers repeatedly to birth and youth — the spawning run of smelt, the puppy's behavior, the vegetables planted and sprouting, the arrival of the coon "heavy with young," the delivery of goose eggs, the swallows beginning their nests, the grandchildren clutching wildflowers. Nonetheless there is also considerable reference to mortality — "when the tide is a late one, smelting is for the young"; "our old coon came down the tree in defeat"; images of drought, decay, the death of the goose, and the purge of Achillea-the-Pearl from the perennial border. At the end of the draft White's concluding paragraph centers on a spring image:

It is wonderful what memories one
has, returning to the city. What I most vividly
                    3-year-old
and longingly recall, is ~~the~~ my grandson & his
  ~~brown~~ sunburnt
little sister, returning to their kitchen door, with
spoils of the meadow — she with a couple of violets,
                    as in vice
he clutching dandelions ~~in the tight grip of~~
                    spring   in the hand
~~childhood.~~   Children hold wildflowers so tightly —
the way adults ~~hold chil,~~ who are less sure of
each succeeding spring, hold it in their hearts.

When White began to write the ending, his focus was on the children, but in the immediate revision he refers back to the sense of mortality with which he opened the piece.

The printer's draft reveals changes that are more in line with this discovery; the section on the coon adds the sentence: "I was sorry for her and felt a twinge of sympathetic understanding toward any who are evicted from their haunts by the younger and the stronger — always a sad occasion for man or beast"; the section on the puppy in the middle of the piece adds a description of his diet, including "well-rotted cow manure, . . . a dead crocus bulb, . . . a bloody feather from the execution block." The new concluding paragraph reads:

> One never knows what images one is going to hold in memory, returning to the city after a brief orgy in the country. I find this morning that what I most vividly and longingly recall is the sight of my grandson and his little sunburnt sister, returning to their kitchen door from an excursion, with trophies of the meadow clutched in their hands, she with a couple of violets, smiling, he serious and holding dandelions, strangling them in a responsible grip. Children hold spring so tightly in their brown fists — just as grownups, who are less sure of it, hold it in their hearts.

In this revision the somber more equally offsets the celebratory. This balance in the piece White had only discovered at the end of the first draft.

The published text of 25 March, however, differs still from the printer's draft, which was set in slugs 13 May, three days after the ostensible original draft was written. It may have been a matter of confusion about the location of the piece — like a letter to familiar friends White makes references to locations as if readers already know their circumstances — i. e., that they own a farm in Maine and also live in a New York apartment in Turtle Bay — but in the two drafts discussed the city references are obscure and dislocating. It may also have been a matter of recognizing the darker side of the piece and wanting to soften it. The published text revises the opening paragraph on the puppy into two paragraphs, one about making the decision in the first place, and the second about going to fetch the dog. The new first paragraph is much lighter in tone than the earlier one:

> I bought a puppy last week in the outskirts of Boston and drove him to Maine in a rented Ford that looked like a sculpin. There had been talk in our family of getting a "sensible" dog this time, and my wife and I had gone over the list of sensible dogs, and had even ventured once or twice into the company of sensible dogs. A friend

had a litter of Labradors, and there were other opportunities. But after a period of uncertainty and waste motion my wife suddenly exclaimed one evening, "Oh, let's get a dachshund!" She had had a glass of wine, and I could see that the truth was coming out. Her tone was one of exasperation laced with affection. So I engaged a black male without further ado. (*Points* 111)

White's wife has a larger role throughout, both in the decision making about the dog and in the travel — where the printer's draft had read, "When I took him from the kennel, a week ago today, his mother kissed us both goodbye," the published text reads, "When my wife and I took him from the kennel, a week ago today, his mother kissed all three of us goodbye." White also makes it clearer that the setting of the piece is Maine as remembered in New York: "At present, I am a so-journer in the city again, but here in the green warmth of Turtle Bay I see only the countenance of the country." However, the major change in the two paragraphs is to shift the focus from the intimations of mortality, with broodings on his own interment, to the acquisition of the dog. The tone suggests comically that acquiring a puppy will cause disruption and hides the issue of life expectancy in those amusing spec-ulations: "from our window we could gaze, perhaps for the last time, on a world of order and peace. I say 'for the last time' because it oc-curred to me early in the proceedings that this was our first adoption case in which there was a strong likelihood that the dog would outlive the man. It had always been the other way around. The Garden had never seemed so beautiful. We were both up early the next morning for a final look at the fresh, untroubled scene" (*Points* 111). The effect of these changes is to brighten the tone and make the issue of mortality more of an undercurrent in the piece than a theme equally important with the celebration of spring.

The greater irregularity of his composing and the demands of the longer-form Letter encouraged White to rely more heavily on his ten-dencies toward discovery through writing and reliance upon revision. "A Report in Spring" is a transitional piece in this regard, working its way through multiple drafts to a form that emerges only in the final draft. In the past White's habit with revision had been more to use it to give grace and clarity to the prose than to discover structure. Be-cause he was writing less frequently, he had more time to compose drafts, but he also had greater need to work through multiple revisions.

"The Eye of Edna" and "A Report in Spring" both have a sense of immediacy about them. They were written hard upon the events they describe and have structures influenced by the structures of the experiences. The manuscript evidence shows that White had greater difficulty finding the structure and reaching a conclusion that satisfied him when he turned to less immediate pieces, such as his piece on Will Strunk. It also demonstrates how distinct from one another the sections of an individual letter could be.

🐛 The Strunk item can be traced fairly extensively. White had included three items about English usage in his Notes and Comment page for the 23 February 1957 *New Yorker* issue; possibly in response, on 20 March Howard A. Stevenson, a friend from Cornell University, sent him an early edition of Strunk's *The Elements of Style*. Perusing the book, White saw a possible piece in it and wrote Stevenson on 2 April 1957, thanking him for the book and asking for background information:

> Last night I went through it, seeing Will in every word and phrase and line — in Charles's friend, in Burns's poems, in the comma after each term except the last. What a book, what a man! Will so loved the clear, the brief, the bold — and his book is clear, brief, bold.
>
> It may be that I'll try to do a piece on "The Elements of Style" for the *New Yorker*. Perhaps you can fill me in on a few matters on which I am vague or uninformed. (*Letters* 434)

White's questions had to do with the name and number of the course Strunk taught, whether students were required to buy the book and whether it was sold in bookstores, and whether Strunk himself or the university had paid for it to be printed (White had been sent a copy of the privately printed 1918 edition; Harcourt, Brace and Company had published it in a somewhat revised form in 1920 and in various revised editions through 1938). He doubted that the book was in current use anywhere — "it would be considered too arbitrary, too cocky, too short. ('Omit needless words. Vigorous writing is concise.')" (435). White revealed to Stevenson considerable unfamiliarity with the book itself, although not with the principles behind it:

> For some reason that escapes me, I think I never had a copy of the book, even when I was a student in the course. I could be wrong about this, but I seem to remember being somewhat baffled (at first) by frequent references to "the little book," not knowing what the "little book" was. Even now, I am not certain whether these pages

come back to me as pages that I studied, or whether I simply remember the contents as they were reproduced in class by Will himself, who must have followed the book pretty closely. ("Make definite assertions.") (435)

As the quotation from Strunk suggests, White was interested in having accurate data so that he could make definite assertions, and many of the issues he raises in the letter, as well as his sense of unfamiliarity with the book, would be resolved by the time the final draft was published.

White's comments and quotations from the book throughout the letter to Stevenson suggest that he was already taking notes about the book; whether before or after the letter was written, he wrote a series of notes on a 5″ × 8″ unruled pad, citing reference points for later use and recollections of Strunk's classroom behavior.

> *P. 9 : "He saw us coming — "*
> *Contrary to NYer style.*
>
> ---
>
> *Will: "If you don't know*
> *how to pronounce a word,*
> *say it loud."*
>
> ---
>
> *P. 8 —*
> *3. Enclose parenthetic*
> *expressions between commas.*
> *P. 10 (2 pages later)*
> *   "It is of course equally*
> *correct to write the above.*

Some of the notes attempted description or reflection:

> *His lips nibbling each*
> *other like the ~~g~~ mandibles*
> *   ~~learned~~*
> *of a grasshopper, his smile*
> *shuttling to & fro in*
> *   carefully*
> *a ~~casually~~ trimmed*
> *mustache.*

Five out of five would be
the perfect score, leaving
             beautiful, unbroken
the world in silence.

Others predicted the order of events in a prospective text, such as a long section drafting a possible conclusion and headed by a reference to a period when Strunk worked on MGM's 1936 production of *Romeo and Juliet* (White tried to draft this passage but eventually left it out of the finished piece):

The Hollywood interlude

The way a book — any book —
preserves, restores, & illumines
the face & form & character
of the man who wrote it.

If I were ever faced with the
(to me) impossible assignment
of facing a class of students,
I ~~would~~ think I would just
say, "Now you boys & girls
get your hooks in a copy of
the "little book" & you go
home & come back in 2
weeks. ~~Re Learn~~ Memorize
the rules, & see if you can
understand some of the
explanations. Come back
in 2 weeks, & we will go on
from there."
     But I doubt that
the "little book" will ever
circulate again. Every
teacher, as Will said, has
his own body of theory."
Cornell, I am sure, has
gone to longer & lower
~~bodies of chassis~~ of English

designs of rhetoric.
I still like the little book.
I love to read: "In especial,
the expression "the fact that"
should be revised out of
every sentence in which it
occurs." I must have written
"the fact that" a thousand
times in my life, revised it
out maybe 500 times,
failed 500 times. It may
even appear in this
very piece — God forbid,
proofreader forbid.

"If you don't know how to
pronounce a word, say
it loud." Will was
full of ~~little~~ comical
nuggets of wisdom.
May he rest in the sort
of peace that has not a
~~a word extra~~.

These notes then were expanded upon in another series of longhand pages, and some of the reference points were expanded into draft paragraphs reflecting on the rule recorded.

By the time he began to draft the piece he had already rehearsed some of the language and familiarized himself thoroughly with the book. Reading the book helped him retrieve memories of Strunk in the classroom (they had corresponded after White graduated from college, as well), and he had received a response from Stevenson about some of the background of *The Elements of Style*. When he turned to the composing of an actual draft as a "Letter from the East" in July, he had already been both working on and incubating the item since the beginning of April. Compared to "The Eye of Edna" and "A Report in Spring," this was a very long incubation period.

When White began drafting on the typewriter, he intended to use two items in this particular "Letter from the East": a comment on the behavior of mosquitoes in their Turtle Bay apartment and a reflection on Will Strunk and his textbook. In the first typewritten draft, dated 9 July, the mosquitoes item runs two pages and turns its attention midway through to house sparrows. The section ends:

> But the house sparrow stay ~~st,~~ ~~h~~nesting in the eaves and the under the gutters and in the chancy but delightful spots. They seem be enjoying a second courtship these days — on a more subdued note, in keeping with the ~~greater~~ great heat, love in summertime — relaxed and abandoned.
> ~~We are going to give up the apartment, and~~

The casualness with which words are left out or left in without strikeovers suggests the tentativeness of this draft in White's mind. When he begins the section on Strunk on the third page, it starts off abruptly, with no transition from the mosquito piece.

on

or what used to be known ~~all over~~the Cornell campus as "little book2.

The book I am ~~reading these~~ days is "The Elements of Style", by William Strunk, Jr. I must have once

little or big,

owned a copy of it, but I'm not good at hanging on to books, and this copy came to me in the mail the other day, — a gift from a fellow who took the course called English 8 under Strunk the same year I did — it must have been ~~the~~ 1919–1920. ~~Anyway,~~ "the "Elements of Style" was Will Strunk's parvum ~~magnum~~ opus

cut

~~an attempt~~ his attempt to ~~reduce~~ the vast tangle of

down to

rhetoric ~~to the~~ size ~~of a golf tee~~ and to write its rules and principles on the head of a pin.

The opening is wordy, rambling, and awkward — White's attempt to give himself something to work with. Only later will it become more direct, less garrulous; the introduction of the book to the reader will become more succinct as well and at least tangentially connected to the mosquito account.

In the next draft of the two items, dated 10 July, White expands the material on the mosquito by adding half a page theorizing on the ways they get into the apartment, then stops halfway through a revision of the sparrows section to further develop the reference to abandoning the apartment that he had alluded to and then struck over in the first draft. He continues the section in longhand through the bottom of the second page and onto the third, then crosses it all out and retypes the whole paragraph from the beginning. The mosquito section now ends with this passage on moving:

Every so often I make an attempt to simplify my life, ~~discarding~~ burning my books behind me, discarding the *masses* ~~welter~~ of accumulated miscellany. I have noticed, though, that

of mine   led to

these purifications have usually resu ted in ~~ever~~ even greater complexity, and I have no doubt that this one will, too. The last time I tried to rid myself of all my earthly goods and purify myself by fire, I managed to acquire a zoo in the process and am still supporting it and carrying ~~water to the~~ heavy pails of water to the ~~cages.~~

animals, a task that is sometimes beyond my strength.

to which my tolerant wife submits with cautious grace,

and that my first as an old horse act ~~after un~~ will get to work be to ~~try~~ and improve the pasture.

On page 4 of the 10 July draft White made three attempts on a single page to connect the ending of the mosquito section with the opening of the Strunk section.

One book I have decided not to burn is a small volume that a friend sent me recently, called "The Elements of Style" by William Strunkm Jr. I must have own a copy of it about thirty-eight years ago, but it disappeared

bouts

— perhaps in one of my ~~periods~~ of catharsis.

a gift from a friend in Ithaca.

One book I have decided not to burn is "~~The~~
that arrived in the mail the other day ~~from a fr~~
a small volume called "The Elements of Style" by William Strunk,
Jr. It used to be known on the Cornell campus as "the little
book", and I must have once owned a copy, but have not seen
it ~~in~~ since 1919, when I took English 8 under Professor Strunk.

A book I have decided not to burn is a small
one that arrived in the mail the other day — a gift from a friend
in Ithaca. It is "The Elements of Style" by William Strunk, Jr.,
and was
~~or what used to be~~ known on the Cornell campus in my day as
with the stress on the word "little".
"the little book." I must have once owned a copy, for I took
English 8 under Professor Strunk in 1919, and the book was
my copy presumably failed to survive an early purge
required reading, but ^ I've not laid eyes on it in thirty-eight
am now
years and ~~was~~ delighted to see it again.

In the typescript White drew a large X over the first two paragraphs.
The third paragraph was now linked more comfortably and casually
with the first piece; if the two were not thematically connected, they
were at least bound together in the kind of conversational linkage that
letters often have.

The revisions demonstrate how independent the items in a letter
could be and the pains White would sometimes take to revise them in
order to generate a minimal, tangential connection. It should be noted
that the two items were revised repeatedly in drafts that present them
as part of the same Letter; the manuscript of the third item that appeared in the issue of the *New Yorker* in which these two were published — the item on the disposal of atomic waste — has the heading
"add Letter from the East" and dates on the top indicating that it was
probably composed 16 July, intended for the 20 July issue as an addition to the mosquito and Strunk items (which were completed 15 July),
and possibly for reasons of room in the issue published a week later,
on 27 July. These circumstances help us to see how independent the
three items were and in particular why the atomic waste item was cut
from the Letter in *The Points of My Compass* — White clearly had com-

posed the mosquito and Strunk pieces at the same time and only added the atomic waste piece at the last moment. The subsequent dropping of the mosquito piece from the Will Strunk section for inclusion in the revised *Elements of Style* further indicates how loosely linked these two items were — only the reference to book burning points back to the close of the mosquito item.

The Strunk piece also indicates how White rehearsed language, using writing as a way of trying out language both for its sound and for its sense. In the letter to Stevenson, White had already used the sentence: "Will so loved the clear, the brief, the bold — and his book is clear, brief, bold" (*Letters* 434). In the drafts he returns to his notes as well as to the phrase in the letter and tries out several versions of the same passage:

> Will Strunk loved the clear, the brief, the bold; and his book is clear, brief, bold. ~~It contains a~~
>
> It is encouraging to ~~any man who~~ see
> how beautifully, how perfec ly a book ~~enshrines the character~~
> *dusty*
> ---even a rule book----perpetuates a man. Will Strunk loved the clear, the brief, the precise, the bold, and his book is
> *It is his mission & his monument.*
> clear, brief, bold. Boldness is perhaps its most distinguishing
> mrk, ~~its greatest virtue~~.
>
> It is encouraging to see how ~~beautifully, how~~ perfectly a book, even a ~~dusty~~ rule book perpetuates the mind and the spirit of a man. Will Strunk loved the clear, the brief, and the bold, and his book is clear, brief, bold. Boldness is perhaps its chief distinguishing mark.

The ideas have come together from separate sources and White keeps adjusting the sentences and the word choice throughout.

Perhaps a better example of White's working through multiple revisions to get a "clear, brief, and bold" passage occurs at the end of the Will Strunk item. In his notes he had imagined being a teacher advocating the use of the "little book"; in his drafts he returned to that theme. His concluding paragraph in the 9 July draft was a combination of typing and, when he broke off from the typing, longhand additions.

~~I gather from my friend's letter accompanying~~

of course

~~his gift that~~ the "little book" has ^ long since passed into disuse.
In these days of longer, lower textbooks it would be consider

crotchetty   ~~elementary~~

too arbitrary, too short, too simple. But if I were ever

he   *from teaching*

Will died in 1946; ~~and~~ had ~~been~~ retired several years

         in English classrooms

before that. Longer, lower textbooks are in style, I

     books

dare say, ~~and~~ with upswept tailfins. ~~The~~
~~Strunk opus is to would be found too eas short,~~
~~too simple, too cocky, cocksure, and [unintelligible]~~

       verbs ~~transitions~~

and automatic ~~transmissions.~~ I hope some

        as   good

of them manage to compress ~~so much~~ ^ sense in

    small   as does "The E. of Style"

~~so small~~ a ^ space, but I can would back "The Elements

      stock model on   track

of Style" against any ~~comer over~~ a modern ~~speedway,~~
manage to get to the point as quickly, & ~~keep to it~~
~~so~~ illuminate it so ~~craf~~ amusingly, &
to the

The draft in longhand breaks off at this point. In later drafts White frequently quits midsentence or midthought when he feels the material is getting away from him and often starts over or waits until the next draft to try to work with the material again. In the 10 July draft he goes back to the material in the notebook that he had been working on in the 9 July draft and runs through it to a more succinct conclusion:

> I gather from my friend's letter that
> accompanied his gift, that the "little book" has long since passed
> into disuse. ~~It is,~~ I have no doubt, been supplanted by bigger,
> longer, lower ~~books~~ textbooks. In these days of longer and
> lower textbooks, it would probably be found too arbitray, too short,
> too crochety, too simple. I think, though, that if I were ever
> in the, to me, unthinkable position of facing a class in English

usage and style, I would lean far over the desk o   the first
      clutch my lapels, blink my eyes, and intone:
day, and say: "Get the <u>little</u> book, Get the <u>little</u> book, Get the
<u>little</u> book." Then I would dismiss the class for two weeks, and
                                       the
tell them to come back when they had learned ~~its~~ rules. *of the game.*

Throughout White is struggling to make the comparison of styles of
usage instruction with faddishness in car design (a later Letter derides
the changes in automobiles of the late 1950s) as well as to make a compelling and effective concluding sentence out of his imaginary instructions to students. This version is less verbose than the version in his
notes but more so than the version in the 15 July draft that follows:

> The "little book" has long since passed into
> disuse. Will died in 1946, and he had retired from teaching several
> years before that. ~~I dare say~~ Longer, lower textbooks are in use
> in English classes nowadays, I dare say — books with upswept
> tailfins and automatic verbs. I hope some of them manage to
> compress as much good sense into as small a space, manage to get
> to the point so quickly and illuminate it so amusingly. I think,
> though, that if I ~~were suddenly faced with the, to me, impossible~~
> suddenly found myself in the, to me, unthinkable position of facing
> a class in English usage and style, I would simply lean far outover
> the desk, clutch my lapels, blink my eyes, and say: "Get the
> <u>little</u> book, Get the <u>little</u> book. Get the <u>little</u> book."

In this version the automobile analogy is less strained, and the final
image (which hearkens back to a description of Strunk's own stance
and habit of repeating commands) raises the echo and makes the impersonation more effective by abbreviating it. White has run syntactical
variations on his final image in order to satisfy his ear — and, it may
be, the reader's ear as well.

White's composing strategies for the "Letter from the ———" series changed according to his topic. The mosquito item, like the "Report in Spring" or "The Eye of Edna," was easier to draft and discover through revision than a work playing with ideas, like the Strunk
item; in this way the two items resemble the distinctions between the
"Twins" and "Sound" pieces in late Comment. But his process was also

becoming more labored as he wrote less frequently in a less predictable form.

The critical reception accorded *The Points of My Compass* was largely positive. Reviewers tended to respond to the persona White presented and the prose style with which he presented it. The question of the literary form seldom was addressed in the reviews, and when it was broached, it usually led back to issues of voice and style. As one critic observed, "The essay writer occupies one of the more exposed of all literary positions. . . .Year in, year out, the essayist is right there with us, bravely talking along, telling us what *he* thinks of things, what *he* sees." The writing of essays "places extraordinary emphasis on the kind of man who is doing it, on the stamp of his mind and his character, which is probably as good a reason as any one can think of why so few people have ever done it well" (Arlen 24). Yet the reviews seldom actually addressed the pieces in the book as essays and sometimes responded to other aspects of the writing. For example, one critic felt that White's "essays are not conventional examples of the craft" because of "a thread of memoir in them, an accumulation of concrete experience from which the theme emerges without raising its voice" (Nordell 9); another took seriously the premise of the collection as "Letters from the East, the West, the North, the South" (as the subtitle read) and responded to it in that manner, observing that "the letter form is particularly adapted to Mr. White's personal tone, and every reader is likely to feel that the author is corresponding directly with him" (Barrett 172).

For some critics an interest in the style outweighs an interest in the ideas. One reviewer went so far as to declare, "Whatever his subject or mood, however slight the piece, White is one of the true American masters of style" (Fuller 2), and another identified the collection as evidence for why "White has been praised for his wisdom, his seemingly casual approach, his curiously unobtrusive but effective humor, and above all for the ease and clarity of his style" (Walker 5). The sense of White as a prose stylist allowed one critic to identify him as the "most influential of living American prose writers," whose writing had been "of paramount importance in American prose over the last two generations" as "an example of how to approach the writing of English and the responsibility of the journalist." He continued: "His style, usually so relaxed in its precision, can stiffen with contempt as eloquently as it can dance with delight over the prospect of a fine day on the farm.

His use of language mirrors its meaning with a closeness rare in the history of English prose and almost unique today in this time of telegraphic ad-man communications. He takes no liberties with the basic elements and yet still manages to make his style jauntily contemporary" (Weatherby 14). Another critic claimed that White was "one of the great prose writers of our language" and explained that he "writes sentences the way writers ought to write sentences, but almost never do, which is to say with pain and care, and a sense of the warmth and precision and jauntiness of English words" (Arlen 24). These critics see style as very close to tone of voice — as Stanley Walker writes, "In an age of exhortation, acerbity, tantrums, obfuscation, and foggy syntax, Mr. White is here to remind us that there is a civilized way of saying things that ought to be said" (5).

For some critics this "civilized" voice is suspect. The reviewers who had misgivings about the collection struggled with the voice projected throughout. While Wilfrid Sheed acknowledged that it was "elegantly written, obsessively mild and archly humanistic throughout," he undercut his description of White as "the most accomplished prose writer" (of White, Thurber, and Wolcott Gibbs) by adding, parenthetically, "the prettiest, anyway," and objecting that he was also "the most self-conscious." Sheed's objection is clearly to his persona: "He projects non-stop a person who is gentle, level-headed, doesn't take himself too seriously, is full of rustic good sense that may be (although he would be the last to say so) the only real wisdom" (48–49). Sheed was objecting in part to what he took to be a tone that predominated at the *New Yorker*, which he identified as "the spiritual home of the graceful writer with nothing to say." Of such writers, according to Sheed, "White must be the archetype and all-time champion — and this is not meant abusively; he has made some fine things out of his nothing. It is only when he brings his 'the chipmunks are getting scarcer' approach to bear on something like disarmament or the U.N. that it grates seriously. . . . His essays on country-life are, so long as he lays off the sophisticated folksiness, excellent and right in line with the magazine's galloping de-urbanization" (Sheed 49). Surely this is the observation of someone who sees language as performance — Sheed himself can be fairly described as using his own "I'm not really being as nasty as you think I am" approach throughout the review. Yet even Herbert Gold, who held the view that "the burden of grafting a Thoreauvian blend of stoical abstention and poetic concern onto the *New Yorker's* peculiarly discreet diction has weighed heavily on White," acknowledged that "nevertheless, his real quality as a man and a writer has managed to survive" and concluded, "Wit and understatement and a contained rage result in a considerable achievement in this new collection" (30).

The complaints about the collection — that it was "brilliant sentence by sentence, convincing paragraph by paragraph, but occasionally fades out into whimsy over the long stretch of an essay" (Gold 30) or that "a few [pieces] have aged awkwardly in spite of the reflective wit that transcends topicality in almost everything he writes" (Fuller 2) — were relatively minor. Most often the positive comments were connected to the reviewer's appreciation of the voice in the collection. In one of the comparisons of White to Thoreau, a critic concluded that "the sum of his work is probably as close to a contemporary *Walden* as we are likely to get — the similarity being not so much in the subject as in the attitude and the sense of a style completely reflecting the man" (Weatherby 14). Another also linked the style and man: "The qualities for which we know him are all on display: judgments firm but temperate, a patient, gently satirical wryness about the way of the present world, whether in the halls of nations, the city streets, or the back woods, and sharp, fresh ways of seeing and saying" (Fuller 2). Yet another found the book to be "a first-rate collection of pieces wise and funny and perceptive and altogether interesting, and written with that special magic which only people trying to write truthfully now and then attain" (Arlen 24).

Such remarks show a trust in the honesty of the voice of the texts, which the less favorable reviews doubted or did not value. Both reactions seem to reinforce White's view in *The Elements of Style* that "every writer, by the way he uses the language, reveals something of his spirit, his habits, his capacities, his bias. This is inevitable, as well as enjoyable. All writing is communication; creative writing is communication through revelation — it is the Self escaping into the open. No writer long remains incognito" (53). Whether that is true of every writer, it was certainly true of White himself.

The Points of My Compass was White's last collection of new material. From the early 1960s onward, working with Katharine to catalog and donate his manuscripts and memorabilia to the Cornell University Special Collections (Katharine's material went to Bryn Mawr), selecting from among his letters and previously published work for new collections, preparing new editions of earlier collections, White's chief activity was retrospection.

10

"I HAVE WORN MANY SHIRTS"
White as Essayist

By the time E. B. White completed the material collected in *The Points of My Compass*, he was writing less frequently than at any time since 1926. Although he would write yet one more children's book (*The Trumpet of the Swan*, 1970), his regular production of original material was finished; new Comments, new Letters, and new essays appeared only intermittently. There was a ten-year interval between "The Years of Wonder" and the next two "Letters from the East" (reprinted as "The Winter of the Great Snows" and "The Geese") in 1971. The only other "Letter from the East" after those (and reprinted under that title) was dated 8 February 1975. In addition, White also wrote occasional independent essays — one published in *Ford Times* in 1963, two in the *New Yorker* in 1966. He wrote a few short pieces for the *New York Times* between 1967 and 1974. Occasional poems, Comments, Answers to Hard Questions, and letters to various editors make up the rest of his output.

Writing irregularly affected White's methods of composing. For one thing, he did not have to worry as much about being timely, except with some of the Comments. Most of the Comments he wrote after retirement were commemorative or eulogistic, like his final Comment page published 5 July 1976 on the nation's Bicentennial. The evidence of some of those pages suggests that the editorials came with greater difficulty as White grew unaccustomed to writing them. Regular writing in the same format creates a rhythm, almost a momentum, a habit of length and depth and focus, a characteristic voice; infrequent writing demands more effort adopting a persona that has grown unfamiliar, pacing oneself through the composition, and discovering what to say about the topic, particularly if the topic, as in a commemorative Comment, is chosen for the writer rather than by him.

In the case of the Letters, White had the attitude of the letter writer to fall back on. As his collection *Letters of E. B. White* shows, White was a graceful, careful writer of both personal and professional letters; the "Letter from the ————" series had sometimes drawn upon that habit when White needed to put on the shirt of a correspondent. After the completion of *The Points of My Compass*, such a "Letter from the East" as the final one adopts the casual tone and the associative structure of a letter meant to catch the reader up on the letter writer's recent experiences. Interestingly enough, in later years White frequently limited his publication to letters to editors of local newspapers. He was still writing in response to the news. Equally interesting is the scarcity of independent essays after the Letter series — the two for the *New Yorker* drew upon familiar techniques: "What Do Our Hearts Treasure?" is virtually a Christmas "Letter from the South," and "Annals of Birdwatching: Mr. Forbush's Friends" is a celebration of Edward Forbush's ornithological trilogy on the birds of Massachusetts, much in the manner of the very early "St. Nicholas League."

Most of White's writing throughout his career was timely and deadline driven, but after retirement a certain portion of his writing opened up — it did not need to concern itself with current events, it was not dependent on an established structure, and it had no particular due date. As liberating as that may seem, it was also problematical because it offered little in the way of habitual resources to fall back on.

It is a commonly held view that work expands to fill the time available to perform it. Some people get a number of things done in the same time that other people take to do only one thing, because they alter their view of what is an acceptable level of performance to fit the amount of time and the number of responsibilities they have. Writing prolifically on deadline means developing a willingness to let things go into galley at a certain level of professionalism or competence that might not be acceptable or readily attainable when one is writing infrequently without a deadline. Regular journalism also requires that writing be sufficient for the day; as Tom Wicker has observed, "Something that you do now, this week, may be really quite good in the context of this week and a year from now have no relevance to anything" (Root, *Working* 103). Writing that is designed to reverberate with immediacy may lose its resonance over time; writing that does not reverberate against passing events often acquires resonance over time, sometimes inadvertently. The columnist and the regular journalist often have to choose between immediacy and durability, and the nature of magazine publishing ranks immediacy as the first priority.

White's choice of material to fill his clipbooks suggests some of the problems of writing for the immediate deadline. *Every Day Is Saturday* contains paragraphs that he culled from a much larger number published in the magazine. They are very specific in references to current events, as well as witty, whimsical, and succinct. As weekly journalism they had an important role to play in expanding the popularity of the magazine and developing its overall persona, but they have not aged well — White could take it for granted that his readers could identify figures, events, and issues when he wrote about them, but a good many have evaporated from public awareness at the end of the century. The later Comment collected in *The Second Tree from the Corner*, covering a broader span of time, offers less topicality, more depth and timelessness. When White had the opportunity to select material from the span of his entire career for retrospective collections such as *Essays of E. B. White* and *Poems and Sketches of E. B. White*, he tended to draw from material previously collected in clipbooks and unreprinted material written after the publication of *The Points of My Compass*; none of it comes from *Every Day Is Saturday* or *The Wild Flag*, and only a little comes from *Quo Vadimus? or The Case for the Bicycle*, essentially a clipbook of humorous and satirical material — it may be a sign of how ephemeral White understood his editorial and comment writing to be and how much he was capable of separating it, finally, from his other work — the children's books, the Letters, the infrequent essays. Yet this other work is the work anthologized in the two retrospective collections, which are the sources of White's material reprinted in classroom anthologies and analyzed in scholarly criticism — in other words, the work that has tended to be the most enduring.

White wrote in his foreword to *Essays* that he had "chosen the ones that have amused me in the rereading, along with a few that seemed to have the odor of durability clinging to them" (viii). Most were either from *Points* or *Second Tree* or previously uncollected, including the final three letters and the three essays from *Ford Times* and the *New Yorker*, mentioned earlier. White explained that "except for extracting three chapters, I have let *One Man's Meat* alone, since it is a sustained report of about five years of country living — a report I prefer not to tamper with" (ix). The three chapters are "Once More to the Lake" and "On a Florida Key" from *Harper's*, and "The World of Tomorrow" from the *New Yorker*. Part of White's motive in excluding other pieces may well have been their relevance to their time, the elements that make the pieces more powerful in relationship to the events and atmosphere of

World War II — it surely is not country living as a topic that White is reluctant to reprint. But the decision also eliminates all the multiple-item columns and the columns broken up into separate independent miniatures for the book. In the retrospective collection, all the essays read as single-item pieces, even the most rambling and associative. The collection sets limits on what among White's writing he thought of as "essays."

If retirement set White free of both the restraints and the supports of writing in a more-or-less-specific form, even one self-selected, as the "Letters" series was, the consequence was greater complication of his composing processes. Perhaps the piece that best exemplifies White's difficulty with a general essay at this time of his life is "The Sea and the Wind That Blows," published in *Ford Times* in June 1963. The Cornell manuscripts show that this essay was a long time in process.

The piece had its origins in an article that appeared in the 30 January 1957 *New York Times*, recounting the transatlantic solo crossing of a German physician named Hannes Lindemann, who had spent seventy-two days in a sail-driven kayak. White clipped the article and placed it in his work folder, adding to it a list of sailing books he had read or consulted and notes on other sailors and boats. He dated a draft 1 February (two days after the article) and began typing a two-and-a-half-page opening that he eventually abandoned. It started with a reference to Lindemann and took the tone of a celebration of the desire to sail solo; the second paragraph referred to White as "something of a student of small boat voyages," identified Joshua Slocum's voyage on the *Spray* as the starting point for books on circumnavigation of the globe, and mentioned one sailor who crossed the Pacific because "he simply wanted to get to a certain girl in Australia." In addition to the typescript beginning, he wrote a page and a half in longhand about Joshua Slocum. He got no further on this draft.

It may have been illness that drew him away from the piece — White's first Comment of 1957, the entire multiple-item page for 16 February 1957, includes three items on a recent stay in the hospital — or it may have been the sense that the piece was not going to develop as he hoped. He wrote several Comment pages in a row. His next Comment page contained four items on English usage, perhaps the prompt that encouraged Howard A. Stevenson to send him Strunk's textbook; he also contributed both his last multiple-item comment, with linked paragraphs on the railroad, published 3 March, and his initial single-item editorial, published a week later. He published two more Comments in 1957, as well as "The Rock Dove" and three items in his Letter series. The press of other writing and discouragement with the direction of the sailing piece left it abandoned. Over the years White had written many paragraphs inspired by something in the news that either never developed into something usable on the Comment page or was stalled by more timely, urgent, and interesting paragraphs until it became stale. The solo crossing of Hannes Lindemann rapidly became old news.

White returned to the sailing essay again in the summer of 1960. He started a new draft as a typical epistle, with a "Letter from the East" heading, and proceeded through a paragraph about the governor of Maine's appearing in town, a paragraph on playing croquet with his grandchildren, a paragraph on the death of the local village blacksmith, a paragraph on the decline of rail travel (which he crossed out later as having already been used in his January Letter on the railroad), and a long section about trying to decide whether to give up his boat. In this closing passage he recalled how he learned to sail, hinted at some of the difficulties he had in sailing, and alluded again to all the books on sailing he had read. We can date the draft by mention of the age of Joel White's "yearling" third child and of the campaign trip in which Senator John F. Kennedy spoke of a new frontier. White abandoned this draft as well.

When White returned to the sailing theme once more, in February or March 1963, he initially thought of it, again, as another "Letter from the East," even though *The Points of My Compass* had already been published with all the earlier Letters. He began the draft, wrote up a separate page on Humphrey Bogart's funeral, drafted another page in longhand on the fear the sea engendered in him, and struggled with the title: "~~The Dream of~~ The Sea and the Dreaming"; "An End to ~~the Wind~~ Voyaging"; "The Fear of the Sea"; "The Sea and the Summons"; "The Sea Is a Summons"; and, finally, "The Sea and the Wind That Blows." Drawing on the opening of the previous attempts to begin, he took three drafts to get through it, each draft building on the draft before it and advancing steadily to the final draft. It had become a reminiscence of his own experience sailing, no longer tied to current events, reading, or the Letter format, and that is the way it was published in *Ford Times*.

Begun in 1957 and completed in 1963, "The Sea and the Wind That Blows" went through an unusually long period of incubation and development — at least for White. Only a handful of his published works, usually his longest and most intimate pieces, were similarly a long time in coming. Toward the end of his active writing life he wrote less frequently off the top of the news and more often from his personal experience. The work came more slowly and with greater difficulty. More and more he had the time to let ideas develop slowly. It is not surprising then that the final essays in *Points* are either reminiscences like "The Years of Wonder" or "Will Strunk," reflecting back on White's youth, or essays on themes like television, the motorcar, the railroad, and the United Nations — topics he had written on in earlier essays and Comment pieces in the past. Even his final children's book, *The Trumpet of the Swan*, drew very much on White's childhood.

The effect of White's movement away from regular composing can also be seen in the literary form with which he was most familiar. His 1969 Comment on the moon landing was only his second Comment of that year, and it did not come easily. In the appendix of his biography of White, Scott Elledge describes the progress of the editorial:

> White watched the moon-walk on television at his home in Maine on Sunday night from about 11 P.M. till 1 A.M. Since press time at *The New Yorker* was Monday noon, he wrote under some pressure. On Monday morning, when he had typed what he thought was his final draft (No. 3 of the series here reproduced), he sent it by telegraph to *The New Yorker*. Shortly afterwards, he decided that he did not like what he had written, and he composed a new version (No. 4), revised it (No. 5), made a fair copy of the revision (No. 6), and then sent Shawn [*New Yorker* editor, William Shawn] a telegram (No. 7). When Shawn phoned and, having heard the new version, agreed that it was better than the first, White dictated it to Shawn, who sent it at once to the printer. The paragraph was published on Thursday, in the issue dated Saturday, July 26. (359)

Elledge reproduces the series of drafts and observes — in accord with Thurber's comment that the "art of paragraphing is to make something that was ground out sound as if it were dashed off" — that the drafts illustrate White's practice of writing a thing first and thinking about it afterward, then grinding it into a finished piece.

Douglas Hunt, in the introduction to his textbook, uses this Comment as an example of "The Evolution of an Essay," identifying "comment" as "unsigned essays in miniature" and acknowledging that, despite "more than forty years of experience with them," the moon-landing Comment was "a particularly difficult assignment" (6). Drawing on Elledge, he reprints the first three drafts and the published version, and analyzes White's motives for the major changes over the series of drafts. He concludes: "This is certainly not the best comment White ever wrote, but like all his comments it is compact and lively. . . . It isn't merely White's *recording* of his reaction to the moon landing that changes from first draft to last: the reaction itself changes to something more generous and complete" (10). Dauntingly, for the college students to whom his anthology is directed, Hunt emphasizes that only 15 of the original 305 words survive to the finished draft.

In some ways the moon-landing piece is typical of White's later composing — the survival rate from early work was much higher, and in his most prolific period extensive multiple revisions would have been impossible. Even in the apparatus for *The Points of My Compass* seven years earlier (and at the same time that the drafts of "The Sea and the Wind That Blows" were accumulating), White exhibited difficulty carrying little projects through to completion. The foreword to the collection went through several drafts, including multiple drafts of a section eventually inserted into a previously almost-completed text.

Part of the apparatus includes a series of "postscripts" to the Letters from the east, north, and south. The postscript idea fit the conceit of correspondence running through the book and gave White an opportunity to respond to the outdatedness of some of the entries. The postscript to "Will Strunk" went through three drafts in March 1962 and a fourth in April; he attempted several drafts of a postscript to "A Slight Sound at Evening," working on comparing the costs of Thoreau's house at Walden with those of a ceremony accepting Thoreau into a Hall of Fame for Great Americans (a device he had used in "Walden" and "Movies"), but abandoned the postscript for that essay altogether.

A more compelling example comes from the drafts of "The Winter of the Great Snows." Sometime in February 1971, White wrote a longhand note to himself, on 5 × 8 personal letter paper, trying out some ideas for another Letter:

Some people read with their minds, but I read with my lips & have to hear a word, not just see it. This takes forever but is worth it. I don't have much of a feeling for words, but I have a strong feeling
      certain words.   *care for*
against ~~them~~ For instance, I don't ~~like~~ the word "genre." I know
  I don't   *wide of the mark*
why too: I can't pronounce it. I call it John, which I know is ~~incorrect~~

but it's the best I've ever been able to do. ^ I avoid all writers who
use the word — and this takes in almost all literary critics, who seem

and I let them alone.

to love it. I call them John writers. When the Sunday Times arrives,
I glance at the Book section and then discard it. "Just a bunch of john
writers," I grumble. My wife can say the word and she likes the

how

john writers. I don't know ~~*whether*~~ *the Famous Writers School*
would look on ~~*such a*~~ *my narrow, prejudicial approach to words.*
~~*There are probably*~~ *Some of the board may be john writers.*

From this note White developed a first draft, which he dated 23 February 1971 and which opens with comments on shifting the date of Washington's birthday, the end of rail passenger service, and the mail, before launching into a section in which he receives "a letter from the Director of Admissions of the Famous Writers School, wanting to know if I had a feeling for words, or perhaps an undeveloped aptitude for writing." White kids about this, claiming to have given up after starting their test:

> My feeling for words varies greatly with the time of day. Right after lunch I have no feeling for words at all — not the slightest. Around six o'clock, after a couple of drinks, I sometimes have a feeling for
>
> am always suspicious of it   makes things seem a
>
> words but it ~~leaves me suspicious~~ as I know ~~what alcohol can do the~~ whole lot more inspired and beautiful than they really are.
>
> ~~imagination warp a man's judgment~~ and pervert his dreams.

He *likes* the original passage the test asks him to edit and imagines a fable using story elements from the editing test. Then he claims to know someone who joined, cheated, and dropped out. It is a three-page draft.

The second draft, also dated 23 February, follows those three pages but claims the story about the man who joined was a fictional piece. White elaborates on it and has his hero drop out of the Famous Writers School, publish an issue-length piece in the *Atlantic*, and, based on his success, get hired by the school as a subeditor. All his homework had been done by a teenage boy. White continues: "I showed this piece to my wife, and she said it wasn't funny, so I threw it away — which is what I do with more than half of everything I write anyway. *Sometimes I think I'd be doing better if I were married to Faith Baldwin.*" He then incorporates the "feeling for words" section and the extended "genre-john" joke before turning to items on smelt and gulls, the cold weather and daily life (pages four through six of the draft), and a new section about three topics of conversation: the weather, the schools, and oil. The draft ends with part of a paragraph on schools.

In preparatory notes separate from the first notes on writing, White had tried various starts for the rest of the Letter. A sentence about gulls and smelt was the second start on a legal-pad sheet dated 10 February. The first start was about winter, one sentence long, crossed out; the draft extended from the second start about gulls and smelt into two paragraphs about winter. When White was working on the second draft, he shifted from writers to gulls ("But enough of words and writers, a dull subject. Somebody told me recently that a seagull won't eat a smelt") and continued for two paragraphs from the preparatory note.

The third draft, dated 8 March 1971, starts with "Somebody told me the other day that a sea gull won't eat a smelt," follows with the two paragraphs from the second draft, develops the winter subject at length, and then elaborates on the chief topics of conversation. This draft is ten pages long and ends talking about how the town can "regulate the taking of shellfish" but cannot "regulate the discharge of the waste that makes the shellfish inedible." In a longhand addition he talks about the Constitution.

The fourth draft, dated 9 March, with proof marks from 11 March, is a revision of the third draft, and discusses sea gulls, smelt, winter, weather, schools, oil, and ends with a revision of the regulation sentence and White's later addition about being not only "impractical" but "unconstitutional." The last line is "And I still don't know whether a gull will eat a smelt." The piece then was published in this form in the *New Yorker* on 27 March.

None of the early material about the genre writers and the Famous Writers School makes it into the later drafts. It may be that White discovered a greater unity to the items he used in the later drafts (all connected to place and season, an appropriate unity in a Letter), or it may be that he recognized the aptness of Katharine's advice about the genre-john joke and the strained levity of the satire on the Famous Writers School — its brochure is the kind of material that in the past had produced memorable Comment in "Calculating Machine," "Two Letters, Both Open," and "Dear Mr. ⑂0214ᵐ⅃063⑂⊪0 2ᵐ10730ᵐ8⊪ "

(all reprinted in *Poems and Sketches*). White may have indeed thrown out half his writing in the past, but he had also produced pieces of this length with less wasted effort over shorter periods of time.

When we trace the course of a writer's career through a trail of manuscripts, we are likely to find some constants in the approach to composition as well as a number of differences from youth to old age, from decade to decade, from one literary form to another, from one set of composing circumstances to the next. Like many writers who expect to be writing constantly, White had habitual approaches to rely on. For example, he engaged in various forms of string saving. He kept a journal regularly, as we know from whole sections lifted from it in "First World War" and other references in personal and public writing. The journal was a place to rehearse language, record events, respond to experience and ideas. He also kept a folder of notes on what he read and observed, and clippings and articles that potentially could be used in his own writing. Although it may not have been his intention, his letters to other people — including his wife, his colleagues, his friends, and his readers — also served as occasions to make trial runs of language and ideas; we can trace specific phrases and sentences in published works to letters written considerably earlier.

Much of the material in White's string saving never made it into his writing or was abandoned at an early stage. It might have become outdated before he could use it; it might have been pushed aside by more lively, more provocative, or more relevant material; it might not have connected to other material in a way that led to drafting. The early drafts of "The Sea and the Wind That Blows" are pertinent as an example of material failing to coalesce. In the early Comment days, the items on Hannes Lindemann's solo sailing or Humphrey Bogart's funeral or "john" writers might have easily made a quick paragraph, but in the context of longer pieces they needed some solid way of connecting to other material. Often a writer stores material away — in memory, in a folder, or in some other storage area — until current events or chance occurrences trigger associations that provoke a desire to explore the connections. For topical pieces in particular, such as "The Railroad" essay in *The Points of My Compass*, actual storage of clipped news items is important — data from outside sources is vital in such a piece — but even in a more personal piece, such as the reminiscence on Will Strunk, circumstances need to provide a prompt to memory and reflection. In this case, White's reading of *The Elements of Style* helped him call up recollections of Strunk. The portrait that emerges from the details re-called by the specific teachings of the textbook probably could not have been generated as readily without rereading the book itself (and doing further string saving on it as he read). We can note other in-stances in White's career in which similar connections are prompted: the memoir on the Model T is prompted by a piece on the subject by Richard Lee Strout; the essay "Once More to the Lake" is generated by White's return to Belgrade Lake with his son, Joel.

A writer who intends to write and publish weekly looks at the world around him with a writer's eye, on some subconscious level constantly searching for and evaluating potential topics; when he writes less fre-quently, likely topics are arrived at more deliberately, more cautiously, more tentatively. Much of White's composing was engendered by im-mediate response to what he experienced, observed, or read. The hab-its for this grew out of the relentless need to be prolific prompted by the deadlines of the Notes and Comment page, in which many of White's paragraphs were inspired by "trivial events of the day," the juxtapositions of observed city life he found while strolling the streets. For material out of his reading, think of the early paragraphs on the promotional material from his Lake Placid in-the-Adirondacks corre-spondent or May Day events at Bryn Mawr, or his later editorial on a judicial decision involving sound trucks; for material out of his obser-vations, think of the paragraph on the chauffeur and the pink lingerie, the Comment on the twin fawns, or the "Sabbath Morn" column or the "Eye of Edna" Letter or the first half of "The Ring of Time." In most of these examples the description itself carries much of the weight of the text, and the writer's side comments and reactions to what he describes add breadth and depth.

White also had habitual ways of approaching the actual drafting. Whether the material was a long time gestating or provoked by imme-diate events, White tended to begin his attack on it by using the writing as a way to prompt thinking rather than the reverse, as a means to record it. In effect White wrote discovery drafts to begin with, some-times drafts too rough to be considered first drafts, sometimes rough drafts that helped him discover his theme or his perspective, some-times drafts advanced enough to need mostly sharpening of focus or tightening of rhythm or tuning of voice. The difference in the amount of labor the drafting took and the number of revisions that would fol-low depended upon two factors that influence all composing. One was his work circumstances, including his familiarity with the topic, its degree of concreteness or abstractness, and the exigencies of length and time he needed to consider. The other was the form in which he was working, including his familiarity with its demands. In more personal items, such as "Twins," which tended to focus on description and narration, White's attention in composing was more readily on tone and detail; in more editorial items, such as "Sound," which tended to focus on persuasion and information, the need for a sustained argument on abstract issues complicated and extended the composing. In either case the material was easier to work with — because it was brief and focused and designed for a specific magazine page — than a piece like "The Sea and the Wind That Blows," which had no certain publication site and no specific limitations. Even writers of vast experience and expertise may be thrown back into the situation of less-accomplished writers when facing unfamiliar composing circumstances. Writers who hope to use White as a model for their own composing should make allowances for the differences between White's work circumstances and their own.

The way White revised — "by ear," as he said — should also be noted. Many of the revisions in the manuscripts show a writer struggling to say the words on paper not simply in a serviceable way or a plain, clear way or a correct way but rather (or also) in a way in which the rhythms and sounds of the language capture and reinforce the meaning. White's endings never trail off — they conclude, they end, they linger in the ear and the imagination. Writing is not simply a matter of recording sentences and ideas that the mind has stored perfectly formed; neither is it pouring language and ideas into universal syntactical molds. So White wrestles with not only ideas and images but also the word choice and sentence arrangement that will make them come across to the reader most forcefully or most memorably or most entertainingly — and perhaps make them most carry the resonances reverberating in the author himself. "Once More to the Lake" ends: "Languidly, and with no thought of going in, I watched him, his hard little body, skinny and bare, saw him wince slightly as he pulled up around his vitals the small, soggy, icy garment. As he buckled the swollen belt, suddenly my groin felt the chill of death" (*One Man's Meat* 203). The description of the boy pulling on his wet bathing suit prolongs the action, draws it out, almost puts it into slow motion, emphasizing vulnerability, discomfort, coldness, the long, languid sentence both preparing us thematically and lulling us syntactically for the impact of the short, startling final sentence. He ends the first segment of "Songbirds"

(*One Man's Meat* 227): "The unseasonable warmth invests the night with a quality of mystery and magnitude. And in the east beyond the lilac and beyond the barn and beyond the bay and behind the deepening hills, in slow and splendid surprise, rises the bomber's moon." The peacefulness of the scene is disturbed by the ominous final image, and the sentence has been inverted to hold that image off until the very end while keeping the active voice it needs to make it forceful. Benjamin DeMott, in his review of *Essays of E. B. White*, identified the language as the key ingredient in this "resourcefully melodic collection": "what is beyond criticism in a White essay is the music. The man knows all the tunes, all the limited lovely music that a plain English sentence can play — the affordable balances ('It took an upheaval of the elements and a job at the lowest level to give me the relief I craved'), the affordable vowel songs ('the tonic smell of coon'), everything. On nearly every page, there are subtleties of rhythm and pace, interweavings of the sonorous and racy rare in most contemporary writing" (77). The qualities of White's style arise from a deep-seated and intrinsic way of perceiving his world, but they are achieved through painstaking revision to get the sense into the sound.

White tended to be a solitary writer. Thurber made much of White's shyness and elusiveness in his profile of his friend, but the image he depicts was based on observation. While it is not difficult to discover in White the influences of the writers whom he read and reread with pleasure — particularly Thoreau and Marquis, but a number of others as well — he relied on himself as the judge of his own interests and as the editor of his own work. He said of his wife Katharine once, "She is a truly gifted writer-helper, and I have had to do my own work in secret for twenty-eight years in order to maintain any feeling of personal accomplishment" (*Letters* 445). Identifying her in another letter as an editor, he explained, "An editor is a person who knows more about writing than writers do but who has escaped the terrible desire to write. . . . A writer, however, writes as long as he lives" (391). One of the recurring themes in his writing, particularly when he was encouraged to be a propagandist or accused of being one, was his insistence on writing for himself. That was part of his motive in accepting the column assignment from *Harper's*, titling it "One Man's Meat," and insisting, in response to a writer who had vowed to write nothing that was not significant, that "a writer should cultivate only what naturally absorbs his fancy, whether it be freedom or cinch bugs, and should write in the way that comes easy" (*One Man's Meat* 34). In the twentieth anniversary issue of the *New Yorker* White observed that "the deepest instinct of a creative person is not to promote the world's cause but to keep the minutes of his own meeting." The observation foreshadows his later assertion in *The Elements of Style* that "the whole duty of a writer is to please himself and the true writer always plays to an audience of one" (70) and his view in the *Paris Review* interview that a "writer should concern himself with whatever absorbs his fancy, stirs his heart, and unlimbers his typewriter" (Plimpton 85). His most powerful and enduring work in Comment, Letter, and essay was achieved by following those principles.

When we talk about White the essayist, we have to remember that as a literary form the essays were either separate from the regular writing he did — the Comment, the column, the editorials, the Letters — as "Farewell, My Lovely!" and "Death of a Pig" were, or they were anomalous exceptions within the regular writing, as "Once More to the Lake" and "The Ring of Time" were. In terms of genre or subgenre it more often makes sense to see specific examples as paragraphs stretched into miniature essays or essaylike letters than to see them as essays per se. In the long run, however, jumbling all the nonfiction work White did under one vague umbrella term not only obscures the nature of the essay but also ignores White's achievement in very distinct literary forms. As we have seen, his most prolific output was in the form of paragraphs for Notes and Comment. I want to insist that the paragraph was a literary form in itself that reached, in Morris Bishop's term, its "apotheosis" in White's hands. The paragraph — like an epigram or perhaps a haiku in poetry — is a prose form that concentrates itself within narrowly circumscribed limits, centering on observed events or found language to which the paragraphist gives a droll, trenchant, and/or witty interpretation or response. White accomplished brilliant results within the constraints of the short paragraph. He also stretched the limits of the form in both length and attitude, not only with such experimental Comments as "Grace Notes" and "Chair Car," which ran like stream-of-consciousness meditations the length of the entire Comment section, but also with linked paragraphs that sometimes only winked at linkage but sometimes developed into a prototype of the modern "collage" essay.

White's work on the Comment page should be seen as not only the most constant employment of his writing talents but also the most persistent influence on the rest of his writing, even when he turned to other forms. For example, his retreat from Comment writing and subsequent involvement in the "One Man's Meat" column allowed him to alter his writing voice and to develop his reflections beyond the limits of first-person-plural paragraph writing but, as we have seen, in practice during the life of that column he drew frequently on the habits of the Comment page. Most of the "One Man's Meat" columns in the magazine are subdivided into distinct items, sometimes very short essays unrelated to one another ("Movies" and "Boston Terrier" come readily to mind), sometimes nothing more than a disjunctive series of paragraphs (such as "Compost" or the column from which "Goose's Return" is taken); only a relatively few "One Man's Meat" items are distinctly fully developed essays: "Once More to the Lake," "Walden," and "On a Florida Key." Yet such is the persistence of the essayist's presence in even the most segmented of columns that his ability to make items reverberate off one another generates columns that are clear precursors of the contemporary disjunctive or collage essay.

White blurs the boundaries between subgenres, and it gives his nonfiction prose a persistently different tenor from the work of most other essayists. But, of course, when we talk of White as an essayist, we are talking of attitude, of temperament, outlook, expression. In terms of literary form White has written a small body of essays compared to the volume of nonfiction work he produced — I would insist on identifying most of the Notes and Comment work as paragraphs or editorials, most of the "One Man's Meat" work as columns, and I would emphasize the epistolary construct of the Letters as much as the essayistic. However, I would insist that his approach to most of his nonfiction writing was essayistic, and it is the voice, the presence, of the essayist that distinguishes his work in all these forms from the work of others in the same forms.

The essayist in White took some time to emerge. It may have been there from the beginning, providing a certain distinctive timbre, but it did not become central to his writing until the period of the *Harper's* column — "I was a man in search of the first person singular, and lo, here it was — handed to me on a platter before I even left town," he wrote in the introduction to the 1982 edition of the book (xiii). It did not predominate in his writing until the final decades of his career. Yet the form in which he works or the ideas that he espouses are less central to the reader's response to his writing than the person he seems to be. Scott Russell Sanders, one of our best contemporary essayists, in an essay that seems redolent of White's own foreword to *Essays of E. B. White,* has noted, "It is the *singularity* of the first person — its warts and crotchets and turn of voice — that lures many of us into reading essays, and lingers with us after we finish" (196); he cites White as his foremost example. It is precisely this sense of the essayist's identity that Eudora Welty pinpointed in her own review of White's essays: "What joins all these essays together is the love held by the author for what is transitory in life. The transitory more and more becomes one with the beautiful. It is a love so deep that it includes, may well account for, the humor and the poetry and the melancholy *and* the dead accuracy filling the essays to the brim, the last respects and the celebrations together" (43). She notes that there is "a melancholy running through nearly all these pieces" that does not leave the reader depressed: "This may be due to the lyric quality irrepressible in Mr. White's writing, it may be due also to its prevailing sanity." She observes that the "writing is itself dateless as a cloudless sky, because the author has dateless virtues" (7). Cautioning against the assumption that an essayist has a single identifiable voice rather than a range of voices or distinctly different voices playing off against one another, Carl Klaus has suggested that "the capacity and willingness" to, in White's words, "pull on any sort of shirt" may be "essential to the creation of authentically personal essays — essays, that is, in which a personality comes to life in something like the rich variety of its actual being. The drama of one's personality depends, after all, on the *dramatis personae* one is capable of performing" ("Chameleon" 128).

Reviewers of White's clipbooks have long associated him with his forebears in literary nonfiction. A review of *Every Day Is Saturday* was actually titled "Thoreau on a Roof Garden," and many critics have readily responded to the Thoreauvian echoes in his sentences and in his attitudes; among writers Thoreau surely had the deepest impact on White. But in the long run such allusions are not particularly apt in terms of the kind of essayist White was, nor are comparisons to Montaigne, Addison, Lamb, Hazlitt, or Twain, all of whom have been cited in one or more reviews. Among essayists no one else wrote in the forms White did; among journalists writing in his typical forms no one else drew so thoroughly upon the essayistic impulse. The frustrations for literary classifiers in locating White in the essayist tradition arise in part from his stance apart from rather than astride that tradition. Only rarely, as in the introduction to the collected essays, does White embrace the tradition; for the most part he can be found strolling along just off the path, intersecting with it only occasionally for a literary essay ("Walden — 1954," the introductions to *the lives and times of archy & mehitabel* and *A Subtreasury of American Humor*) or a personal essay ("Once More to the Lake," "On a Florida Key," "Farewell, My Lovely!") but more often meeting the path where it arches out into *his* trajectory. As critics have observed of White's style, it may also be said of his essays: To write like White you have to become White. With a good many other practicing essayists, to write in the form is to write like other essayists; they are true enough to the traditions of the form (as protean as they may seem) that to work within the form is to assume common elements of identity. Or, to work within White's metaphor, to don one of the many shirts in the essayist's closet is to assume an attitude within a traditional design; to don the mantle of White is to assume an identity that is sui generis, and for anyone else, will not be a good fit.

The essayist that emerged out of the career of E. B. White was the essayist that was submerged throughout his career, a self-liberated man recognizable by the individual voice within the forms in which he wrote — that is, the voice of the essayist within the writer of paragraphs, editorials, Letters, columns, and Comments who pushed those constricted forms toward the freedom of the essay. White in his own time was a principal exemplar and exponent of the first person singular, and his work gives authority to those who in our own time would find in the essay a place to express the "authentically personal" in singular or multiple voices, to find the music in the language, to listen for the "faint squeak of mortality."

E. B. WHITE'S WRITING, 1926–1976

In the tables below the first two columns on the left refer to the contributions to Notes and Comment, following Katharine Romans Hall's designations of holdings in the E. B. White Collection at Cornell University. They give the number of weeks each year White contributed either all or part of the Notes and Comment page. In the first table the third column refers to items republished in clipbooks; the "Talk" column refers to casuals in Talk of the Town; the other headings are self-explanatory. Footnotes explain specific contents of some table cells.

1926–1936

Year	Comment			Talk	Other Forms of Writing					
	All	Part	Clip		Humor	Articles	Fiction	Reviews	Letters	Poetry
1926		3			21					17
1927	29	22		27	32[a]			4		15
1928	41	7		32	18	3		5		23
1929	29	11	2[b]	24	17					12
1930	39	14		12	14	1		2		12
1931	39	12	1[c]	15	11	2		6		8
1932	47	4	1[d]	4	8	3		7		10
1933	50	2	1[e]	6	10	2		6		14
1934	52		1[f]	7	11	3[g]				17
1935	52			3	9	1		1		12
1936	51	1	1[h]	9	11	1[i]		1		7

a. Includes ten satirical advertisements featuring Sterling Finney.
b. *The Lady Is Cold* and *Is Sex Necessary?*
c. *Ho Hum*, a collection of newsbreaks.
d. *Another Ho Hum*, a second collection of newsbreaks.
e. *Alice through the Cellophane*, a 3-part satire from the magazine.
f. *Every Day Is Saturday*, a collection of Notes and Comment paragraphs.
g. Includes an early essay, "The St. Nicholas League."
h. *Farewell to Model T* (first published as "Farewell, My Lovely!").
i. Includes the essay "Farewell, My Lovely!"

| Year | Comment | | Clipbooks | | Other Forms of Writing | | | | | | |
	All	Part	One Man's Meat	The Wild Flag	Children's Books	Humor	Articles	Fiction	Reviews	Letters	Poetry
1937	32	0				7		3		I	4
1938	3	11	4			9	I		2		6
1939	0	16	14			10		2			2
1940	1	9	12			12			1		1
1941	0	2	12			3					4
1942	0	22	11			6					1
1943	0	40	3	12 [a]		5					1
1944	4	40		12 [a]		3	I		1		7
1945	13	33		27 [a]	1 [b]	3	3		1		3
1946	1	30		12 [a]		3			2		4
1947	0	12				3	3	2	1	2	4
1948	23	20				3	I		2		5
1949	2	21				5	I			I	4
1950	7	9				2		1	1	I	3
1951	20	11					I	I			1
1952	25	6								2	3
1953	24	6			1 [c]	I	I			I	1

a. Items in *The Wild Flag* are also counted in Comment.
b. *Stuart Little*, White's first children's book.
c. *Charlotte's Web*.

Year	Comment			Clipbooks		Other Forms of Writing						
	All	Part	Obits	Essays of E. B. W.	Points of My Compass	Children's Books	Humor	Articles	Other	Reviews	Letters	Poetry
1954	22	5			2 [a]		3		1	1		0
1955	8	6			1		3	2				3
1956	1	0	1		5		2	2				2
1957	5	1			3		5 [b]					2
1958	0	0	1		2		3					1
1959	0	0			0		2		13 [c]		1	1
1960	0	0	1		3				4 [c]			0
1961	1	0	1		1		1				1	1
1962	0	0					2					0
1963	1	0	1	1 [d]			4				1	1
1964	4	0	1				4				1	0
1965	3	0					1				1	0
1966	0	1		2 [e]			1					1
1967	0	0					1	1	2 [f]		1	1
1968	0	0					1		1 [f]			0
1969	3	0					2				1	1
1970	0	0				1 [i]	1				2	1
1971	0	1		3 [g]							2	
1972	1	0					3					
1973	0	0					1				2	
1974	1	1					2	1			1	
1975	0	0		1 [h]			1				3	
1976	1	0					1				1	

a. "Walden—1954" and "The Eye of Edna."

b. "The Rock Dove."

c. "These Precious Days" clippings (*New Yorker*).

d. "The Sea and the Wind That Blows."

e. "What Do Our Hearts Treasure?" and "Annals of Birdwatching: Mr. Forbush's Friends."

f. Topics in the *New York Times*.

g. "Letters from the East" ("Winter of Great Snows," "Geese"); "Riposte."

h. "Letter from the East."

i. *The Trumpet of the Swan.*

WORKS CITED

Adams, Franklin P. *Column Book of F. P. A.* Garden City: Doubleday, 1928.

Adams, J. Donald. "Speaking of Books." *New York Times Book Review*, 3 June 1945: 2.

Arlen, M. J. "World of E. B. White." *New York Times Book Review*, 28 October 1962: 24.

Barrett, William. "Reader's Choice." *Atlantic Monthly*, December 1962: 172.

Beck, Warren. "Call for Immediate World Government." *Chicago Sun Book World*, 15 December 1946: 3.

Benét, William Rose. "For Future Historians." *Saturday Review of Literature*, 27 October 1934: 40.

Bishop, Morris. Introduction to *One Man's Meat*, by E. B. White. Harper's Modern Classics. New York: Harper, 1950.

Blair, Walter, and Hamlin Hill. *America's Humor: From Poor Richard to Doonesbury.* New York: Oxford University Press, 1978.

"Brave New Scanties." *Time*, 11 November 1946: 109–110.

Bromfield, Louis. *Malabar Farm.* New York: Harper, 1948.

Canby, Henry S. ". . . But No Man's Poison." *Saturday Review*, 13 June 1942: 7.

Chapman, Arthur. "The Colyum Conductor." *Scribner's Magazine*, August 1916: 210–223.

Chase, Mary Ellen, and Margaret Eliot MacGregor. *The Writing of Informal Essays.* 1928. Reprint, Freeport, N.Y.: Books for Libraries, 1970.

Colby, Frank Moore. *The Colby Essays.* 2 vols. Edited by Clarence Day, Jr. New York: Harper, 1926.

"Colyums." *Saturday Review of Literature*, 15 August 1925: 37, 43.

Comley, Nancy R., David Hamilton, Carl H. Klaus, Robert Scholes, and Nancy Sommers, eds. Introduction to *Fields of Writing: Readings Across the Disciplines.* 4th ed. New York: St. Martin's, 1994.

DeMott, Benjamin. "Books 1. Pick of the List." *Saturday Review*, 20 August 1977: 62–64.

DeVane, William C. "A Celebration of Life." *Yale Review* 32:1 (1942): 163–165.

Edman, Irwin. "Earthy, Humorous, Accessible." *New York Herald Tribune Books*, 14 June 1942: IX:2.

———. "The Wonder and Wackiness of Man." *New York Times Book Review*, 17 January 1954: 7:1.

Edson, C. L. *The Gentle Art of Columning*. New York: Brentano's, 1920.

Elledge, Scott. "Coda to Foreword." In *E. B. White: A Biography*. New York: W. W. Norton, 1986.

———. *E. B. White: A Biography*. New York: W. W. Norton, 1985.

Epstein, Joseph. "E. B. White, Dark & Lite." *Commentary* 81:4 (1986): 48–56.

———. "Writing Essays." *New Criterion*, June 1984: 26–34.

Fadiman, Clifton. "In Praise of E. B. White, Realist." *New York Times Book Review*, 10 June 1945: 1.

Flanner, Janet ("Genêt"). "Letter from Paris." *New Yorker*, 10 September 1955: 82, 84–88.

Fuller, Edmund. "Multitude of Topics Touched by a True Master of Style." *Chicago Tribune Magazine of Books*, 21 October 1962: 2.

Fuller, John Wesley. "Prose Styles in the Essays of E. B. White." Ph.D. diss., University of Washington, 1959.

Gold, Herbert. "Hearth and Hurricane." *Saturday Review* 45:47 (24 November 1962): 30.

Grayson, David. *Adventures in Contentment*. New York: Phillips, 1906.

Greene, Graham. *In Search of a Character: Two African Journals*. London: Bodley Head, 1961.

Hall, Katherine Romans. *E. B. White: A Bibliographic Catalogue of Printed Materials in the Department of Rare Books, Cornell University Library*. New York: Garland, 1979.

Haskell, Dale Everett. "The Rhetoric of the Familiar Essay: E. B. White and Personal Discourse." Ph.D. diss., Texas Christian University, 1983.

Heydrick, Benjamin A., ed. *Types of the Essay*. New York: Scribner's, 1921.

Hoagland, Edward. "The Voice of the New Yorker." *New York Times Book Review*, 8 November 1981: 3, 36–37, 39.

Holmes, Charles S. *The Clocks of Columbus: The Literary Career of James Thurber*. New York: Atheneum, 1972.

Howarth, William L. "Successor to *Walden*? Thoreau's 'Moonlight — An Intended Course of Lectures.'" *Proof* 2 (1972): 89–115.

Hunt, Douglas, ed. "Introduction: About Essays and Essayists." In *The Dolphin Reader*. 2nd ed. Boston: Houghton, 1990.

Ingersoll, Ralph. "The New Yorker." *Fortune*, August 1934: 72–86, 90, 92, 97, 150, 152.

Jefferson, Bernard L., ed. *Essays and Essay Writing.* New York: Thomas Nelson, 1929.

Klaus, Carl H. "The Chameleon 'I': On Voice and Personality." In *Voices on Voice: Perspectives, Definitions, Inquiry*, edited by Kathleen Blake Yancey. Urbana: NCTE, 1994.

———. "Essayists on the Essay." In *Literary Nonfiction*, edited by Chris Anderson. Carbondale: Southern Illinois University Press, 1989.

———. "Excursions of the Mind: Toward a Poetics of Uncertainty in the Disjunctive Essay." In *What Do I Know?: Reading, Writing, and Teaching the Essay*, edited by Janis Forman. Portsmouth: Boynton, 1995.

Kramer, Dale. *Ross and the New Yorker.* New York: Doubleday, 1951.

Krutch, Joseph Wood. "The Profession of a New Yorker." *Saturday Review*, 30 January 1954: 15–16.

Kunkel, Thomas. *Genius in Disguise: Harold Ross of "The New Yorker."* New York: Random, 1995.

Lane, Lauriat, Jr. "Thoreau at Work: Four Versions of 'A Walk to Wachusett.'" *Bulletin of the New York Public Library* 69:1 (January 1965): 3–16.

"Last Look Around." *Time*, 22 June 1942: 91–92.

Lopate, Phillip. "Whatever Happened to the Personal Essay?" In *Against Joie de Vivre.* New York: Poseidon, 1989.

———, ed. Introduction to *The Art of the Personal Essay: An Anthology from the Classical Era to the Present.* New York: Anchor, 1994.

Marquis, Don. "Confessions of a Reformed Columnist," *Saturday Evening Post*, 22 December 1928: 6–7, 53; 29 December 1928: 50–51, 62.

———. *The Almost Perfect State.* Garden City: Doubleday, 1927.

———. *the lives of archy and mehitabel.* Introduction by E. B. White. Garden City: Doubleday, 1950.

———. "Speaking of Prefaces." In *The Gentle Art of Columning*, edited by C. L. Edson. New York: Brentano's, 1920.

Marvel, Ik [Donald Grant Mitchell]. *My Farm at Edgewood: A Country Book.* New York: Scribner, 1863.

Montaigne, Michel de. *The Complete Essays of Montaigne.* Translated by Donald M. Frame. Stanford, Calif.: Stanford University Press, 1948.

Morley, Christopher. "Confessions of a Colyumist." In *Pipefuls.* Garden City: Doubleday, 1921.

———. *Inward Ho!* Garden City: Doubleday, 1923.

———. *Pipefuls.* Garden City: Doubleday, 1921.

———. *The Romany Stain.* Garden City: Doubleday, 1926.

———, ed. *Modern Essays.* New York: Harcourt, 1921.

———, ed. *Modern Essays, Second Series.* New York: Harcourt, 1924.

Neumeyer, Peter F. "The Creation of Charlotte's Web: From Drafts to Book," parts 1 and 2. *Horn Book Magazine*, October 1982: 489–497; December 1982: 617–625.

———. "The Creation of E. B. White's The Trumpet of the Swan: The Manuscripts." *Horn Book Magazine*, January–February 1985: 117–128.

———. "Stuart Little: The Manuscripts." *Horn Book Magazine*, September–October 1988: 593–600.

Nordell, Roderick. "The Safekeeping of . . . Enchantment," *Christian Science Monitor*, 18 October 1962: 9.

Opdycke, Mary Ellis. "Colyumism." *New Republic*, 29 August 1923: 15–17.

Panter-Downes, Mollie. "Letter from London." *New Yorker*, 8 October 1955: 121–125.

"Paragraphs Culled from the New Yorker." *New York Times Book Review*, 7 October 1934: 9.

Perrin, Noel. *First Person Rural: Essays of a Sometime Farmer*. Boston: David R. Godine, 1978.

"Personal and Otherwise." *Harper's* 177 (1938): 561–562.

Plimpton, George A., and Frank H. Crowther. "The Art of the Essay I: E. B. White." *Paris Review* 48 (Fall 1969): 65–88.

Poore, Charles. "Pointers for Statesman or Skeptic." *New York Times Book Review*, 17 November 1946: 3, 58.

Review of *One Man's Meat. Catholic World*, August 1942: 627–628.

Root, Robert L., Jr. "Once More to the Essay: Prose Models, Textbooks, and Teaching." *Journal of Teaching Writing* 14 (1995): 87–110.

———. *Working at Writing: Columnists and Critics Composing*. Carbondale: Southern Illinois University Press, 1991.

———, ed. *Critical Essays on E. B. White*. New York: G. K. Hall, 1994.

Rosenfeld, Isaac. "Chopping a Teakettle." *Nation*, 28 December 1946: 762–763.

Sampson, Edward C. *E. B. White*. New York: Twayne, 1974.

Sanders, Scott Russell. "The Singular First Person." *Secrets of the Universe: Scenes from the Journey Home*. Boston: Beacon, 1991.

Scholes, Robert, and Carl H. Klaus. *The Elements of the Essay*. New York: Oxford University Press, 1969.

Shanley, J. Lyndon. *The Making of "Walden" with the Text of the First Version*. Chicago: University of Chicago Press, 1957.

Sheed, Wilfrid. "*The New Yorker* Code." *Jubilee* 10 (March 1963): 48–54.

Sherwood, Robert E. "E. B. White: A Treasury of that Modest, Wise, and Witty Master." *New York Herald Tribune Book Review*, 17 January 1954: 1.

Smith, Ken. "Contesting Discourses in the Essays of E. B. White." In *Critical*

Essays on E. B. White, edited by Robert L. Root, Jr. New York: G. K. Hall, 1994.

Smith, Logan Pearsall. *Trivia*. London: Constable, 1918.

Steinbeck, John. *Journal of a Novel: The "East of Eden" Letters*. New York: Viking, 1969.

———. *Working Days: The Journals of "The Grapes of Wrath" 1938–1941*. Edited by Robert DeMott. New York: Viking, 1989.

Stoddart, Alexander McD. "Journalism's Radium, the Colyum." *Independent*, 16 February 1918: 274, 289–293.

Strunk, William, Jr. *The Elements of Style*. Ithaca: privately printed, 1918.

Strunk, William, Jr., and E. B. White. *The Elements of Style*. New York: Macmillan, 1959.

Thoreau, Henry David. *Walden*. Edited by J. Lyndon Shanley. Princeton: Princeton University Press, 1973.

"Thoreau on a Roof Garden." *New York Herald Tribune Books*, 14 October 1934: VII: 23.

Thurber, James. *The Years with Ross*. Boston: Little, Brown, 1959.

Trilling, Diana. "Humanity and Humor." *Nation*, 8 August 1942: 118.

Van Doren, Carl. "Day In and Day Out — Adams, Morley, Marquis, and Broun: Manhattan Wits." *Century Magazine*, December 1923: 308–315.

Walker, Stanley. "E. B. White's Civilized Way of Saying Things." *New York Herald Tribune*, 21 October 1962: 5.

Warshow, Robert. "Melancholy to the End." *Partisan Review* 14 (January–February 1947): 86.

Watson, Mark S. "Mr. White Surveys the World." *Saturday Review* 9 (November 1946): 14–15.

Watt, W. W. "E. B. White: An Appreciation." In *The Second Tree from the Corner*, by E. B. White. Modern Classics Edition. New York: Harper, 1962.

Weatherby, W. J. "A Modern Man of Walden." *Manchester Guardian Weekly*, 14 February 1963: 14.

Weeks, Edward. "First Person Singular." *Atlantic Monthly*, July 1942: 100.

Welty, Eudora. "Dateless Virtues." *New York Times Book Review*, 25 September 1977: 43.

White, E. B. *Alice through the Cellophane*. New York: John Day, 1933.

———. *Another Ho Hum: More Newsbreaks from The New Yorker*. New York: Farrar & Rinehart, 1932.

———. *Charlotte's Web*. New York: Harper, 1952.

———. "Child's Play." *New Yorker*, 9 May 1925: 14.

———. "Defense of the Bronx River." *New Yorker*, 26 December 1925: 17.

————. Introduction to *the lives of archy and mehitabel*, by Don Marquis. Garden City: Doubleday, 1950.

————. *Essays of E. B. White*. New York: Harper, 1977.

————. *Every Day Is Saturday*. New York: Harper, 1934.

———— [Lee Strout White, pseud.]. *Farewell to Model T*. New York: Putnam, 1936.

————. *The Fox of Peapack and Other Poems*. New York: Harper, 1938.

————. "From Sea to Shining Sea." *Ford Times*, July 1953: 8–12.

————. "Garter Motif." *New Yorker*, 5 June 1926: 33.

————. *Here Is New York*. New York: Harper, 1949.

————. *Ho Hum: Newsbreaks from The New Yorker*. New York: Farrar & Rinehart, 1931.

————. *The Lady Is Cold*. New York: Harper, 1929.

————. "Letter from the East." *New Yorker*, 27 July 1957: 35–36, 41–45.

————. *Letters of E. B. White*. Edited by Dorothy Lobrano Guth. New York: Harper, 1979.

————. "The Lobsterman." *Boston Sunday Globe*, 12 December 1954: 8A.

————. "The Manuscript Club." *Cornell Era* 53:15 (11 June 1921): 9.

————. "No Hat." *New Yorker*, 7 November 1926: 28.

————. "Notes and Comment." *New Yorker*, 2 October 1926: 17; 26 February 1927: 17; 2 May 1936: 11–12.

————. "One Man's Meat." *Harper's Magazine*, October 1938: 553–556; September 1939: 441–444; July 1940: 217–220; June 1941: 105–108; October 1943: 498–501.

————. *One Man's Meat*. New York: Harper, 1942.

————. *One Man's Meat*. New and Enlarged Edition. New York: Harper, 1944.

————. *One Man's Meat*. New York: Harper, 1985.

————. "Open Letter to My Burglar." *New Yorker*, 11 December 1926: 52–54.

————. *Poems and Sketches of E. B. White*. New York: Harper, 1983.

————. *The Points of My Compass*. New York: Harper, 1962.

————. *Quo Vadimus? or The Case for the Bicycle*. New York: Harper, 1939.

————. "The Sea and the Wind That Blows." *Ford Times*, June 1963: 2–6.

————. "A Step Forward." *New Yorker*, 18 April 1925: 21.

————. *The Second Tree from the Corner*. New York: Harper, 1953.

————. *Stuart Little*. New York: Harper, 1945.

————. *The Trumpet of the Swan*. New York: Harper, 1970.

————. "Walden — 1954." *Yale Review* 44 (Autumn 1954): 13–22.

————. *The Wild Flag*. New York: Harper, 1946.

————. *Writings from the New Yorker 1925–1976*. Edited by Rebecca M. Dale. New York: HarperCollins, 1990.

———. "You Can't Resettle Me." *Saturday Evening Post* 209:25 (10 October 1936): 8–9, 91–92.

———, ed. *Four Freedoms*. Washington, D.C.: Office of War Information, 1942.

White, E. B., and James Thurber. *Is Sex Necessary? or, Why You Feel the Way You Do*. New York: Harper, 1929.

White, E. B., and Katherine S. White, eds. *A Subtreasury of American Humor*. New York: Coward-McCann, 1941.

Wicker, Tom. *On Press*. New York: Viking, 1978.

INDEX